Studies in the History of Medieval Religion

VOLUME XXXVI

JOCELIN OF WELLS
BISHOP, BUILDER, COURTIER

Studies in the History of Medieval Religion

ISSN 0955–2480

General Editor
Christopher Harper-Bill

Previously published titles in the series
are listed at the back of this volume

JOCELIN OF WELLS
BISHOP, BUILDER, COURTIER

Edited by
ROBERT DUNNING

THE BOYDELL PRESS

First published 2010
The Boydell Press, Woodbridge

ISBN 978-1-84383-556-1

The Boydell Press is an imprint of Boydell & Brewer Ltd
PO Box 9, Woodbridge, Suffolk IP12 3DF, UK
and of Boydell & Brewer Inc.
668 Mt Hope Avenue, Rochester, NY 14620, USA
website: www.boydellandbrewer.com

The publisher has no responsibility for the continued existence or accuracy
of URLs for external or third-party internet websites referred to in this book,
and does not guarantee that any content on such websites is,
or will remain, accurate or appropriate.

A catalogue record for this book is available
from the British Library

This publication is printed on acid-free paper

Printed in Great Britain by
CPI Antony Rowe, Chippenham and Eastbourne

Contents

List of Illustrations   vii

Preface and Acknowledgements   ix

List of Abbreviations   xi

Introduction   *Robert Dunning*   1

Bishop Jocelin of Wells

1   Jocelin of Wells: the making of a bishop in the reign of King John   9
    Nicholas Vincent

2   Jocelin of Wells and the role of a bishop in the thirteenth century 34
    Jane Sayers

3   Jocelin of Wells and his cathedral chapter   53
    Diana Greenway

4   The bishop and his cathedral cities   67
    Sethina Watson

Bishop Jocelin the Builder

5   Jocelin of Wells as a palace builder   101
    Tim Tatton-Brown

6   Bishop Jocelin and his buildings in Wells   110
    Jerry Sampson

The Bishop's Palace at Wells

7   Geophysical and geoarchaeological survey at the Bishop's Palace,   125
    Wells
    Alex Turner, Christopher Gerrard and Keith Wilkinson

8   The location of Bishop Jocelin's palace at Wells   137
    Mark Horton

9   Lichens on the stonework of the Bishop's Palace, Wells   154
    David J. Hill

10 Robert Burnell and the transformation of the Bishop's Palace   169
    Matthew Reeve

Index   197

Illustrations

Colour plates *(between pp. 114 and 115)*

1 Crozier head found at Wells and now ascribed to the time of Bishop Jocelin.
2 The election of Bishop Jocelin, 1206.
3 The consecration of Bishop Jocelin, 1206.
4 Seal of Bishop Jocelin, attached to the declaration of his consecration.
5 Jocelin, bishop of Bath, grants to the dean and canons of Wells the church of Congresbury.
6 Wells Cathedral, west front: hot mastic repairs.
7 Wells Cathedral: the west doors and the painting scheme of 1239.
8 The Bishop's Palace.
9 Bishop Jocelin's range from the south-east.
10 The Bishop's Palace: two blocked windows.
11 a and b The Bishop's Palace: ashlar lining and decoration in the roof-space of Bishop Jocelin's range.
12 Extract from the plan by John Carter of the 'General Plan of the Monastical Buildings' at Wells.
13 Excavations on the south side of Bishop Burnell's Great Hall.
14 Culvert to carry water from gardens to moat
15 *Caloplaca polycarpa* growing on *Verrucaria baldensis*.
16 *Sarcogyne 'pruinosa'* with *Caloplaca variabilis*.
17 The rare *Catapyrenium rufescens*, *Physcia* sp. and *Caloplaca aurantia*.
18 *Collema confertum*, *Candelariella medians* and *Caloplaca citrina*.
19 Capping stone of rampart wall east of the north tower, showing the weathered surface with solution holes.
20 Bishop Burnell's Great Hall and chapel from the north-west.
21 Bishop Burnell's chapel from the north.
22 The solar end of the Great Hall.

Figures

1 Bishop Jocelin, Bishop Richard Poore of Salisbury and Hugh de Tournai, chancellor of Chichester, give absolution to those about to fight for the liberation of England and praise God for the victory over the French off Sandwich in 1217   39

2   Ordinance of Bishop Jocelin, changing the common payments of the   62
    canons and vicars of Wells from bread to money; 17 October 1242

3   The Wells brothers. Hugh, bishop of Lincoln, grants to Jocelin,   92
    bishop of Bath and Glastonbury, half a knight's fee in Rowberrow
    and Draycott; 11 July 1214

4   Bishop Jocelin's range: plans of ground and first floors   106–107

5   Bishop Jocelin's range: extract from the engraving of 1733 by Samuel 120
    and Nathaniel Buck

6   Plot of the resistivity data for the Bishop's Palace   128

7   Plot of the magnetometry data for the Bishop's Palace   128

8   Annotated interpretation of the resistivity data for the Bishop's Palace   129

9   Annotated interpretation of the magnetometry data for the Bishop's 129
    Palace

10 Location of boreholes drilled in 2003 and 2004   130

11 The percussion drilling equipment being used to sample an area of   131
    the present croquet lawn

12 North-west to south-east composite stratigraphic transect   132

13 North–south composite stratigraphic transect   132

14 Engraving of the Bishop's Palace by Samuel and Nathaniel Buck, 1733 138

15 Extract from the map of Wells by William Simes, 1735, showing   140
    details of the palace grounds

16 Drawing of the Bishop's Palace by C.A. Buckler   142

17 General plan of the Bishop's Palace by C.A. Buckler   143

18 Extract from the map of Canon Grange manor, before 1827, showing   146
    Horse Pond and Upper (or Palace) Mill

19 Relieving arches along the north wall of the palace enclosure   147
    indicating the line of the earlier stream

20 Detail of the southern hearth on the south side of the Great Hall   150
    with a crescent of stones and internal charcoal spreads

21 Reconstruction of the topography of the palace at the time of   152
    Bishop Jocelin

22 Plan showing locations of the sites referred to in Table 9.1.   162

23 Windows of Bishop Burnell's Great Hall   178

24 Window in the church at Nantwich, Cheshire   179

25 The Great Hall: elevation and section of the south-west turret,   184
    sketched and measured by A.W. Pugin

26 Junction between the south-east turret of the Great Hall and the   186
    south-west corner of the chapel

27 Windows of the palace chapel of St Etheldreda, Holborn   190

Preface and Acknowledgements

This collection springs from two main initiatives.

In the mid-1990s some linear features appeared in the lawn of the Bishop's Palace at Wells, which were investigated by the archaeologist Dr Lucy MacLaurin. Subsequently, recognising their importance, the then bishop of Bath and Wells, Jim Thompson, asked Dr MacLaurin to form a committee of local experts. With advice from the Somerset County Archaeologist, Bob Croft, and with the bishop's enthusiastic encouragement, she gathered together a group of archaeologists and others interested in the history of the building and its site. Some of the work commissioned by this committee is now published here for the first time.

Peter Price, who succeeded Jim Thompson in 2001, and his wife Dee immediately saw the immense potential of the palace and continued to support the committee in its wish to examine their home and garden in detail and to explain the site, the ruins and the buildings still in use so that visitors might be attracted in greater numbers and receive increased satisfaction from their experience. The year 2006 provided a convenient one for drawing attention to the palace, for it marked the 800th anniversary of the election and enthronement of Bishop Jocelin, sometimes known as Jocelin Trotman, more often as Jocelin of Wells, as bishop of Bath. It may not have been in 1206 that Jocelin put up the first buildings on the present site but without question it was the beginning of his significant rule as bishop, significant both for the palace he clearly built, for the great minster church to the north which was to become his successor's cathedral, and for the diocese that he presided over for nearly forty years. Such an anniversary needed to be marked so that the great bishop and his palace could be worthily celebrated.

Thus, during a busy week of celebrations in September 2006, actively inspired and supported by the bishop and his wife and organised under the leadership of Brigadier John Hemsley, two days were given over to a conference where an enthusiastic audience heard experts talk on historical, archaeological, liturgical, cultural and architectural aspects of the history of the cathedral, palace and city of Wells, set in both national and international contexts. Dr Lucy MacLaurin most successfully organised the conference and a large debt of gratitude is owed to her.

The thanks of the planning committee are due first to the contributors to the conference and to this volume; and second to a number of people who made significant contributions in so many ways: Mrs Judy Bloom-Davis; Mrs Elizabeth Cairncross and the pupils of Wells Cathedral School; Mrs Marian

Shaw and her team of workers and administrators at the palace; and especially to Miss Philippa Hemsley, whose fund-raising activities gathered the necessary finance to pay for (among other things) a significant contribution to this publication. Particular thanks are due to Mendip District Council and Natwest Bank for financial support given for archaeological investigations.

Abbreviations

Acta of Hugh of Wells	*Acta of Hugh of Wells, Bishop of Lincoln, 1209–1235*, ed. D.M. Smith, Lincoln Records Society 88 (2000)
Annales Monastici	*Annales Monastici*, ed. H.R. Luard, 5 vols, Rolls Series 36 (London, 1864–69)
Bath Charts	*Two Chartularies of the Priory of St Peter at Bath*, ed. W. Hunt, Somerset Record Society 7 (London, 1893)
Buckle, 'Wells Palace'	E. Buckle, 'Wells Palace', *Proceedings of the Somersetshire Archaeological and Natural History Society* 34 (1888), 54–97
Carter's plan, 1784	'General Plan of the Monastical Buildings', plate 1 in *John Carter's Architectural Records of Wells, 1784–1808*, ed. W. Rodwell and G. Leighton, Somerset Record Society 92 (Taunton, 2006)
CChR	*Calendar of Charter Rolls*, 6 vols (London, 1903–27)
CCR	*Calendar of Close Rolls*, 47 vols (London, 1900–63)
CFR	*Calendar of Fine Rolls*, 24 vols (London and Woodbridge 1911–)
Cherry and Draper, 'Excavations'	J. Cherry and P. Draper, 'Excavations in the Bishop's Palace, Wells', *British Archaeological Association Conference Transactions 1978* (1981), 52–3
Church, *Chapters*	C.M. Church, *Chapters in the Early History of the Church of Wells* (London, 1894)
Collectanea I	*Collectanea I: A Collection of Documents from Various Sources*, arr. T.F. Palmer (including 'Historia Minor' ed. J.A. Robinson), Somerset Record Society 39 (1924)
Councils and Synods	*Council and Synods with Other Documents Relating to the English Church*, i. 871–1204, ed. D. Whitelock, Martin Brett and C.N.L. Brooke (Oxford, 1986); ii. ed. F.M. Powicke and C.R. Cheney (Oxford, 1964)
CPL	*Calendar of Papal Letters 1 1198–1304*, ed. W.H. Bliss (London, 1893)
CPR	*Calendar of Patent Rolls*, 72 vols (London and Woodbridge, 1903–86)
CR	*Close Rolls*, 14 vols (London, 1902–38)
Cur. Reg. R.	*Curia Regis Rolls*, 20 vols (London, 1922–2006)
Domerham	*Adami de Domerham Historia de rebus gestis Glastoniensibus*, ed. T. Hearne, 2 vols (Oxford, 1727)

DB	*Domesday Book. A Complete Translation*, ed. A. Williams and G. H. Martin (London, 2002)
Dunning, 'Bishop's Palace'	Robert W. Dunning, 'The Bishop's Palace', in *Wells Cathedral: A History*, ed. L.S. Colchester (Shepton Mallet, 1982), 227–47
Edwards, *Eng. Secular Cathedrals*	K.E. Edwards, *English Secular Cathedrals in the Middle Ages* (Manchester, 1967)
EEA	*English Episcopal Acta*: vi. *Norwich 1070–1214*, ed. C. Harper-Bill (Oxford, 1990); viii. *Winchester 1070–1204*, ed. M.J. Franklin (Oxford, 1993); ix. *Winchester 1205–38*, ed. N. Vincent (Oxford, 1994); x. *Bath and Wells 1061–1205*, ed. F.M.R. Ramsey (Oxford, 1995); xviii. *Salisbury 1078–1217*, ed. B.R. Kemp (Oxford, 1999); xix. *Salisbury1217–28*, ed. B.R. Kemp (Oxford, 2000); xxv. *Durham 1196–1237*, ed. M.G. Snape (Oxford, 2000); xxvi. *London 1189–1228*, ed. D.P. Johnson (Oxford, 2003)
Fasti 1066–1300	John le Neve, *Fasti Ecclesie Anglicane 1066–1300*, revised D.E. Greenway: iii. *Lincoln* (London, 1977); vii. *Bath and Wells* (London, 2001)
Gesta Pontificum	William of Malmesbury, *Gesta Pontificum*, ed. Michael Winterbottom and Rodney Malcolm Thomson (Oxford, 2006)
Glast. Chart.	*The Great Chartulary of Glastonbury*, ed. A. Watkin, Somerset Record Society 59, 63–4 (1947–56)
'Historiola'	'Historiola de primordiis episcopatus Somersetensis' in *Ecclesiastical Documents*, ed. Joseph Hunter, Camden Society 8 (London, 1840)
Mon. Angl.	W. Dugdale, *Monasticon Anglicanum*, ed. J. Caley, H. Ellis and B. Bandinel, 6 vols (London, 1817–30)
ODNB	*Oxford Dictionary of National Biography* (Oxford, 2004)
Parker, 'Bishop's Palace at Wells'	J.H. Parker, 'The Bishop's Palace at Wells', *Proceedings of the Somersetshire Archaeological and Natural History Society* 11 (1861–62), 143–57
Pipe Roll	Publications of the Pipe Roll Society or other
Reg. Drokensford	*Calendar of the Register of John de Drokensford*, ed. Bishop Hobhouse, Somerset Record Society 1 (1887)
Robinson, *Som. Hist. Essays*	J.A. Robinson, *Somerset Historical Essays* (Oxford, 1921)
Rodwell, *Wells Cathedral*	W. Rodwell, *Wells Cathedral: Excavations and Structural Studies 1979–1993*, 2 vols (London, 2001)
Rot. Chart.	*Rotuli Chartarum*, ed. T.D. Hardy (London, 1837)

Rot. Cur. Reg.	*Rotuli Curiae Regis*, ed. F. Palgrave, 2 vols (London, 1835)
Rot. de Oblatis	*Rotuli de Oblatis et Finibus* ed. T.D. Hardy (London, 1835)
Rot. Litt. Claus.	*Rotuli Litterarum Clausarum*, ed. T.D. Hardy, 2 vols (London, 1833)
Rot. Litt. Pat.	*Rotuli Litterarum Patentium*, ed. T.D. Hardy (London, 1835)
Shaw, *Community*	D.G. Shaw, *The Creation of a Community: the City of Wells in the Middle Ages* (Oxford, 1993)
Shirley, *Royal Letters*	*Royal and other Historical Letters illustrative of the reign of Henry III*, ed. W. W. Shirley, 2 vols, Rolls Series 27 (1862)
Simes's map, 1735	*A Plan of the City of Wells by William Simes* (1735)
SRO	Somerset Record Office
TNA	The National Archives
VCH	*Victoria County History*
Wells MSS	*Calendar of the Manuscripts of the Dean and Chapter of Wells*, ed. W.H.B. Bird and W. Paley Baildon, 2 vols, Historical Manuscripts Commission (London, 1907–14)

Introduction

As indicated in the Preface, the papers in this volume have their origin in a conference organised under the auspices of the Archaeological Research Committee of the Bishop's Palace at Wells, held there on 11–12 September 2006. The date was chosen to commemorate Bishop Jocelin of Wells (bishop 1206–42) and to share current knowledge of his enormous contribution to the history of the present cathedral and diocese and of the buildings that he erected which still form the heart of the Bishop's Palace. Not all the papers included here were actually delivered at the conference. The additional contributions represent work, most of it archaeological, which had been undertaken over several years to understand the origins of what is one of England's most iconic collection of buildings; and more recently as necessary preliminaries in preparation for developments that will enable the palace to take its proper place among the accessible sites of our national heritage. The more traditional historical and architectural papers were mostly composed for the conference; some of those delivered on those two days have been modified by their authors, while others remain very much as they were heard and thus offer a flavour of a most enjoyable and significant occasion. Together they provide a wide-ranging examination of what Pevsner called 'without doubt the most memorable of all bishop's palaces in England'[1] and of the man who created its earliest surviving fabric and made of it, of the great collegiate church he was completing a few yards to the north and of the city adjoining to the west the heart of his developing diocese.

Jocelin, the local boy who had come to the centre of power in his native place and wielded considerable influence far beyond, achieved by the fifteenth century some kind of immortality. According to a note added to a copy of Higden's *Polychronicon* in reference to Jocelin's exile, the bishop had slain a dragon that lurked in his park near Wells. Four-legged, winged and with a face like a man's, it was said to have been deadly; but Jocelin, dismissing his followers, attacked it single-handed and cut off its head. The version of the *Polychronicon* in which this story appeared is now Eton College MS 213 but was formerly among the books that the scholar John Blacman took with him when he entered the Carthusian house at Witham

---

[1] N. Pevsner, *North Somerset and Bristol*, Buildings of England (Harmondsworth, 1958), 313.

in 1458–59. Whether the note was added by Blacman himself is not known, but he was a Somerset man, probably aware of local traditions.[2] Who knows but that the dragon in the park represents a folk memory of some kind of dispute that preceded or accompanied Jocelin's adoption of the land south of Wells minster church for which licence was obtained from the Crown in 1207? It was a move, as Nicholas Vincent points out in chapter 1 of this volume, that marks the transfer of episcopal power from Bath back to Wells and the clear opportunity to establish both a domestic and an administrative base.

Jocelin's origins were not simply local; he was, as Nicholas Vincent reveals, a rarity in his time, the first Englishman to put an end to a tradition of Anglo-Norman prelates, and yet one whose family connections linked him with some of its most distinguished, and Somerset-based, members – the Poore brothers and their father Richard of Ilchester.

Birth and education contributed to notice by a potential patron. Was it Simon de Camera who drew this likely youth to the attention of the ubiquitous Prince John in his frequent visits to the Mortain estates in the West Country? But competence and loyalty were not enough; a king needed a man with personal charm and finesse, though not necessarily theological expertise or sanctity, to be acceptable as a bishop.

Jocelin's election by the monks of Bath and the canons of Wells together set a local precedent, though co-operation between the two bodies seems to have remained strictly formal, consultations between them after the bitter dispute following Jocelin's death being usually held between representatives half-way between Bath and Wells at Farrington Gurney, one of the 'indifferent places' suggested by the Wells chapter.[3] But Jocelin's election was of wider significance. Ostensibly endorsed by all the bishops of the southern province as a way of establishing a hoped-for precedent over the rights of the monks of Canterbury in an archiepiscopal vacancy it was, inevitably, used by the Crown successfully to restate its control of appointments in the face of papal claims. The local boy found himself on the international stage.

The election, whatever its wider significance, was to the see of Bath and Glastonbury. The latter was rather a poisoned chalice bequeathed by the greed of his predecessor, Savaric. It was a political situation which might have been handled with much more serious consequences, perhaps because Jocelin's ambition for the 'quasi-cathedral' (to use Diana Greenway's phrase) at Wells was to establish it not just as a building but as an institution that

---

[2]   The discovery of the legend in the Eton MS was brought to Wells by Dean Armitage Robinson and was retold by L.S. Colchester in the *Friends of Wells Cathedral Report 1973*, 18–19. See also *Medieval Libraries of Great Britain*, ed. N.R. Ker (London, 1964), 205. For Blacman as a native of Somerset: *The Register of John Stafford, Bishop of Bath and Wells 1425–1443*, ed. T.S. Holmes, Somerset Record Society 31–2 (1915–16), 395.

[3]   *Wells MSS* i. 94–7, 101–2, 111, 116–17, 128, 529–30; ii. 121, 123.

made its full cathedral status three years after his death entirely inevitable. In that ambition Jocelin followed the examples of Robert of Lewes and Reginald FitzJocelin and established a chapter at Wells, as Diana Greenway so ably explains in chapter 3, that continues to this day.

To these fine Wells traditions must be added Jocelin's work as a royal administrator, a commanding and stabilising figure in the early years of Henry III's reign and one who, in the turbulent times of King John, was seen as a man 'devoid of political ambition' who, in Nicholas Vincent's phrase, 'walked the tightrope that joined *regnum* to *sacerdotium*'. As a diocesan bishop he was clearly active and organising if not, as Jane Sayers observes in her clear summary of his recorded diocesan actions (chapter 2), in the vanguard of reform. With the sole exception of Walter de Grey of York, Jocelin was the most experienced bishop among his contemporaries. One personal and tangible survival of his episcopate is the head of a pastoral staff (Plate 1) once ascribed to Bishop Savaric but now to the early years of Jocelin's rule.[4] Jocelin's figure in brass inlaid in his marble tomb in the middle of the cathedral quire, might have done the same, but it did not survive the sixteenth century. It would, if made at the time of Jocelin's death in 1242, have been not much later than the earliest such memorial known in the whole of Europe.[5] Might this be seen as a measure of the public appreciation of the man?

The Somerset diocese provides for Sethina Watson, in chapter 4, an opportunity to study the relationship of a bishop to his cathedral city and to follow the changes in both Bath and Wells that made the 'shifting, often controversial uses' of the two (Glastonbury, the third in the title, was never of urban significance) in the context of urban developments in the county as a whole. Jocelin's role as co-founder of the hospital at Wells with his brother Hugh was clearly of personal concern, and his enthusiastic development of his regional estate which began with the creation of the park to the south of the site that was to become his home and headquarters spread to industrial and commercial enterprises, wealth that his successors were to enjoy until the sixteenth century.

Jocelin the church and palace builder is another aspect of this multi-faceted man. The memorable west front of Wells cathedral, still spectacular though bereft of its original colour, was the culmination of work on the building begun by Reginald FitzJocelin in the 1180s. Construction by Jocelin's time as bishop had reached the western piers of the central tower and

4   Church, *Chapters*, 391–3; J. Alexander and P. Binski, eds, *Age of Chivalry: Art in Plantagenet England 1200–1400* (London, 1987), no. 257.
5   J. Leland, *Itinerary of England and Wales*, ed. L.T. Smith (London, 1964), 293; F. Godwin, *Catalogue of the Bishops of Bath and Wells* (1595), cited by S.H. Cassan, *Lives of the Bishops of Bath and Wells* (1829), 128; J. Mann, *Monumental Brasses* (Harmondsworth, 1957), 7 and plate 32.

the building was then, as he was to recall at the end of his life, on the point of collapse. How far he personally was responsible for progress from this low point is not possible to say, but the reorganisation of the chapter there certainly assisted in the financing of the work. From the mid-nave break in construction, a planned interlude that happened to coincide, as Jerry Sampson explains in chapter 6, with the rigours of the Interdict, the work was taken up again and triumphantly concluded. Jocelin 'must have been intimately involved' in the great west elevation. Sampson's careful study of the different stones used and his successful search for the marks of the masons allow him not only to date precise progress on the church but also to suggest with confidence that Jocelin's surviving range in the palace complex was the work of those same masons who completed the nave and west front, work that was proceeding after 1213.

Tim Tatton-Brown, in chapter 5, sets the scene for this secular work when most other bishops, following royal example, were creating similar residences across the country. What survives of Jocelin's work is 'an exceptionally large chamber block' that he suggests may have been built alongside and to the west of an aisled hall perhaps built by Reginald FitzJocelin.

The position of that hall and any service buildings must now necessarily be within the province of archaeologists, though the limits set on their intervention are strict. Mark Horton, in chapter 8, concludes that a possible kitchen to the west of the present ruined Great Hall, and the original topography as revealed by the work described by Alex Turner, Chris Gerrard and Keith Wilkinson in chapter 7, points to the site of an earlier hall on the very spot later selected by Bishop Burnell at the end of the thirteenth century. The earlier topography, before the moat and later ground-raising measures took the place of a network of streams, does not at first sight suggest an area where building of any scale would be sensible. The sites of Winchester and Salisbury cathedrals provide amazing parallels, and the east end of the cathedral at Wells seems perilously near the shifting springs in the Bishop's garden. The water table on the palace site is only just below the pavement in the bishop's chapel.

David Hill, in a fascinating contribution (chapter 9), offers a study of lichens as a way of understanding building sequence with no dangerous interventions. His chapter serves as a model where documentary and stylistic evidence is far less useful.

For many people, the ruined Great Hall of the Bishop's Palace is its most memorable feature, and Matthew Reeves's contribution to this volume (chapter 10) introduces another bishop, Robert Burnell, whose awareness of the increasing social and political power of bishops overtook their pastoral role; regnum and sacerdotium were not, at least in Burnell's case, in balance. The elusive hall of Jocelin or Reginald (if on the site Mark Horton proposes) was now replaced by a chapel and hall, the whole within a walled enclosure that was not exactly a castle constructed for a serious military purpose but nevertheless offered aristocratic display of an obvious kind. There was about it, perhaps a touch of the romance that contemporaries associated with King Arthur. The more limited needs of Bishop Jocelin were of the past.

Robert Dunning, Taunton

BISHOP JOCELIN OF WELLS

1

Jocelin of Wells:
The Making of a Bishop in the Reign of King John

NICHOLAS VINCENT

Strange as it may seem to open an account of the election of Bishop Jocelin of Wells with personalities of the twentieth rather than the thirteenth century, it would be an act of *lèse-majesté* were I to fail to acknowledge that what follows is not so much my own work but a mere précis of that of two of the greatest of twentieth-century ecclesiastical historians. The first of these giants was a local man, Joseph Armitage Robinson, born at Keynsham, professor of divinity at Cambridge, dean of Westminster and after his controversial removal from that (still controversial) office, dean of Wells from 1911 to 1933.[1] Although principally remembered today as a patristics scholar, famed for his rediscovery of early Christian manuscripts in libraries from London to Vienna, in turning his attention to the thirteenth-century church Robinson not only brought into commission all, or very nearly all, of the relevant unpublished sources relating to Bishop Jocelin's election, but supplied a quite masterly reconstruction of Jocelin's background and early career. Robinson's essay 'Bishop Jocelin and the Interdict', first delivered in 1913 and published a decade or so later, remains a definitive statement of the facts.[2] Besides elucidating the circumstances of Jocelin's election, Robinson also sought to explain the ins and outs of that most vexed and perplexing of jurisdictional disputes, between the bishops of Bath and Wells and the monks of Glastonbury abbey, that will necessarily occupy us in part of what follows. What little Robinson left unsaid here was comprehensively stated in the work of the second of my twentieth-century giants: Christopher Cheney, himself professor at Cambridge, mentor to several of the contributors to this present volume and, in his *Pope Innocent III and*

---

1 For Robinson (1858–1933), see T.F. Taylor, *J. Armitage Robinson: Eccentric, Scholar, and Churchman* (Cambridge, 1991), with a shorter life supplied by Taylor for the *ODNB* xlvii. 376–8.
2 Robinson, *Som. Hist. Essays*, 141–59, which carries only a bare minimum of footnote references: a lack which I have taken the opportunity to remedy below.

England, author of a definitive account not only of Anglo-papal relations but of the wider history of the English church in the early years of the thirteenth century.[3]

With Robinson and Cheney already ahead of me in the field, what then remains for me to do here save to draw attention to the magnificence of their contributions? In what follows, I shall attempt two tasks. Spared by Jane Sayers and Diana Greenway from the need to supply an outline of Jocelin's career as bishop, I shall attempt to explain why Jocelin still matters to our wider understanding of the early thirteenth-century church. Secondly, I shall do my best to throw some light upon what we know of English kingship at this time and, in particular, of what we know, or do not know, of the personality and ecclesiastical policy of England's King John. From this basis, I shall try to expound – 'vulgarise' might be a better term – the insights that Robinson and Cheney have already supplied into Jocelin's election as bishop.

Let us begin then with Jocelin. The first thing that we need to understand about him was that he was an intensely 'local' man, in all probability born at Wells or within a few miles of the city. Certainly he was raised there 'from his first milk', as his fellow canons were to declare on electing him as bishop.[4] The Glastonbury chronicler, Adam of Domerham, even refers to Jocelin as being 'of the nation of Wells' ('natione Wellensi, fratre Hugonis Lincolniensis presulis').[5] As bishop, of course, Jocelin was called upon to play a not insignificant role in national politics. From 1215 to 1217, rather than attend the great Lateran Council that summoned the majority of his fellow bishops to Rome, he remained in England throughout the period of civil war, apparently as a loyal subject of the king, attending the coronation of the nine-year-old Henry III at Gloucester in the autumn of 1216 and being present, albeit on shore, in the following year when the French fleet, and with it the last hope of a rebel victory, was dispatched to the bottom of the Channel in the battle of Sandwich.[6] In 1219, he served as justice in eyre for the south-western counties of England, clearly once again as a loyal servant of the king and his court.[7] If his interventions on the national political stage thereafter remain somewhat overshadowed by those of his greater contemporaries – the scholar archbishops of Canterbury, Stephen Langton and Edmund of Abingdon, the great reforming bishop of Salis-

---

3   C.R. Cheney, *Pope Innocent III and England* (Stuttgart, 1976), esp. 220–5, and see M. Chibnall's biography of Cheney, in *ODNB* xi. 303–4.
4   *Wells MSS* i. 63: *a primo lacte*.
5   *Domerham*, ii. 441.
6   For his role in the coronation of Henry III, see *The Letters and Charters of Cardinal Guala Bicchieri Papal Legate in England 1216–18*, ed. N. Vincent (Canterbury and York Society 83, 1996), 28 no. 36. For his presence at the Battle of Sandwich, see Figure 1.
7   D. Crook, *Records of the General Eyre* (London, 1982), 73.

bury Richard Poore, and even by that demon-king amongst the thirteenth-century English church hierarchy, Peter des Roches, bishop of Winchester – Jocelin's part in national politics and the ordering of the English church was still a very substantial one. Without being a trimmer, he maintained a personal role and hence an episcopal presence at court throughout the 1220s and 1230s, signalling a new level of co-operation between the more enlightened and 'reforming' amongst the English bishops and the central processes of English royal government. By his very longevity – thirty-six years a bishop, exceeded in his lifetime only by Walter de Grey, archbishop of York – he contributed wisdom and stability to royal counsels. Like Walter de Grey, indeed, who had begun as King John's chancellor but who later proved himself a conscientious pastor and diocesan administrator, Jocelin's career stands as a demonstration of the fact that not all courtiers made bad bishops and that not all bishops found the demands of the court and of Christ mutually exclusive. Probably more than any other medieval bishop of his diocese, with the single exception of Bishop Burnell in the 1280s, Jocelin played a long and distinguished role not just upon the local, but upon the national stage. Caroline Marino Malone perhaps comes closest to expressing the reality of Jocelin's career when she writes of the west front of Jocelin's cathedral at Wells as a great summation both of the triumphalism of the church in the aftermath of the Fourth Lateran Council and of the compromise between *regnum* and *sacerdotium*, state and church, effected by Jocelin and his fellow bishops in English politics during the twenty years after 1215.[8] Not everything in Malone's account is to be accepted as the unvarnished truth. The decision to relocate the seat of the bishop from the Roman imperial and later distinctly royal city of Bath to the relatively unroyal Wells, much like the almost simultaneous decision by Richard Poore and his brother, Herbert, to relocate their see from the royal enclave at Old Sarum to its new site at Salisbury, can in fact be read as a deliberate severing of the ties that had previously bound together *regnum* and *sacerdotium*.[9] Nonetheless, as a summing up both of the way that Jocelin managed to walk the tightrope between the demands of church and state and of why his career still resonates both at a national and a local level, Malone's reading of the cathedral's significance has much to recommend it.

It is from the national to the local scene that we must now return, and specifically to Jocelin's early years, before ever he took up his responsibilities as a bishop. The date of Jocelin's birth, and of that of his elder brother, Hugh, remain unknown, but can probably be located at some point in the late

8   C.M. Malone, *Facade as Spectacle: Ritual and Ideology at Wells Cathedral* (Leiden, 2004), 41ff.
9   For the translation to Salisbury from Old Sarum see *Letters and Charters of Guala*, 140–1 no. 170; *VCH Wiltshire*, iii. 164–5.

1160s. Likewise, we know nothing certain of Jocelin's education, though it is natural to suppose that he was first taught in the grammar school already attached to the newly resurgent collegiate church at Wells. He first appears in the late 1180s or early 1190s, as a witness to charters of Bishop Reginald of Bath, on one occasion – a charter relating to the market at Wells – in company with Edward of Wells, his father.[10] Thereafter, he rose to become a canon of Wells, probably under Bishop Savaric, occurring together with his brother Hugh as a representative of the chapter of Wells before the king's court in June 1199 and again in January 1200, sent to impose the bishop's will upon the recalcitrant monks of Glastonbury.[11] By c.1204 he had also acquired the Hampshire church of Dogmersfield in return for service to Robert, prior of Bath, originally recompensed with an annual pension of £5, and he had also, before 1205, acquired the prebend of Leicester St Margaret in Lincoln cathedral, perhaps as a result of his service, apparently as deputy to Hugh his brother, as royal keeper of the vacant see of Lincoln (1200–3) preceding the election of Bishop William of Blois.[12] By 1206, Jocelin was referred to with title as 'Master' Jocelin, a title which seems at this date to have been more than merely honorific, implying some period of higher study, where we cannot say, though in all probability not at Wells itself but at some other centre of learning, Oxford perhaps, or Lincoln, possibly even Paris.[13] How was it that a local man from Wells, of no great social standing, could pursue such studies and even, in time, come to obtain promotion to a bishopric? Here, Jocelin's family background was no doubt crucial.

Jocelin, his brother, Hugh of Wells, and their father, Edward of Wells, are all described in the sources under one or other toponymic version of their name, 'of Wells', that ties them to England and specifically to one narrow corner of the English south-west.[14] On at least two occasions, however, both Jocelin and Edward are referred to by another surname – 'Trotman' or 'Tortesmains', literally 'Twisted Hands' – that although it may have begun as a purely descriptive nickname seems to have developed as a local Somerset surname several generations before Jocelin's birth.[15] A Ralph Tortesmains is

[10] *EEA* x. nos 72, 80, 177.
[11] *Rot. Cur. Reg.* ii. 179; *Domerham*, ii. 387; *EEA* x. no. 234, and in general see *Fasti 1066–1300* vii. 87.
[12] *Bath Charts.* 2, 15 nos 64–6; *Fasti 1066–1300* iii. 77, and for Jocelin and his brother Hugh as keepers of the vacancy at Lincoln, see *Rotuli de Liberate ac de Misis et Praestitis*, ed. T.D. Hardy (London, 1844), 97; *Pipe Roll 8 John*, 22.
[13] *Wells MSS* i. 63.
[14] For Jocelin's family, the essential collection of references remains that made by Robinson, *Som. Hist. Essays*, 156–9, most crucially citing Wells Cathedral Library, charter 13 (whence *Wells MSS* ii. 549 no. 13), witnessed by Hugh son of Edward and Jocelin his brother.
[15] For Edward, Jocelin's father, as Edward Trotem(an), see Wells Cathedral Library, charter 12, whence calendared (without witness list) *Wells MSS* ii. 548 no. 12.

recorded in the Domesday Survey (1086) as holding land at Banwell from the bishops of Bath. He also held land at Winscombe, Pilton and Alhampton from the abbots of Glastonbury.[16] Land at Pilton and Alhampton was still in the possession of a Henry Tortesmains by 1189: a significant fact this, since Hugh, Jocelin's brother, was later to bequeath money in his will to his poor kinsmen at Pilton.[17] In the late 1150s we find an Elias Tortesmains also holding land in Somerset.[18] Elias may be important to our story, since he seems also to have held property in the Gower peninsula: an enclave of English or rather of Anglo-Norman lordship in South Wales, and a reminder of how, in the twelfth century, Somerset was in many ways far more closely tied into the politics and economy of South Wales than for those, today, who pay extortionate fees on the toll bridges.[19] Wales and the Gower lay only a short boat ride from the Somerset coast, with the Bristol Channel serving, much as the Thames estuary served at this time, more as a vector of communication and contact than as a barrier to movement.[20] Elias Tortesmains is particularly significant to us because he occurs as a benefactor of the Hospitaller preceptory at Slebech in Gower. Our only reference to Jocelin of Wells under the surname Trotman or Tortesmains likewise occurs in a South Welsh source: the annals of Margam abbey, recording Jocelin's election as bishop in 1206.[21]

If Jocelin was indeed an offshoot of the Tortesmains family then this would cast a significant light on his later career, since the Tortesmains were knights, not merely urban freeholders.[22] Their ultimate origin, whether

---

[16] *Domesday Book: Somerset*, ed. C. and F. Thorn, Phillimore Domesday Edition 8 (Chichester, 1980), sections 6, 9; 8, 2; 8, 29; 8, 30, where Ralph's surname, missing in Great Domesday, is supplied from the Exon Domesday.

[17] For the Henry Tortesmains of 1189, apparently deprived of his land at Churchill (*Cercell'*) held of the bishopric of Bath in 1197, but himself still living in 1199, see *Surveys of the Estates of Glastonbury Abbey c.1135–1201*, ed. N.E. Stacy, Records of Social and Economic History n.s. 33 (Oxford, 2001), 84; *Pipe Roll* 9 Richard I, 139; *Pipe Roll* 10 Richard I, 219; *Pipe Roll* 1 John, 134. For the will of Bishop Hugh, see *Acta of Hugh of Wells*, 193 no. 408: 'lego pauperibus parentibus meis apud Well' et circa Pilton' lx. marcas ubi dominus frater meus <et> alii executores mei viderint expedire.'

[18] *The Great Rolls of the Pipe for the Second, Third and Fourth Years of the Reign of King Henry the Second*, ed. J. Hunter (London, 1844), 99 where, in 1157, Elias is recorded owing half a mark 'pro recto de terra episcopi Bath'.

[19] *St Davids Episcopal Acta 1085–1280*, ed. J. Barrow, South Wales Record Society 13 (1998), 71 no. 46: 'ex dono Heliae Tortesmains duodecim acras et parvum angulum augmentationis'.

[20] For the concept of 'Severnside' as a distinct regional identity, first propounded by Professor Ralph Griffiths, see B. Golding, 'Trans-Border Transactions: Patterns of Patronage in Anglo-Norman Wales', *The Haskins Society Journal*, 16 (2006), 37–8.

[21] *Annales Monastici*, ed. H.R. Luard, 5 vols, Rolls Series (London, 1864–69), i. 28: 'Jocelinus Troteman consecratur in episcopum Bathoniensem.'

[22] For a Thomas Tortesmains in 1190 fining 15 marks together with Richard of Kent to have their right in a single knight's fee in Allerton (*Alenc'*) and in three parts of a knight's fee in Churchill (*Cercell'*) (Somerset) against Henry Tortesmains, a debt that was summoned in

English or Norman, remains unknown. The Ralph Tortesmains of 1086, like Jocelin himself, bore a Christian name that was more continental than English. By contrast, Jocelin's father Edward was named in such a way as to suggest descent from one of the Anglo-Saxon families that had managed, albeit in reduced circumstances, to survive the Norman Conquest of 1066. Here we might reflect more generally upon Jocelin's apparently sudden rise in royal favour and his credentials to be considered one of those 'new men' – 'men risen from the dust' as one contemporary put it – who are supposed have thronged the courts of twelfth- and thirteenth-century England. Jocelin, who by 1205 had risen to become a middling member of the king's itinerant chancery staff, responsible for the drafting and issue of royal letters, might at first sight seem to fit into the mould of the 'new men', risen from humble obscurity to influence and ultimately to great wealth through service to the king.[23] In reality, whenever the evidence permits us to probe behind the scenes, we almost invariably find that such 'new men' were kinsmen or satellites of older men, long established in royal service, as members of that great chorus of indigent and ambitious cousins, nephews and relations that perched in the branches of any well-connected family tree.[24] One of the most telling examples of this phenomenon concerns another Somerset man, Richard of Ilchester, successively scribe in the king's chancery, archdeacon of Poitiers, leading royal advocate in King Henry II's dispute with Archbishop Becket and thereafter promoted, as bishop of Winchester, ruler of one of the wealthiest sees in medieval Europe.[25] Long supposed to have been of entirely obscure birth, Richard was in fact part of a vast family network that extended back to John of Tours, bishop of Bath in the early 1100s, and which comprehended connections, some of them distinctly aristocratic, extending across south-west England and northern

Kent each year until Michaelmas 1197 whereafter it disappears from account, suggesting that the fine was never paid, see *Pipe Roll 2 Richard I*, 150; *Pipe Roll 9 Richard I*, 27. Nonetheless, at Michaelmas 1203, Hilaria, the widow of Henry Tortesmains, now remarried to Hilary of Bathampton, sued Thomas Tortesmains and Richard de Keu *alias* Ken' for her right in two hides of land and a mill at Allerton, eventually obtaining seisin: *Cur. Reg. R.* iii. 10, 13, 215. For a Robert Tortesmains and Matilda his wife, sued over land at Allerton in 1196, sued over land at Alfoxton in Holford (Somerset) in 1201, and in the same year successfully establishing Matilda's claim to land at Allerton held of Ralph de Conteville see *Cur. Reg. R.* i. 23–4, ii. 2, 37; *Pedes Finium Commonly Called Feet of Fines for the County of Somerset, Richard I to Edward I*, ed. E. Green, Somerset Record Society 6 (1892), nos 1, 49. For the heir of a John Tortesmains, apparently with lands in Hampshire in 1204, see *Pipe Roll 6 John*, 129.

23 For Jocelin's early career as canon and royal clerk, see below.
24 See here R.V. Turner, *Men Raised from the Dust: Administrative Service and Upward Mobility in Angevin England* (Philadelphia, 1988); N. Vincent, 'Warin and Henry fitz Gerald the King's Chamberlains: The Origins of the FitzGeralds Revisited', *Anglo-Norman Studies*, 21 (1999), 251–2.
25 See the recent biography by J. Hudson, in *ODNB* xxix. 195–8.

France.[26] Richard of Ilchester is directly relevant to our story, since the very earliest appearance made by Edward of Wells, the father of Bishop Jocelin, occurs as witness to a charter issued in the 1160s or early 1170s, by which the abbot of Westminster granted Richard property in London to add to his already extensive portfolio of manors and churches in Somerset.[27] If there was some connection between Richard of Ilchester and Jocelin's father then this would be doubly interesting. In many ways the English bishop closest to Bishop Jocelin and his brother Hugh, bishop of Lincoln, was to be Richard Poore, bishop of Salisbury, himself the illegitimate son of Richard of Ilchester and the brother of his immediate predecessor as bishop of Salisbury, Herbert Poore.[28] As the promotion of these two sets of brothers – Jocelin and Hugh of Wells, and Richard and Herbert Poore – should further demonstrate, there was a sense in which the English church hierarchy at the beginning of the thirteenth century operated as a semi-closed oligarchy, in which sons could follow their fathers into episcopal promotion, and brothers followed brothers.

The qualifications for episcopal office were many and various but in by no means all cases involved perceived sanctity or great theological learning. Richard Poore was a very considerable scholar, most likely the man responsible for propagating the Sarum liturgy throughout England. Jocelin's brother, Hugh of Wells, became bishop of Lincoln in succession to a very formidable saint, Hugh of Avalon, formerly prior of the Carthusian priory of Witham in Somerset and a member of that small and select band of English bishops who in the thirteenth century were to earn canonisation. Neither Jocelin nor Hugh his brother, however, was to be remembered either for learning or sanctity. Rather, they possessed qualities that were regarded as almost equally significant for episcopal promotion: keen practical intelligence and a network of contacts at court sufficient to bring them to the attention of the king and hence in due course to their election as bishops. The court contacts of Jocelin and Hugh came partly, we must suppose, through their families, partly from their circles of acquaintances at Wells. In particular, it has been suggested that a man named Simon de Camera (of the king's chamber), by the late 1190s archdeacon of Wells, regular witness to royal charters from 1198 and thereafter appointed datary and *de facto* vice-chancellor to King John, may have been the talent spotter who first drew both Jocelin and Hugh of Wells into the orbit of the king's court.[29] Yet Simon himself, of course, must have found ways of his own of gravitating to court,

26 V.D. and R.S. Oggins, 'Richard of Ilchester's Inheritance: An Extended Family in Twelfth-Century England', *Medieval Prosopography*, 12 (1991), 57–129, esp. pedigrees 2–5, 123–8.
27 *Westminster Abbey Charters 1066–c.1214*, ed. E. Mason, London Records Society 25 (1988), 137–8 no. 277.
28 See the biographies of Richard and Herbert Poore *alias* Poer, in ODNB xliv. 853–7.
29 David Smith, introduction to *Acta of Hugh of Wells*, xxviii–ix.

and in due course was to end his life as bishop of Chichester.[30] Nor was he necessarily the only or principal connection between Jocelin, Hugh and the king. Hugh's first will and testament, drawn up in exile at St-Martin-de-Garenne in November 1212 with Jocelin as its principal executor, suggests that by this date, Hugh and presumably his brother had established a widespread network of contacts, with both the religious and the secular aristocracy of the south-west.[31] Hugh left substantial benefactions to five monasteries, including the notable sum of 100 marks to Plympton priory in Devon, as well as a further 80 marks or more to commemorate the soul of the widow of Geoffrey de Mandeville and legacies to other members of the Mandeville family, perhaps more likely to be the Mandeville barons of Marshwood in Dorset rather than the Mandeville earls of Essex.[32] Five hundred marks were bequeathed to establish a hospital at Wells. But perhaps the most notable of Hugh's intended bequests was a gift of 300 marks to establish a hospital or other alms for the commemoration of the soul of a man named Jordan de Turri. Although it is possible that this represents Hugh's discharge of an obligation placed upon him as bishop of Lincoln after rather than before 1209, it may nonetheless suggest that there was a closer and more personal association between Hugh and Jordan. Jordan de Turri, whose name appears to have derived from the Tower of London, and who certainly possessed extensive property in and around London, had once been a leading member of the household of Richard of Ilchester, bishop of Winchester, and had gone on to serve as overseer of work on the Tower under King Richard I.[33] He died at some time early in 1205, apparently on

30 For Simon fitz Robert, *alias* Simon de Camera or Simon of Wells, clerk of Hubert Walter, archbishop of Canterbury, prebendary of Salisbury and London, archdeacon of Wells by 1198, provost of Beverley by 1202, witness to charters of Richard I from June 1198 onwards, datary from September 1199 at the latest, elected bishop of Chichester in April 1204, consecrated 11 July 1204, see *Fasti 1066–1300* vii. 33; L. Landon, *The Itinerary of King Richard I* (Pipe Roll Society n.s. 13 (1935), 129ff; *Rot. Chart.*, 21ff.
31 *Acta of Hugh of Wells*, 3–5 no. 2.
32 The religious, other than those of Lincoln and Wells, were the Cistercians of Stanley in Wiltshire (30 marks), of Quarr in the Isle of Wight (20 marks) and of Poulton in Cheshire (30 marks), the Cluniacs of Monkton Farleigh in Wiltshire (10 marks) and the Augustinians of Plympton (100 marks). Further, for the most part much smaller bequests were promised to a series of Somerset houses, including the leper hospital at Selwood (3 marks), the nuns of Barrow Gurney (10 marks), the Augustinian priory of Barlinch (2 marks), the fabric of Buckland priory (20 marks), the nuns of Cannington (5 marks), two hospitals at Bath (10½ marks), the leper hospital outside Ilchester (3 marks) and to the nuns of Studley Priory in Oxfordshire (7½ marks). For the distinction between the two Mandeville families, the earls of Essex native to Manneville (dép. Seine-Maritime), the barons of Earl's Stoke and Marshwood to Magneville (dép. Manche), see L.C. Loyd, *The Origins of Some Anglo-Norman Families*, Harleian Society 103 (1951), 57–8.
33 For his service as witness and clerk under Richard of Ilchester from at least 1174, see *EEA* viii. nos 141, 144, 151, 154, 161–2, 166, 171 (as 'magister'), 172, 186 (as Jordan 'clericus de Turre'), 188, 190, 192–3; *Pipe Roll* 23 Henry II, 25 (accounting for the Mohun lands

a pilgrimage or embassy to Rome.[34] Besides supplying a further hint that it was in the train of Richard of Ilchester, Jordan's patron, that Hugh and Jocelin may first have been drawn from local into national affairs, we might note here the way in which Jordan was able to move easily between the world of the episcopal household and that of the court, acting in turn as bishop's clerk after 1174, overseer of supplies and building-work at London from 1189 to 1192, and in 1202, as a royal justice in eyre, serving under the king's justiciar Geoffrey fitz Peter.[35] A similar general competence was to mark the early careers of both Jocelin and Hugh.

Whatever the precise means by which Jocelin and Hugh were recruited into royal service, there were already strong links between Wells, Somerset and the royal court which may help to explain why we have already been able to discover an entire network of men from, or once resident in, Somerset – Richard of Ilchester, Richard and Herbert Poore, St Hugh of Lincoln, Jocelin and Hugh of Wells, Simon de Camera – scaling the heights to episcopal office. From at least the time of King Alfred, Somerset had been not only home to a series of monastic houses with close connections to the kings of England, but also a favoured location for that most royal of sporting activities, the king's hunt. Not only this, but for a decade before he succeeded to the throne of England in 1199, King John had controlled extensive estates in Somerset and the south-west by virtue of his posses- sion of the lands of the honour of Mortain, scattered across Somerset, Dorset, Devon and Cornwall. It was in the south-west that John seems to have passed much of the 1190s, with a particular fondness for his castles and hunting lodges at Marlborough, Bristol, Dorchester, Shaftesbury and

---

in the south-west as Richard's clerk). For his service under Richard I at London from 1189 to 1192, see *The Great Roll of the Pipe for the First Year of the Reign of King Richard the First*, ed. J. Hunter (London, 1844), 225; *Pipe Rolls* 3–4 Richard I, 136, 140, 149, 301. For his land in and around London, see *Pipe Roll* 2 Richard I, 49; *Cur. Reg. R.* i. 121, 131, 162, iii. 215, 248, 275; *The Great Register of Lichfield Cathedral Known as Magnum Registrum Album*, ed. H.E. Savage, William Salt Arch. Society (1926 for 1924), no. 59; C.N.L. Brooke and G. Keir, *London 800–1216: The Shaping of a City* (London, 1975), 271; *The Cartulary of Holy Trinity Aldgate*, ed. G.A.J. Hodgett, London Records Society 7 (London, 1971), nos 199–200, this latter suggesting, perhaps misleadingly, that he was succeeded by sons named Robert and John.

[34] He last appears as a litigant in the Easter term of 1205 (*Cur. Reg. R.* iii. 275), and by June 1205 part of his London estate had been awarded by the king to Thomas Lovell of Evercreech in Somerset: *Rot. Chart.*, 155; *Rot. Litt. Claus.* i. 35b. In this context, it is worth noting that an unnamed 'boy' of Evercreech is mentioned in Hugh of Wells's will of 1212, promised the substantial sum of 40 marks 'ad eum exhibendum', presumably so that he might receive a proper education (*Acta of Hugh of Wells*, 4 no. 2). For the claim that Jordan had died on pilgrimage to Rome, related to the claim of his nephew Robert to succeed to part of his estate, see *Cur. Reg. R.* ix. 72, 334.

[35] For his service as justice in eyre between June and November 1202, see *Pleas Before the King or his Justices*, ed. D.M. Stenton, 4 vols, Selden Society 67–8, 83–4 (London, 1952–67) iii. clxxxvi–vii, clxxxix.

Cranborne.[36] As count of Mortain in the 1190s, John had granted at least half a dozen charters to the canons of Wells.[37] Although neither Jocelin nor Hugh of Wells appears as witness to any of John's pre-1199 charters, it is by no means fanciful to suppose that they may both, as early as the 1190s, have been brought into contact with the future king.

As to the details of their rise, Hugh of Wells, the elder brother, seems to have preceded Jocelin into royal service by several years. Hugh is to be found witnessing royal charters at York as early as the first year of King John's reign, and thereafter, from the summer of 1202, briefly substituted for Simon de Camera as chief datary to the king's charters issued in Normandy, an office in which he definitively succeeded Simon in 1203.[38] Jocelin's first recorded mention as royal clerk was delayed until February 1204, whereafter he makes occasional appearances as a royal justice, being one of those set to preside over litigation in the king's presence in the court *coram rege*: service which may suggest that his early training had been more legal than theological in orientation and which, from February 1204, was rewarded with presentation by the king to the Herefordshire churches of Lugwardine and Archenfield to which he was subsequently permitted to present a vicar, Master Alardus.[39] In this or the following year he was charged with imposing tallage upon the counties of south-west England including his own native Somerset.[40] From February 1205, he succeeded his brother Hugh as chief datary to charters issuing from the itinerant royal chancery, and by this time is to be found transacting other routine business in and around the chancery.[41] Besides bringing him his churches in Herefordshire, his service to the Crown as keeper of the vacant bishopric of Lincoln may already have

---

36 See here N. Vincent, 'Jean, comte de Mortain: le futur roi et ses domaines en Normandie 1183–1199', in *1204: La Normandie entre Plantagenêts et Capétiens*, ed. A.-M. Flambard Héricher and V. Gazeau (Caen, 2007), 37–59, esp. 42.

37 For five charters issued by John, before his coronation as king to the canons of Wells or Bishop Reginald, chiefly concerning the gift of the manor of North Curry, see *Wells MSS* i. 7–8, nos vi–x. For three further charters issued by John to Bishop Reginald or his church at Bath, including a quittance to the bishop, monks and citizens of Bath from toll and customs payable at Bristol, see London, British Library MS Egerton 3316 (Bath Cartulary) fos 18v–20r, 51r.

38 *Rot. Chart.*, 39 (25 March 1200). The charter rolls for the years 3 and 4 John (May 1201–May 1203) are missing. Nonetheless, Hugh is to be found as datary to charters issued at Argentan in August 1202, at Rouen and Pont-Audemer in February–March 1203, and thereafter on a permanent basis after July 1203: TNA C64/15 m.21; *Cal. Chart. R.* i. 44, iii. 46; *Cartae Antiquae Rolls*, ed. L. Landon and J. Conway Davies, 2 vols, Pipe Roll Society n.s. 17, 33 (1939–60) i. no. 238, ii. no. 494.

39 For a list of his appearances as justice *coram rege*, beginning in Yorkshire and Nottinghamshire in February 1204 and lasting until February 1205, see *Pleas Before the King*, iii. ccxv, ccxvii, ccxxi, ccxxiv. For the Herefordshire churches, see *Rot. Chart.*, 119b; *Rot. Litt. Pat.* 38b.

40 *Pipe Roll 7 John*, 3, 24, 142–4, 167; *Pipe Roll 8 John*, 130.

41 *Rot. Chart.*, 106b, 107b; *Rot. Litt. Claus.* i. 9, 17; *Rot. de Oblatis*, 296.

brought him a prebend in Lincoln cathedral.[42] Given his family's landed interests in and around Wells, and his appearance many years earlier as witness to an episcopal charter concerning the markets and fairs at Wells, it is also worth remarking that the charter which King John granted in 1201 to the men of Wells, confirming their status as burgesses of a free borough and granting them rights to fairs and a market, including a new eight-day fair around the feast of the translation of St Andrew (9 May), was in fact solicited by Hugh of Wells, Jocelin's brother, who offered three palfreys valued at 15 marks in return for the charter.[43] This strongly suggests that Jocelin and Hugh's family already occupied a prominent position within the commercial life of the city: a fact that we might guess from the regularity of the appearance of their father, Edward, in local property transactions. It suggests too that Wells's first royal charter and with it the later prosperity of the borough was owed in no small part to the role played by the two brothers, Jocelin and Hugh, as local men able to bend the ear of King John.

Recruitment as a royal clerk did not in itself ensure that a man would rise to the lofty eminence of a bishopric. Many clerks, some of them very powerful figures at court, remained no more than clerks, perhaps lucky enough to acquire an archdeaconry or a rich haul of prebends and benefices but denied the ultimate reward of a bishops' mitre. To obtain a bishopric, something other than mere competence was required: a quality of courtliness, of smoothness and civility that can already be observed as a prerequisite of episcopal office-holding at least as early as the time of the tenth-century Ottonian emperors of Germany and that is indicative, in twelfth-century England, of the rise of a new code of manners which historians have described, in its secular manifestations, as 'the rise of chivalry'.[44] Bishops were expected to be men of bearing. If they could not all be saints, they could at least be expected to possess a certain dignity and a command of courtly good manners from which the squat, the lame and the downright ugly were necessarily excluded. Just as today those who decide such matters as the appointment of public school headmasters or regius professors work in often mysterious ways, occasionally plucking a diamond from amongst the rough not always so lustrous or adamantine as at first sight it appears to be, so the selection of bishops in the twelfth and thirteenth centuries remains a difficult process to fathom and was not conducted without occasional

---

[42] Above n. 12.

[43] For the charter, which survives as an original still in the Town Hall at Wells and in which no mention is made of Hugh or Jocelin, see *Wells City Charters*, ed. D.O. Shilton and R. Holworthy, Somerset Record Society 46 (1932), 4 no. 4, issued with Simon of Wells as datary, at Chinon, 7 September 1201. For Hugh's fine, see *Rot. de Oblatis*, 179; *Pipe Roll* 4 John, 91.

[44] C.S. Jaeger, 'The Courtier Bishop in "Vitae" from the Tenth to the Twelfth Century', *Speculum*, 58 (1983), 291–325.

mishap. Undoubtedly, however, it favoured bishops capable of serving as advocates of their cathedral chapters with the court and the king. I shall return in due course to the precise role played by King John in Jocelin's election as bishop of Bath. Here I wish merely to point out that Jocelin already by 1205 must have possessed qualities of courtliness that rendered his election feasible. One of these qualities was undoubtedly a fondness for hunting, another a taste for conspicuous consumption. One of the first recorded actions performed by Jocelin on being made bishop was to obtain a royal licence for a park at Wells (in other words a hunting park), and the Bishop's Palace at Wells more than amply testifies to Jocelin's taste for luxury and the correct display of his episcopal dignity.[45] As Dean Robinson long ago pointed out, the licence for the park, obtained whilst the king himself was at Wells in September 1207, and coinciding with Jocelin's surrender to the king of the bishop's former house at Bath, almost certainly marks the point at which bishop and king agreed upon the transfer of Jocelin's see from Bath to Wells and hence the moment from which work on the Bishop's Palace at Wells can be said to have begun.[46] Jocelin clearly possessed an ability to rub shoulders with the royal court that lay beyond the capacity of many a thirteenth-century Dr Thorne or Mr Slope. One hint of why this may have been so was noted by Robinson with his observation that, before he became bishop, Jocelin may have fathered a son: a man named Nicholas of Wells who appears at court at much the same time as Jocelin, who addressed Jocelin in one charter as his 'father', and who Jocelin himself addressed as 'my son' in a context that might imply that the relationship in question was more than that between a mere father and son in God.[47] The evidence here is far from certain (and for a contrary view see the chapter by Jane Sayers in this volume). What Robinson apparently did not know was that Jocelin's elder brother, Hugh of Wells, is also reputed to have fathered children, the evidence here being far more convincing than that for Jocelin's supposed paternity. One of the accusations levelled against Hugh following his election as bishop of Lincoln in 1209 was that he was the married father of at least two, and possibly of more than two daughters.[48]

---

[45] *Rot. Chart.*, 169, followed on 26 November 1207 by licence to divert the king's highway around the park; *Rot. Litt. Pat.* 77. For an earlier gift of 100 deer to restock the bishop's park at Dogmersfield, made by the king on 30 December 1206, see *Rot. Litt. Claus.* i. 75b.

[46] Robinson, *Som. Hist. Essays*, 149, and cf. *Rot. Litt. Claus.* i. 93 for the surrender of the bishop's house to the king before 6 October 1207.

[47] Robinson, *Som. Hist. Essays*, 158–9, citing charters merely calendared in *Wells MSS* i. 18.

[48] Letters of Innocent III to Stephen Langton, 21 June 1209, printed from the papal register in J.-P. Migne, *Patrologia Latina cursus completus*, ccxvi (Paris, 1891), cols. 62–4, whence *The Letters of Pope Innocent III (1198–1216) Concerning England and Wales*, ed. C.R. and M.G. Cheney (Oxford, 1967), 140–1 no. 851, as cited by Cheney, *Innocent III and England*, 157. The pope refers here to rumours that Hugh 'de carnis incontinentia sit suspectus, cum filias habeat matrimonio copulatas', but orders the archbishop to proceed

To judge from his earliest appearance, in a property transaction involving his father Edward, Hugh of Wells may originally have been intended for a secular career as heir to his father's estate.[49] In Hugh's will of 1212, there are various substantial gifts assigned to women who might or might not have been his kin, his daughters or his former wife: most notably the 300 marks assigned to the daughters of William de Stratton 'so that they may marry' and the 150 marks assigned with the same intention to an unnamed 'girl' of Shaftesbury, presumably resident in the Benedictine nunnery there.[50] None of this should surprise us. Clerical celibacy, at least for the secular clergy as opposed to those in monastic orders, was still a relatively recent development by 1200 that had as yet to make much impression upon English cathedral chapters.[51] Jocelin was still only in deacon's orders at the time of his election as bishop, and deacons, unlike priests, were not as yet invariably or canonically vowed to celibacy.[52] Even as late as the 1230s, three decades after Jocelin's election, we can still find cathedral canons openly acknowledging their paternity of children. Simon of Walton, elected bishop of Norwich in 1257, had at least one son whom he treated as the legitimate heir to part of his estate.[53]

One final reflection before we pass on. We have seen that Jocelin was sprung from a local family, almost certainly kin to the family bearing the name Tortesmains or 'Twisted Hands'. The progenitor of this family – the Ralph Tortesmains of 1086 – may have been of Norman extraction. Nonetheless, it is worth remarking that by the time of Jocelin's birth in the 1160s or early 1170s, the Tortesmains had been established in Somerset for close on a hundred years. To this extent, and bearing in mind the distinctly English Christian name, Edward, carried by Jocelin's father, the family was as English by the late twelfth century as virtually any other landholding family could claim to be. Here for the first time we discover something about Jocelin that was truly out of the ordinary. As an Englishman, Jocelin stands apart from at least five of his six predecessors as post-conquest bishops of

---

with tolerance should Hugh have fathered no children recently, or should his marriage be dissoluble by penance: 'quodque incontinentia eius sit recens, maxime si parvulam prolem non habeat recentis incontinentie sue testem, cum premissam incontinentiam vel excusare coniugium vel penitentia potuerit abolere.'

49 Wells Cathedral Library charter 9, whence *Wells MSS* ii. 548 no. 9, and cf. 549 no. 13 for his appearance as Hugh 'son of Edward' witnessing, presumably as the elder sibling, ahead of Jocelin his brother.

50 *Acta of Hugh of Wells*, 4 no. 2.

51 For examples here, see J. Barrow, 'Hereford Bishops and Married Clergy, c.1130–1240', *Historical Research*, 60 (1987), 1–8.

52 See here the testimony of the dean and chapter of Wells: *Wells MSS* i. 63.

53 As cited, with further examples, by N. Vincent, 'New Light on Master Alexander of Swerford (d. 1246): The Career and Connections of an Oxfordshire Civil Servant', *Oxoniensia*, 61 (1996), 297–309.

Bath. All five of these men, even including Giso, bishop from before 1066, had been of foreign descent, be it Anglo-Norman, Flemish, Lotharingian or Burgundian as the case might be.[54] At the time of his election in 1206, Jocelin would have stood apart not only from his predecessors in the see of Bath, but from the majority of England's fourteen ruling bishops, most of whom were of Anglo-Norman or entirely French birth. England in 1206 was still intimately linked to the traditions of cross-Channel, Anglo-French rule that had predominated since 1066 and for whose continuation many, not least the Plantagenet kings of England, were to labour long after King John had abandoned his Norman lands in the face of French invasion, a momentous event that had occurred in 1204, only two years before Jocelin was elected bishop of Bath. Jocelin's election indeed marked the beginning of a trend towards the election of English bishops that, by the 1230s, was to see Frenchmen ousted from all but a handful of English sees.[55] To this extent, not only was Jocelin the first bishop of Bath in more than 150 years who could legitimately claim to be a native-born Englishman, but the first such English bishop to have been elected following 1204 and the collapse of Plantagenet rule over northern France.

Our mention here of King John and of his problems in France invites us to look, albeit briefly, at the king under whom Jocelin was raised to his new dignity. John's tomb at Worcester shows us a conventional image of a pious ruler, flanked by portraits of two bishops, perhaps saints Oswald and Wulfstan of Worcester, but representative nonetheless of the episcopate to which both Jocelin and his brother Hugh aspired.[56] Born in 1164, John was an almost exact contemporary of Jocelin, and had spent much of his early life, as we have seen, in precisely those same parts of the English West Country where Jocelin was to be most active. In history, however, whereas Jocelin is remembered as a good pastor and a keen 'reformer', John has been set down as the very worst of England's kings, 'a mean reproduction of all the vices and of the few pettinesses of his family ... savage, filthy, and blasphemous in his wrath', as William Stubbs, himself a bishop, was to declare in the most influential nineteenth-century account of John's reign.[57] To those raised on the poetry of A.A. Milne, John will be remembered as the king so unpopular that he had to send himself Christmas cards, for lack of any other friends

---

[54] For brief biographies, see Ramsey in *EEA* x. xxi–xxii. For a brief notice of the Flemish descent of Bishop Robert of Lewes (1136–66), see Ramsey in *ODNB* xxxiii. 569.

[55] For comparative figures here, see N. Vincent, *Peter des Roches, An Alien in English Politics, 1205–1238* (Cambridge, 1996), 34–5.

[56] Reproduced several times, for example as the dust-jacket to S.D. Church, ed., *King John: New Interpretations* (Woodbridge, 1999).

[57] 'Preface' to *Memoriale fratris Walteri de Coventria*, ed. W. Stubbs, 2 vols, Rolls Series (London, 1872–73), xiv–xv.

prepared to write to him.[58] Why did John acquire this sulphurous reputation, and why does it still so cling to his reign?

By losing his family's ancestral estates in Normandy in 1204, and by thus bringing an end to nearly 150 years of the Anglo-Norman 'Empire', John certainly did himself no favours either with his Anglo-Norman contemporaries or with later historians. The collapse of Plantagenet rule in northern France was as sudden as it was shocking and was to lead to the king's frantic attempts to raise money to mount an unsuccessful bid for reconquest, which in turn helped set England on the road to baronial rebellion and the negotiations that were to lead to Runnymede and the issue of Magna Carta. The loss of Normandy, however, and the events of the later part of John's reign were merely the most obvious outcomes of personal and political failings for which John had become notorious from his very earliest years. Normandy was lost in the first place because, in 1201, by marrying a southern French heiress, Isabella of Angoulême, previously betrothed to the Poitevin baron Hugh de Lusignan, John had forfeited the support of the Lusignans and of many of the greater men of Anjou and Aquitaine. When the Lusignans rebelled and threw in their lot with the king's eighteen-year-old nephew, Arthur of Brittany, John captured Arthur and had him imprisoned: an imprisonment from which he was never to emerge and during which he was almost certainly done to death, probably at John's direct command. In turn, the disappearance of Arthur allowed the Lusignans and others to appeal directly to the king of France against the tyranny of John, leading inexorably to the Capetian invasion of Normandy mounted in 1203.[59] With these crimes already stacked in the account against him, John did little thereafter to redeem his reputation. John's court was an insalubrious and dangerous place, rife with rumours of the king's violence up to and including the murder of his own nephew; with stories of his adulteries, including the seduction of the wife of his own half-brother, the earl of Salisbury; with the threat that hostages might suddenly vanish in the king's keeping and that he would stop at nothing to extort money or obedience from his increasingly hostile barons.

It was into this atmosphere that Jocelin of Wells was propelled through his promotion to office within the royal chancery: an atmosphere which can be best recaptured from the very chancery records over which Jocelin for a period presided. Of the various transactions and royal letters to which Hugh and Jocelin stand witness, there are none that appear to speak directly of

[58] A.A. Milne, *Now We Are Six* (London, 1927): 'King John was not a good man – He had his little ways. And sometimes no one spoke to him for days and days and days.'

[59] There are several standard biographies of the king, amongst which that by W.L. Warren, *King John* (London, 1961), remains the most balanced and concise. For recent reassessments, see Church, ed., *King John*.

the seamier side of John's court. Elsewhere, however, amongst the records of John's chancery and exchequer, we find ample evidence both of the king's sense of humour and of the suspicions and violence that characterised his court. The roll of fines made with the king, for example, occasionally comes to resemble a clubland wagers book, as in the notorious fine by which the wife of Hugh de Neville, the king's chief forester, offered 200 chickens 'so that she may lie one night with her lord'.[60] On other occasions, the chancery rolls preserve coded correspondence or references to the king's taste for passwords and secret instructions, none more remarkable than a letter of 1202, following the capture of Arthur and his Lusignan allies, in which instructions were issued for Geoffrey de Lusignan, then held in fetters, to speak with one of the king's messengers, revealing *inter alia* that the king himself had forgotten the secret passwords without which he had forbidden access to the prisoners. Should the interview pass off successfully, Geoffrey was to be taken out of his fetters and held instead 'in the place where the restraining rings are'.[61] Writing of the bishops in office after 1208, an anonymous satirist records nothing of Jocelin's part in the violence or scandal of the court. He does, however, refer to Jocelin's perceived role as a loyal instrument of John's financial administration:

> If the bishop of Bath is ever asked how many marks of the king's money have arrived at the exchequer, he will freely tell you 'A thousand, a hundred and so forth, I collect for the king's purse'. Learned in this decalogue, he is nonetheless blind to canon law.[62]

In many ways King John conformed to the very worst expectations of a church already keen to break free from the influence of secular rulers, be it in England or anywhere else in Europe. By those who in the 1180s and 1190s fashioned clerical opinion, kings were characterised as violent, unlettered modern successors to Saul, Belshazzar and the tyrants of Old Testament history. It was precisely this view of kingship that Stephen Langton had taught at Paris, before his election as archbishop of Canterbury in 1207; a view in which kings were instituted by God not for the protection and glory of their people but in punishment for the people's sins. As God himself is said to remark in the book of Hosea (13:11), 'I will give thee a king in my wrath': a sentence which Langton and his fellow Parisian masters were

---

[60] *Rot. de Oblatis*, 275.

[61] *Rot. Litt. Pat.* 17b: 'ponatur extra boias et ponatur in partibus boiorum annulorum'. For examples of coded letters, see N. Vincent, 'Isabella of Angoulême: John's Jezebel', in *King John*, ed. Church, 195–7.

[62] *The Political Songs of England, from the Reign of King John to that of Edward II*, ed. T. Wright, Camden Society 6 (London, 1839), 10: 'Si praesuli Bathoniae fiat quandoque quaestio, quot marcae bursae regiae accedant in scaccario, respondet voce libera, "Mille, centum, et caetera, ad bursam regis colligo". Doctus in hoc decalogo, caecus in forma canonis.'

only too ready to quote.[63] Kings, and not least the Plantagenet kings of England, were charged with a role in the supervision of the church and in both authorising the election of bishops to vacant sees and in granting (or, if necessary, witholding) assent to candidates so elected. Even despite the Becket conflict of the 1160s which, in theory, had guaranteed the liberties of the English church, above all the liberty to exercise free elections, John's control over the election of bishops after 1200 was more or less unchanged from that which his father, King Henry II, had exercised in the 1150s and 1160s. The pope might claim the right as universal ordinary to adjudicate in all disputed elections bolstered by a newly emerging body of canon law in which due process was defined in ever greater detail. In practice, however, kings continued to exercise a control over episcopal elections in England in a way that would have been envied by secular rulers elsewhere in thirteenth-century Europe, not least by the Capetian kings of France.[64]

Thus, when the bishop of Bath, Savaric fitzGeldewin, died in 1205, King John was necessarily poised to play a role in the election of his successor. The ensuing events were long ago teased out by Dean Robinson. Here I need merely sketch them in the broadest of outlines. The cathedral church of Somerset had been established, before 1066, in the city of Wells, but was moved by the first of its post-Conquest bishops, John of Tours (1088–1122), from Wells to the Benedictine abbey of Bath, the election of future bishops being vested in the monks of Bath. This situation had gravely reduced the fortunes and dignity of the canons of Wells, but had to some extent been remedied, from the 1130s onwards, by Bishop Robert of Lewes (1136–66), who (probably in 1136) granted Wells a constitution equivalent to those of the other English cathedral chapters.[65] Bishop Robert may also have restored to the canons of Wells some role in the election of bishops, henceforth to be conducted in concert with the monks of Bath, although our knowledge of these reforms is clouded by the suspicion that the historical record has been tampered with and that various of the twelfth-century sources for Wells are

---

63 See here the definitive study by P. Buc, *L'Ambiguité du livre: prince, pouvoir, et peuple dans les commentaires de la Bible au Moyen Age* (Paris, 1994), citing the Hosea commentary of Langton at 252–4, with a useful summary for those unable to read French, in P. Buc, '"Princeps gentium dominantur eorum": Princely Power Between Legitimacy and Illegitimacy in Twelfth-Century Exegesis', in *Cultures of Power: Lordship, Status, and Process in Twelfth-Century Europe*, ed. T.N. Bisson (Philadelphia, 1995), 310–28.

64 For episcopal elections from 1170 to 1220, the crucial modern authority remains Cheney, *Innocent III and England*, and *idem, From Becket to Langton: English Church Government 1170–1213* (Manchester, 1956), esp. ch. 1.

65 For details here, see introduction to *Fasti 1066–1300*, vii, and F. Ramsey, 'Robert of Lewes, Bishop of Bath, 1136–1166: A Cluniac in his Diocese', in *Belief and Culture in the Middle Ages: Studies Presented to Henry Mayr-Harting*, ed. R. Gameson and H. Leyser (Oxford, 2001), 251–63, to a large extent rehabilitating the authenticity of Bishop Robert's constitutions for Wells (*EEA* x. 34–6 no. 46), called into question by Robinson.

either forged or heavily reworked.[66] Whatever the constitutional confusion between Bath and Wells, the situation was even further complicated in the 1190s by Bishop Savaric, who in 1193 obtained a distinctly controversial augmentation of his privileges from King Richard I. In reward for his assistance in negotiating King Richard's release from captivity in Germany, and in exchange for an offer by Savaric to make over the city of Bath to the king's control, Savaric was promised future rule over the rich abbey of Glastonbury, with a titular position as abbot and the right to style himself henceforth as 'bishop of Bath and Glastonbury'. These arrangements were highly controversial and were vigorously resisted by the Glastonbury monks. The bishop's grant of Bath to the king reeked of simony – the crime of offering or paying money in return for spiritual office. Although confirmed by the aged Pope Celestine III, the arrangement was, as early as 1198, the subject of an attempted repudiation by the king.[67] Nonetheless, and in splendid illustration of the way in which the tightening of canon law procedures now intruded upon legal process, between the ambition of litigants and their prospect of achieving speedy resolution to their disputes, it was to take a further twenty years before the controversy over the settlement of 1193 could be resolved. Even by the time of Savaric's death in Italy on 8 August 1205, Pope Innocent III and his papally delegated agents in England had gone only part way towards settling the substantive issues at stake. In theory, a division had been agreed, whereby Savaric would retain a portion of the lands and resources of Glastonbury and the monks would secure the rest.[68] Neither party, however, was likely to accept this as a permanent settlement.

Immediately upon Savaric's death, the monks of Glastonbury appealed once again to be released from their subjection to the bishops of Bath, an appeal in which they were supported by King John.[69] The appeal had necessarily to be heard before the pope, in part because the archbishopric of Canterbury stood vacant following the death of Archbishop Hubert Walter in July 1205, in part because the popes had long ago won recognition for their claim to be acknowledged as sole authority in disputes touching upon the alteration or transfer of episcopal sees. However, applying a logic that was more legalistic than commonsensical, in March 1206, and in response

---

66 Doubts most clearly articulated by Armitage Robinson: Robinson, *Som. Hist. Essays*, 71–2 commenting on the apparent absence of the monks of Bath from the historical record of the election of Bishop Reginald (1173–74). Letters of King Henry II to Pope Alexander III, supporting this election, fail to specify the identity of the electors: *Materials for the History of Thomas Becket*, ed. J.C. Robertson, 7 vols, Rolls Series (London, 1875–85), vii. 553–4 no. 790.
67 Cheney, *Innocent III and England*, 220–1, relying here upon the full, but far from unbiased, testimony of the Glastonbury chronicler Adam of Domerham.
68 Cheney, *Innocent III and England*, 221–3.
69 *Domerham*, ii. 425–36; *Glast. Chart.* i. 80–6 nos 128–37 (including letters in Glastonbury's support from the chapter of Wells); Cheney, *Innocent III and England*, 223.

to the previous year's complaints, Innocent III decreed an important ruling, henceforth to enter canon law as a definitive precedent for future action. Although entirely sympathetic to the claims of the Glastonbury monks, Innocent enunciated the principle 'ne vacante sede aliquid innovetur': in essence, that there could be no change in status during the vacancy of a see, since any such change might prejudice the right of bishops as yet to be elected.[70] It is intriguing to consider the thought processes at work here. It would, for example, be very difficult to imagine a ruling in modern English law that forbade, say, parents or property holders from making free provision of their property on the grounds that any such disposition might prejudice the rights of future children, yet to be born. Innocent's ruling of 1205 reveals the extent to which, under canon law, the office of bishop and indeed the church itself had come to be regarded as essentially timeless, undying institutions, embedded in an eschatological rather than a purely time-bound reading of history.

By the time that the pope's ruling reached England, Jocelin of Wells himself had almost certainly already been elected as Savaric's successor to the see of Bath by a joint electoral college consisting of representatives of the chapters of Bath and Wells, his election occurring at some time before 4 April 1206 (Plate 2).[71] The actual date of the election remains unknown, but there is no reference to Jocelin with title as bishop-elect in January 1206 when he was presented by the king to the church of Winsham: a presentation that in itself suggests that Jocelin was still at this time acquiring benefices in plurality, with no clear expectation that he would soon be called upon to relinquish them in favour of a higher dignity.[72] Jocelin, still referred to without title on 9 March, first appears as bishop-elect on 4 April 1206, as witness to a royal charter issued at Romney in Kent, although his election had perhaps occurred some days or weeks earlier.[73] On 23 April the

---

[70] Glast. Chart. i. 86–7 no. 138, whence Letters of Innocent III, ed. Cheney and Cheney, no. 695, and cf. Cheney, Innocent III and England, 223 n. 169 for the later citation of this ruling in the Decretals, most notably in the Liber Extra 3.9.1.

[71] Robinson, Som. Hist. Essays, 145–6. The crucial evidences here, including a proxy from the convent of Bath to their prior and other monks to proceed to an election, and undated testimony addressed to the pope from Prior Robert and the monks of Bath, and from Dean Alexander and the chapter of Wells testifying to Jocelin's canonical election, are calendared in Wells MSS i. 62–3. Robinson (Som. Hist. Essays, 146) refers to the proctors for the election following the king to Nottingham (28 September–2 October 1205), Windsor (1–4 November 1206), to Dorset and Wiltshire in January 1206 and again to Lexington in early February. There is evidence for all of these visits in Rot. Litt. Claus. i. 56, 63b, save for the visit to Lexington, where I have been unable to trace Robinson's source.

[72] Rot. Litt. Pat. 57b.

[73] Rot. Chart., 163b–164b; Rot. Litt. Pat. 60. Robinson (Som. Hist. Essays, 146) errs in suggesting that the pope had already heard of Jocelin's election by 25 March 1206. In fact the papal letters of this date (Letters of Innocent III, ed. Cheney and Cheney, no.

king wrote to the papal legate asking that the election be confirmed,[74] and on 3 May to the tenants of the bishopric, ordering them to obey Jocelin as elect, and to his brother Hugh, who in effect now received the surrender of the bishopric's temporalities.[75] We have no certain evidence here, but it seems highly probable that it was King John, or at least Jocelin's perceived closeness to the king, that proved the most crucial factor in determining the chapter's decision. As we have already seen, cathedral chapters across England were anxious to obtain the election of bishops who could command the confidence of the king and who could hence act as competent advocates for their cathedrals and dioceses in royal councils. In 1205, either Jocelin or his elder brother Hugh might have been considered a suitable candidate for the bishopric. Hugh, indeed, was not only the older of the two brothers, but as archdeacon of Wells and as royal custodian of the vacant see might have seemed the more eligible candidate.[76] That he was passed over in favour of his younger brother may reflect the fact that the temporalities of the see of Wells were not regarded as particularly rich, being valued at something approaching £500 a year, as opposed to the £1,500 or so that Hugh was subsequently to obtain on his election as bishop of Lincoln.[77] Lincoln itself did not fall vacant until the death of Bishop William of Blois on 10 May 1206, a few weeks after Jocelin had been elected to Bath. It may be, however, that Bishop William's death was already imminently anticipated and that Hugh and Jocelin, both of them already canons of Lincoln with experience in the custody of the bishopric during the previous vacancy before 1203, agreed that Jocelin should seek election to Bath and that Hugh be allowed to take his chances in the impending election at Lincoln.[78] It may also be that Hugh was held back at Bath by the matrimonial and other complications that were later to be raised in objection against his promotion at Lincoln.[79]

Be that as it may, in the aftermath of Jocelin's election, an entire dossier was prepared on Jocelin's behalf, in which the monks of Bath, the canons

697) merely instruct the papal legate on what to do should the next bishop, as yet unappointed, agree to a dissolution of the union between Bath and Glastonbury.
[74] *Wells MSS* i. 63 no. 205.
[75] *Rot. Litt. Pat.* 63b.
[76] For Hugh acting together with William of Wrotham, close royal confidant and archdeacon of Taunton, as custodian of the vacant see from at least September 1205, see *Rot. Litt. Claus.* i. 49; *Rot. Litt. Pat.* 57b. The reference to Archbishop Hubert Walter as one-time keeper of the vacancy recorded in *Rot. Litt. Claus.* i. 53, cannot refer to the vacancy of 1205 since Hubert Walter predeceased Bishop Savaric.
[77] For very approximate but nonetheless crucial comparative figures here, see the vacancy accounts digested by M. Howell, *Regalian Right in Medieval England* (London, 1962), 212–13, 224.
[78] See here *Fasti 1066–1300* iii. 3, 77, 129, for Hugh and Jocelin's prebends at Lincoln, both acquired c.1203.
[79] Above n. 48.

of Wells, and his fellow English and Welsh bishops were encouraged to endorse both the canonical nature of the election and Jocelin's own personal suitability for episcopal office: in this instance, declaring that Jocelin was locally known, literate and freely elected.[80] This dossier was doubly necessary because the archbishopric of Canterbury remained vacant, with as yet no clear decision as to where authority lay in the election of a new archbishop: with the monks of Canterbury as diocesan chapter, with the suffragan bishops of Canterbury acting as an electoral college competent to determine the future of their province, or with the pope as universal ordinary?[81] The 1206 dossier over the see of Bath was addressed by the electors and bishops both to Pope Innocent III and to the pope's legate, John of Ferentino, who had arrived in England earlier that year. It is clear that the English and Welsh bishops added their endorsements in the clear expectation that this might help them to steal an advantage over the monks of Canterbury, by demonstrating their capacity for collective action and their role as a duly constituted body, capable of acting in the interests of their metropolitan province *sede vacante*.[82] Almost certainly the bishops were encouraged in this by King John, who clearly believed that the suffragan bishops rather than the monks of Canterbury were best suited to elect his own favoured candidate as archbishop. To this extent, the events at Bath and Wells have to be set within a wider context in which for a brief period, the election of Bishop Jocelin came to symbolise the authority of the king and of Jocelin's fellow bishops in pursuing their claim to a role in the far more significant and far more hotly contested Canterbury election dispute. The dossier over Jocelin's election demonstrates two further significant features of contemporary church politics: the emergence of a new and stricter application of legal principles governed by written precedent and written law, in this case canon law; and the consequent need to match this legal rigour to the production of ever more voluminous and carefully recorded legal testimony in writing. The thirteenth century was to become the century not only of law but of a vast expansion in both writing and the preservation of written records.[83]

To this extent, the dossier over Bath and Wells illustrates some of the very broadest themes in English and European history. In practice, and in the specific circumstances of 1206, it may have played only the most minor

---

[80] Calendared in *Wells MSS* i. 62–5, with various of the episcopal letters published in full, most recently in *EEA* xxvi. 82–5 nos 84–7.

[81] For the disputed right to election at Canterbury, see Cheney, *Innocent III and England*, 147–52.

[82] For the legation of John see C.R. Cheney, 'The Papal Legate and the English Monasteries in 1206', *English Historical Review*, 46 (1931), 443–52; and *idem*, 'Cardinal John of Ferentino, Papal Legate in England in 1206', *English Historical Review*, 76 (1961), 654–60.

[83] See in general here M.T. Clanchy, *From Memory to Written Record*, 2nd edn (Oxford 1993).

part in Jocelin's election. Indeed, it is doubtful whether the bishops' letters had even reached the pope by the time that Jocelin himself was confirmed and consecrated by the bishop of London and other English bishops acting under the authority of the papal legate, at Reading on Trinity Sunday, 28 May 1206 (Plates 3 and 4).[84] Already on 3 May, and clearly in anticipation that the pope was about to rule in favour of a dissolution of the union between Bath and Glastonbury, the king had restored Jocelin, and Hugh of Wells as his deputy, to possession of the city of Bath, surrendered by Bishop Savaric to Richard I in 1193.[85] Having been confirmed as bishop, however, Jocelin himself was in no hurry to abandon his claims over Glastonbury. The episcopal seal which he commissioned following his consecration was struck with his title as bishop of both Bath and Glastonbury, and it was under this joint title that the majority of his letters and charters were henceforth issued.[86] After 1206, and having been restored to possession of the city of Bath, Jocelin was to retain possession of the revenues of both Bath and Glastonbury for a further thirteen years. No resolution of the dispute was to be reached until 1219, and even thereafter, although Glastonbury was restored to its independent status, Jocelin made no attempt to have a new seal struck. Although, as we have seen, within a few months of his election he had already begun to transfer his own residence and his own centre of activities from Bath to Wells, even after 1219 it was as bishop of Bath that he continued to be styled for the remainder of his lifetime.[87]

Since Jocelin's subsequent career is dealt with elsewhere in this volume, we are now approaching the end of our much more limited survey. There are, nonetheless, two further points that I wish to make before closing. The first is that, however harmonious or canonically scrupulous the election of Jocelin might appear in light of the great dossier compiled in his

---

[84] Jocelin's consecration is recorded in his profession, in which he is styled very definitely bishop 'of Bath' rather than 'of Bath and Glastonbury', endorsed with the names of the eleven English and Welsh bishops in attendance (*Canterbury Professions*, ed. M. Richter, Canterbury and York Society 67 (Torquay, 1973), 62–3 no. 146); in letters from the papal legate to the prior and convent of Canterbury assuring them that the consecration at St Mary's chapel, Reading, would not prejudice the future right of Canterbury to serve as the normal place of consecrations (Canterbury Cathedral Library Chartae Antiquae C133, whence *Eighth Report of the Royal Commission on Historical Manuscripts Commission* (London, 1881), appendix 320b), and in letters of William, bishop of London, and of Jocelin himself safeguarding the rights of the Canterbury monks in similar terms to the safeguard issued by the legate (Canterbury Cathedral Archives Chartae Antiquae C107; C126 no. 3, whence EEA xxvi. 102 no. 106).

[85] *Rot. Litt. Pat.* i. 63b.

[86] For the seal (already attached to Jocelin's letters describing his consecration, *c*.May/June 1206, Canterbury Cathedral Archives Chartae Antiquae C107), see P. Binski, *Becket's Crown: Art and Imagination in Gothic England 1170–1300* (New Haven, 2004), 113; Plate 4.

[87] Cheney, *Innocent III and England*, 224–5, and the essay by Jane Sayers below.

favour in 1206, there were aspects to Jocelin's election, not all of them noticed by either Cheney or Robinson, that suggest that canonical process in this instance was tailored to ends entirely engineered by King John. Not only was the dossier of letters summoned on Jocelin's behalf intended to boost the authority of the suffragan bishops and hence of the chances of the king's candidate at Canterbury, but in the aftermath of his election Jocelin demonstrated complete loyalty to the king. In particular, in the year to Michaelmas 1207, he entered into a series of financial transactions with the Crown that cast a distinctly murky light upon the circumstances of his election. All told, in 1207 he offered 1,000 marks at the king's exchequer, divided apparently into two distinct fines. The first of these to be recorded, though not necessarily the first offered, was for 700 marks, described as an offer 'for the thirteenth of his knights and for his gift [*donum*] and to have the liberties which the king granted by his charter to the bishop and his successors'.[88] The reference here to the tax of a thirteenth relates to an aid which the king had attempted to levy from laity and clergy after January 1207, which the clergy had refused but which led to a series of individual proffers from churches, including 1,000 marks from the prior and monks of Canterbury and as much as 600 marks from the abbot of Abingdon.[89] Jocelin's offer of 700 marks was nonetheless much higher than those made by most of his fellow bishops, save for the immensely wealthy bishop of Durham who offered £1,000. Moreover, 550 marks of Jocelin's fine was paid in full, either into the king's chamber or at his exchequer by Michaelmas 1208.[90] The second fine was for 300 marks and three palfreys 'for his liberties and the thirteenth', apparently distinct from the 700 mark fine, and in this instance the entire sum was pardoned by the king, apparently by March 1207, before any payment could be extracted.[91] The precise significance of these arrangements is difficult to fathom, but taken in tandem with the fact that Hugh of Wells and William of Wrotham, although serving as royal keepers of the vacant see during the eight months from the time of the death of Bishop Savaric until May 1206, seem never to have rendered accounts for the vacancy at the royal exchequer, suggests that an original offer of 300 marks made in lieu of the thirteenth was later raised by 400

---

88 *Rot. de Oblatis*, 413.
89 S.K. Mitchell, *Studies in Taxation under John and Henry III* (New Haven, 1914), 84–92; D.M. Stenton, introduction to *Pipe Roll 9 John*, xvii–xxi.
90 For the bishop of Durham's fine, paid in full, see *Pipe Roll 9 John*, xix, 70. For Jocelin's payments, see *ibid.*, 63; *Pipe Roll 10 John*, 109. The residue of the fine continued to be summoned after Jocelin's return from exile in 1213, and was only pardoned him in 1214, as part of the wider settlement of Jocelin's claims from the time of his exile: *Pipe Roll 16 John*, 107.
91 *Pipe Roll 9 John*, 63, and for the exemption of the bishop's land from tax assessment, see *Rot. Litt. Claus.* i. 79.

marks to 700 marks, to take into account both the tax imposed in 1207 and the profits of the vacancy in 1205–6, which were perhaps diverted to Jocelin rather than being accounted in detail at the exchequer. A similar diversion of vacancy receipts to an incoming bishop had already been made by King John in the case of Peter des Roches, elected bishop of Winchester in 1205, and the equality of treatment here afforded the courtiers Peter and Jocelin should remind us of how, at this stage in his career, Jocelin retained the king's friendship and confidence.[92] Whilst hardly proof of a simoniac relation between bishop and Crown in which Jocelin could be said to have 'bought' his bishopric, the fine of 700 marks nonetheless reflects a bishop working hand in glove with royal administration, favoured in respect to the profits from the vacancy and at the same time prepared to pay handsomely to retain both the vacancy receipts and his position in the king's favour. As the poem criticising Jocelin for his role at the royal exchequer has already suggested, Jocelin made no attempt to break with King John even after the dispute over the Canterbury election led to John's condemnation by the pope and the sentence of Interdict imposed upon England in 1208. Rather, the breach, when it came, was inspired by far more personal and self-interested considerations. In the spring of 1209, Jocelin's brother Hugh obtained election to the vacant see of Lincoln. Realising that this election would almost certainly be quashed by the pope if he remained in the service of King John, Hugh sought the king's licence to cross overseas, claiming that he wished to obtain consecration at the hands of the archbishop of Rouen, but in fact to seek out the exiled Archbishop Langton.[93] By doing so, and despite the perhaps justified objections that had been raised to his earlier marriage and his service at John's court, Hugh earned the gratitude of the pope and with it the pope's willingness to turn a blind eye to his alleged disqualifications from episcopal office. He was duly consecrated as bishop of Lincoln by the exiled Archbishop Langton at Melun, south-east of Paris, on 20 December 1209.[94] With Hugh, or crossing shortly after him, Jocelin of Bath also sought exile overseas.

Jocelin was destined to remain in exile for a further four years. When he did return, in 1213, it was as a hero rather than a villain in the eyes of the church, with his previous connection to royal government and to King John washed clean in the purifying springs of exile. But this transformation was dearly purchased and should not blind us to the fact that during his

92 For the Winchester vacancy receipts, see Vincent, *Peter des Roches*, 53.
93 Roger of Wendover, *Chronica sive Flores Historiarum*, ed. H.O. Coxe, 5 vols (London, 1841–44), iii. 231.
94 *Fasti 1066–1300*, iii. 3; Cheney, *Innocent III and England*, 157–8; *Canterbury Professions*, 62 no. 147a, and for the leniency urged by Pope Innocent in commissioning an investigation into Hugh's marriage and alleged fathering of children, see above n. 48; Migne, *Patrologia Latina*, ccxvi. cols. 62–4, 101.

earliest years as bishop, and despite all his later commitment to reform and to a more balanced approach to the relations between church and state, Jocelin had begun his episcopal career very much as a creature of the king. The very process of his election, described above, should remind us that, in the thirteenth century, not every reforming bishop began as an outright opponent of royal authority, and not every royalist bishop was destined to be remembered as a recidivist dinosaur obstructing the march of progress. As Christopher Cheney put it, writing of the bishops of England around 1200, 'no clear-cut division produced two well-organized parties of churchmen: still less could one distinguish between a "good" group of reformers and a "bad" group of unregenerate maintainers of abuse'.[95] Had Jocelin died in 1209, or even 1219, it is questionable whether the memory preserved of him would be quite so tinged with admiration for his ability to walk the tight-rope that joined *regnum* and *sacerdotium*. As it is, and as a local chronicler was to record in writing of Jocelin's death in 1242, amongst the medieval bishops of his diocese he was remembered as one 'who had no predecessor like him and who to this day has been matched by no successor'.[96]

---

[95] Cheney, *From Becket to Langton*, 12.
[96] As stated in the 'Historia Maior' of Wells (c.1408): *Collectanea* I 65: 'qui sibi similem anteriorem non habuit, nec hucusque visus est habere sequentem.'

2

Jocelin of Wells and the Role of a Bishop in the Thirteenth Century

JANE SAYERS

Jocelin of Wells died at Wells on 19 November 1242, 'full of days', as the chronicler Matthew Paris says.[1] A Wells man, probably born in the town or its vicinity, he had seen the creation of a cathedral worthy of a bishop, and had dedicated it to St Andrew in 1239.[2] His marble tomb, surmounted by a brass, was placed in the middle of the quire, flanked by tomb effigies of earlier bishops whose remains had been translated there from Bath a decade or so before Jocelin's election.[3] The tomb, constructed before his death, has not survived, but his elegant nave and incomparable west front stand as his present monuments. He had made Wells the cathedral church of Somerset in all but name, and had prepared the way for his successor to take the title bishop of Bath and Wells. The centre of the see had been restored to Wells, as it had been before the Norman Conquest, and the titles of bishop of Bath, and of bishop of Bath and Glastonbury, were replaced by bishop of Bath and Wells in 1245, three years after his death. Jocelin was the first bishop to be buried at Wells since Bishop Giso, whose successor John of Tours had removed the see to Bath c.1090. In death the bishop of Bath had returned to Wells, where his spirit had been from his cradle, and where he had been brought up *a primo lacte*,'in the bosom' of the church of Wells.[4]

But we concentrate here on 1206 and Jocelin's election to the see of Bath, not his death or his birth, so to that event we must now turn. How had Jocelin come to be bishop of Bath? The short answer is he was elected

---

[1]   *Chronica Majora*, ed. H.R. Luard, 7 vols, Rolls Series 57 (London, 1872–83), iv. 233. I am most grateful to David Smith, who is preparing the English Episcopal Acta volume covering Jocelin's episcopate, for the loan of copies of some of Jocelin's charters.

[2]   *Wells MSS* i. 59, 358 and 359.

[3]   *Collectanea I* 64; P. Binski, *Becket's Crown* (New Haven, 2004), 106. The tomb is described by Leland, who saw it in the sixteenth century, in *Leland's Itinerary in England and Wales*, ed. L. Toulmin Smith, i (1964), 293; and for the brass, see A. Way, 'Sepulchral Brasses', *Archaeological Journal* 1 (1844), 119.

[4]   *Wells MSS* i. 63, no. ccvii.

unanimously by both chapters, if not with the direct intervention of the king, certainly with his approval.

And what were the qualifications for a bishopric at this time?

The advertisement, had there been one, might have read as follows:

Bishopric vacant
The legal requirements – the successful candidate must be:
at least thirty years old
of legitimate birth
of commendable life and learning
(Canon 3 of the Third Lateran Council of 1179)

He will be able to dispose of his own benefices freely. He will be in charge of a community; of which the dean and archdeacons must be at least twenty-five years old and commendable in knowledge and behaviour, and in priest's orders.

The candidate we are seeking is likely to have a background in the royal service with experience of administration at the highest level. He should have a knowledge of accountancy and be able to produce evidence of loyalty to king and country. He will have a generous allowance of lands and perks.

In matters spiritual, he will be responsible to the archbishop of the province, and thence to the pope or his legate. His appointment will need to be confirmed by the pope. He will be expected to attend councils of the church and enforce their decrees, to obey mandates from the pope, hear cases as required, and arrange for the collection of taxes.

He will run a medium-sized diocese; he will be expected to hold synods; carry out ordinations of priests, deacons and acolytes; and bless heads of religious houses; visit the same; collate to benefices; institute clergy; hold courts; and correct clergy and laity where necessary.

Finally, he will be expected to promote the interests of the diocese in every way, to further the local cults, to build and to enhance the already existing buildings.

The personal pronoun 'he' is not used here to cover both sexes.

Jocelin's *curriculum vitae* up to 1206 would have read as follows:

Son of Edward of Wells, small landowner.
Qualifications: clerk of Bath and canon of Wells.[5]
In service of king: clerk in the royal chancery under Archbishop Hubert Walter; acting as vice-chancellor.
Prebendary of Lincoln; in possession of livings of Dogmersfield, Lugwardine, Marden and Winscombe.[6]
Previous administrative experience: Justice in the King's Court, hearing fines

[5] *Wells MSS* i. 63 no. ccix.
[6] *Bath Charts.* ii. 64–6; *Rot. Chart.*, i. pt 1, 119b, 142a, 161.

at Westminster and elsewhere; financial assessor and collector of taxes with experience in the king's chamber and exchequer; custodian of the vacant bishopric of Lincoln.[7]

Jocelin fitted the three requirements of the canon law at this time admirably.[8] Firstly, he was probably between 35 and 40 at the time of his election in 1206. He was a canon of Wells by 1199, possibly as early as 1195,[9] when he could have been expected to be about twenty-five,[10] suggesting that he was born c.1165–70, in which case he would have been twenty-five to thirty when he became a canon and about thirty-five to forty when he was elected bishop, dying perhaps in his late seventies.

Secondly, he was clearly of legitimate birth as no attempt was made to acquire a dispensation from the pope, nor would the legate have approved the election if his legitimacy was in question. Illegitimacy among the ranks of the prospective episcopacy was far from rare; Mauger, bishop of Worcester, King Richard I's physician, for example, was dispensed for illegitimacy by Innocent III, and likewise Richard Poore, dean of Salisbury, the son of a bishop, and later a close colleague of Jocelin in the 1220s.[11] Often the dispensations were for royal servants who had their eye on a bishopric, as was the case with Ralph Neville, the king's vice-chancellor, who was to become bishop of Chichester in 1222.[12]

Thirdly, there was the requirement that the candidate should be of commendable life and learning. Jocelin's life, so far as we know, was without stain. The suggestion that he had a son, Nicholas, cannot be supported: the argument depends on the address of Nicholas's charter, 'venerabili patri meo J. dei gracia Bathonie episcopo', which clearly does not mean *his* father and the opening phrase of Jocelin's charter, 'Cum dilectus filius Nicholaus de Welles', a normal phrase of reference, and not meaning *his* son.[13] On the second point – learning: in all the documents connected with his election, Jocelin is referred to as a master, and as a man who was 'industrious, lettered,

7 *Fines sive Pedes Finium*, ed. Joseph Hunter, 2 vols (1835–44), i. liii–iv, 58; ii. 7–8, 25–6, 63–4, 91–2; F. West, *The Justiciarship in England 1066–1232* (Cambridge, 1966), 248–9; *Rotuli de Liberate ac de Misis et Praestitis*, ed. T.D. Hardy (London, 1844), 97.
8 Canon 3 of the 3rd Lateran Council, in *Conciliorum Oecumenicorum Decreta*, ed. Centro di Documentazione (Basle, 1962), 188–9.
9 *Fasti 1066–1300* vii. 87.
10 Edwards, *Eng. Secular Cathedrals*, 34, says twenty-two was acceptable for a subdeacon.
11 *The Letters of Pope Innocent III*, ed. C.R. and M.G. Cheney (Oxford, 1967), nos 189, 674; CPL i. 24.
12 CPL i. 70; Shirley, *Royal Letters* i. 534.
13 Robinson, *Som. Hist. Essays*, 158–9, citing *Wells MSS* i. 18 no. xlii. A charge against Jocelin's brother, Hugh of Wells, on his election to the see of Lincoln, was that he was incontinent and had daughters; it was ill-founded. See David Smith, *ODNB* lviii. 62.

and honest'.[14] It is only by chance that we know that his fellow bishop and royal servant, Richard Poore of Chichester (subsequently of Salisbury and Durham), was a Paris master, and that he had pursued his studies there under the future archbishop of Canterbury, Stephen Langton. Could Jocelin have spent time studying at Paris or at Oxford?[15] It is, indeed, possible. If Jocelin was more scholarly than has hitherto been recognised however, we have no written evidence for this; no surviving sermons, biblical commentaries, sacramental works or instructions for clergy, such as have been attributed to Richard Poore.[16] The Paris schools did not only produce scholars; as in all universities, then and now, there were those students whose bent was of a more practical nature, who entered the administrations of popes, emperors, kings and bishops. Jocelin might well have fitted into that kind of group of able and business-like men who felt no need to compose or write treatises.

In 1206, when Jocelin was elected bishop, he was primarily a royal servant and as such he had doubtless expected advancement within the church. The king's administrators were clerks, his chancellors often bishops, similarly his treasurers and justices. Together with his brother, Hugh (who was to become bishop of Lincoln), Jocelin had served as a royal clerk under Hubert Walter, chancellor and justiciar, and archbishop of Canterbury, perhaps the greatest of all the medieval English civil servants, for it was he who introduced wide-ranging administrative reforms into the chancery and important new series of records.

All of the previous six bishops of Bath from 1061 onwards, save Robert of Lewes, a monk of Lewes, had experience of royal service. Jocelin was no exception, and this was the predominant experience of the bench of bishops at this time. Unlike his two immediate predecessors, however, he did not come from an aristocratic background, nor from a dynasty of clerics.

On consecration as a bishop, royal duties did not cease, but the tide of political events was such at the time of Jocelin's election that immediately the service of two masters, king and pope, was to colour nearly all his episcopate. Archbishop Hubert Walter's death in the year before Jocelin's election was to change dramatically the relations between the English king and the pope. King John's refusal to accept Pope Innocent III's nominee, Stephen Langton, as archbishop of Canterbury, led to terrible consequences for the English state. Severe penalties were imposed. First of all, a general interdict was proclaimed on 23 March 1208, which withdrew the sacraments of the

---

14 *Wells MSS* i. 62–5 nos ccii–ccxvi and Wells Cathedral, charter 41. He is also referred to as master (twice) in *Fines*, ed. Hunter, ii. 7–8, and 63–4.

15 A.B. Emden, *Biographical Register of the University of Oxford to AD 1500* (Oxford, 1957), included him in the Addenda (uncertain university category) iii. 2226.

16 See R. Sharpe, *A Handlist of the Latin Writers of Great Britain and Ireland before 1540*, Publication of the Journal of Medieval Latin 1 (Turnhout, 1997), 498.

church from the people, except for the baptism of infants and the confession of the dying. Although in time the tough rules were relaxed and the clergy were permitted to celebrate divine service behind closed doors, the with-drawal of the sacraments, followed by the king's threats to confiscate the property of churchmen who would not celebrate divine service publicly, put the country in turmoil. Loyalties were divided; those bishops who were royal servants found themselves in an impossible situation. Bishops and clergy who chose to go abroad sacrificed their lands and revenues, and later, in 1212, the king confiscated the churches and revenues of clerks who had been instituted on the orders of the expatriate bishops.[17] Both Jocelin and Hugh spent the Christmas following the imposition of the Interdict with the king at Bristol; they were still associated with the royal administration. The next weapon employed by the pope against the intransigent king was excommu-nication, banning him from the sacraments but also meaning the possible withdrawal of allegiance of his vassals (laymen as well as churchmen) whose vows of fealty were no longer regarded by the church as valid, and whose association with an excommunicate would imperil their own souls. Jocelin was sent by the king to treat with Stephen Langton at Dover in July 1209, but the king's excommunication was only temporarily stayed. In November 1209, sentence was pronounced; consequently Jocelin could no longer serve the king or remain safely in England. He left for northern France together with his brother Hugh, now bishop-elect of Lincoln, and in the company of the dean and a canon of his cathedral, and several clerks. The bishop-executors of the Interdict (London, Ely and Worcester) had already gone; the bishops of Rochester and Salisbury departed at about the same time as Hugh and Jocelin. The bishop of Winchester, Peter des Roches, was prob-ably the only diocesan to remain in England.[18]

Hugh was consecrated bishop of Lincoln by Langton at Melun in December 1209 and in November 1212 he drew up his first testament, with Jocelin present, at St-Martin-de-Garenne in the Île-de-France and archbish-opric of Rouen.[19] Jocelin, clearly hoping for better times, issued a document concerning the prebends during this period, and we can discount the story of the St Albans chronicler that having left England secretly the expatriates were all living in luxury![20] In May 1213 King John made submission to the

17 C.R. Cheney, *Pope Innocent III and England* (Stuttgart, 1976), 303–25.
18 *Annales Monastici*, iii. 31 (Annals of Dunstable); *Councils and Synods* II. i. 12. The bishop of Norwich, John de Gray, was acting as justiciar in Ireland, but returned to England from the summer until Christmas 1211, see *EEA* vi. 381–2.
19 Because Jocelin was Hugh's executor, the copy has remained in the Wells archives; printed in *Acta of Hugh of Wells*, no. 2. Robinson, *Som. Hist. Essays*, 134, wrongly identi-fied St-Martin-de-Garenne as 'near Bordeaux'.
20 *Wells MSS* i. 58 no. clxxxxii (R I fo. 49v, and R II fo. 13v); *Chronica Majora*. ii. 522–3.

Figure 1. Bishop Jocelin, Bishop Richard Poore of Salisbury and Hugh de Tournai, chancellor of Chichester, give absolution to those about to fight for the liberation of England and praise God for the victory over the French off Sandwich in 1217. Corpus Christi College, Cambridge, MS 16 fo. 52r. Reproduced with permission from the Master and Fellows of Corpus Christi College, Cambridge.

pope, and most of the bishops returned from exile.[21] It appears that Jocelin had maintained his support for the English Crown and was concerned with the re-establishment of firm, if modified, royal government. He was one of the seven bishops and two archbishops present at Runnymede in 1215 at the sealing of Magna Carta,[22] and later his assistance at the coronation of the young Henry III at Gloucester in October 1216 indicates his support for John's heir. The years between 1215 and 1217 were years of civil war and Jocelin with some of the other bishops was present at the battles of Lincoln and Sandwich.[23] He was itinerant justice on the south-western circuit in 1218 and 1219, hearing cases which had accrued during the disturbances. In the same eyre of 1218–22, he was charged with Bishop Richard Poore of Salisbury to visit Wiltshire and Cornwall, but these shires were never reached.[24] From the start of the minority of Henry III, a select group of bishops worked with the papal legates in government, and when the legate Pandulf departed in 1221, it was Archbishop Langton and the bishops of Bath (Jocelin) and Salisbury (Richard Poore) who together with Hubert de Burgh, the justiciar, formed the government.[25]

The Patent Rolls show Jocelin extremely active in the royal administration in the 1220s. He had custody of the castles of Bristol and Sherborne and acted as sheriff of Somerset in 1223.[26] He had a reputation for harsh-

[21] *Councils and Synods* II. i. 37.

[22] *Ibid.*, II. i. 43.

[23] For his presence at Lincoln, see *The Chronicle of Melrose*, facsimile with introduction by A.O. Anderson, M.O. Anderson and W.C. Dickinson (1936), 68; at Sandwich, *Chronica Majora* iii. 28–9.

[24] CPR 1216–25, 259; Shirley, *Royal Letters*, 10–11 no. ix; D. Crook, *Records of the General Eyre*, PRO Handbooks 20 (1982), 71, 73.

[25] See D.A. Carpenter, *The Minority of Henry III* (1990), 400.

[26] CPR 1216–25, 419; Shirley, *Royal Letters*, 510–11.

ness, remarking in 1224, when the rebel garrison at Bedford castle was sent to the gallows, that if the same fate had befallen the rebels at Bytham in 1221, no such action would be necessary now.[27] From at least 1223, in the company of the bishop of Salisbury and Hubert de Burgh, he was in attendance on the king – at Wallingford, Bedford, Marlborough and frequently, of course, at Westminster.[28] If we take the year 1225 alone, we find him and the bishop of Salisbury in charge of special exchequers at London to receive a fifteenth to counteract the French threat – and again in 1229 for a sixteenth[29] – paying out expenses from the New Temple; returning information from the county of Somerset to the King's Bench; acting as justice for the assize of *mort d'ancestor*; and attesting letters of protection for those serving in Gascony, together with Poore and de Burgh.[30] There is no decrease in his activities on behalf of the king until the mid-1230s.[31] He was much at Westminster with the court, and still often in the company of Richard Poore, now bishop of Durham.

The bishop had a London house opposite the church of St Helen in Bishopsgate by 1216 to 1219.[32] By 1230, he had a second London property in the parish of St Clement Danes, which later became the site of Arundel House,[33] and it was probably from this house that the bishop issued a document dated at London in 1237.[34] The Strand area, close to the river, housed an increasing number of bishops as the century progressed, and would have been more convenient for Westminster than further east.[35] Even with a house in London, the amount of travel for a curial bishop was gruelling, in attendance on the court, on royal business, and within his diocese.[36]

Jocelin was high in the royal favour, as he had been in the early years as a bishop under the king's father. Between 1228 and 1235, the liberties

[27] *Memoriale fratris Walteri de Coventria*, ed. W. Stubbs, 2 vols, Roll Series 58 (1872–73), ii. 268.

[28] *CPR 1216–25*, 417–26, 428–41,443–4, 447–61, *CPR 1225–32*, 11, 111, 218, 226, 285, 418.

[29] *CCR 1227–31*, 380.

[30] *CPR 1216–25*, 548, 559–60, 573, 579.

[31] *CCR 1231–34*, 428, 433, 438, 479, 487, 488; *1234–37*, 26, 53.

[32] *Wells MSS* i. 16 no. xl; dated by the witnesses.

[33] See P. Croot in *VCH Middlesex*, ed. P. Croot *et al.*, vol. 13 pt. i (Woodbridge, 2009), 42–3; *Wells MSS* i. 474–5; ii. 553–4 no. 38.

[34] *Two Cartularies of the Augustinian Priory of Bruton and the Cluniac Priory of Montacute*, ed. Members of the Council, Somerset Record Society 8 (1894), Montacute Cart. no. 187. The house was made the property of the see by Jocelin: *CChR 1226–57*, 168–9.

[35] Bishop Ralph Neville of Chichester died in a house he had built not far from the New Temple and so quite close to Jocelin's, but Hugh of Lincoln's house was at the other end of Chancery Lane, adjoining the Old Temple in Holborn (*Chronica Majora* iv. 287); for a transaction there, see *Rotuli Hugonis de Welles*, ed. W.P.W. Phillimore, 3 vols, Canterbury and York Society 1, 3, 4 (1907–9), iii. 54.

[36] Itineraries for his companion Richard Poore as both bishop of Salisbury and bishop of Durham (*EEA* xix. 412–19; *EEA* xxv. 342–3), well illustrate this point.

of his bishopric were confirmed.[37] He was given licences to deafforest, as at Pucklechurch, and to assart, as at Cheddar, and to work iron mines in the Mendips.[38] All his lands were to be free from fines for not hambling (disabling) dogs, and fines for amercements and transgressions exacted by the royal justices were granted to him.[39] There were gifts of stags from the royal forest and of fallow deer in the forest of Selwood.[40] He received land to enlarge his park at Dogmersfield.[41] King John had already allowed him to enclose his park at Wells, and to divert the royal highway in exchange for the bishop's house in Bath, thus enabling Jocelin to build his house at Wells, and in August 1233, when at Wells, King Henry III ordered thirty oaks from the Forest of Dean to be transported to Wells for the bishop's house.[42] The king came to Wells again in August 1235 and Jocelin was present when he approved the extension of a safe conduct.[43] Hugh of Wells, Jocelin's brother, died in February 1235 and Richard Poore in 1237. In June 1237 the king granted Jocelin licence to make a will (or testament) of his moveables.[44]

Servant of the pope

The bishop not only served the king; he also served the pope. The influence of the pope became paramount with the arrival of powerful legates after 1213 and Jocelin found himself in an active role serving two masters, as did many of his contemporaries. Primarily the bishop's duty towards the pope was to enforce the canon law, implement the decrees of general councils, and carry out papal mandates and instructions. The normal contacts with the curia were made by a visit to 'the threshold of the apostles' or by letter to and from the papal court. So far as we know Jocelin never visited the papal curia. King John's attitude to the pope made any such visit unlikely in 1206, and during the Interdict on England, when the administration of the dioceses was largely suspended, there were few contacts between the curia and the bishops. There might have been an opportunity for Jocelin to have visited the pope during the period of his exile, but there is no evidence that he did so. Furthermore, it is certain that he did not attend the Fourth Lateran Council of 1215, unlike his brother Hugh and Richard Poore, the newly consecrated bishop of Chichester, for on 30 November 1215, the date

---

37 *CCR 1227–31*, 177.
38 *Ibid.*, 58; *1234–37*, 149, 86, 92–3.
39 *Ibid.*, *1227–31*, 295–6, 528, 531.
40 *Ibid.*, 459, 572; *1231–34*, 88; *1234–37*, 23.
41 *Ibid.*, *1227–31*, 23.
42 *Rot. Chart.*, i. 1. 169; *Rot. Litt. Pat.* 77; *CCR 1231–34*, 243.
43 *CPR 1232–47*, 114.
44 *CPR 1232–47*, 184; for similar earlier arrangements, see *CChR 1226–57*, 42, 137.

of the Council's third session, he issued a document at Dunster.[45] By no means all the English bishops attended the Council; other absentees were the bishops of London, Salisbury and Winchester; and three sees, Carlisle, Durham and Hereford, were vacant.[46]

The pope corresponded with his bishops mainly by letter, involving them in the settlement of disputes and the raising of taxes, supplying them with indults for certain irregularities, and answering their queries on points of law. Some letters were petitioned for by the bishops, for example, Richard Poore asked Pope Honorius III for empowerment to take action against pluralists, sons succeeding fathers in the same benefices, rectors who refused to be ordained, and non-residents, and Bishop Peter des Roches of Winchester in 1205 had sought similar powers,[47] but there is no record of Jocelin taking such a step. He did, however, receive certain mandates of which we have record. Among the Wells archives is an original letter of Pope Innocent III ordering the bishop to allow M., a poor scholar of his diocese, to minister in the orders which he had already taken, and to proceed to higher orders, if he was found suitable. Apparently M. in his youth had been rather a dangerous fellow, violently attacking fellow students and other clerks; for this crime he had been ordered by the abbot of Saint Victor at Paris, where he was presumably studying, to seek absolution from the pope.[48] Jocelin acted as a judge-delegate of the pope, hearing cases as commissioned,[49] and with the bishop of Salisbury (Richard Poore) and the bishops of Rochester and Ely, was involved in bringing about a settlement between the bishop of Durham and his monks,[50] and with Poore of Salisbury and Neville of Chichester between the abbot and the monks of Westminster.[51] Again with Poore, and presumably because they were regarded as the Crown's officials, he was charged with obtaining a subsidy from the churches of England for the king on 30 January 1226.[52]

---

[45] *Wells MSS* i. 48 no. clxv, providing for payments 'to the service of the Glorious Virgin'.
[46] *Councils and Synods* II. i. 48.
[47] *CPL* i. 105; *Regesta Honorii III*, cal. P. Pressutti, 2 vols (Rome, 1888–95), ii. no. 5816; and see Jane E. Sayers, *Papal Government and England during the Pontificate of Honorius III (1216–1227)* (Cambridge, 1984), 155. *Letters of Innocent III*, nos 643, 645–9, *Die Register Innocenz' III*, ed. O. Hageneder and A. Sommerlechner, viii (Vienna, 2001), 143, 145–9; *EEA* ix. li, lvii. In 1235 Alexander of Stavensby, bishop of Coventry, sought special powers to act against married priests; Shirley, *Royal Letters*, 560.
[48] Wells Cathedral, charter 20.
[49] Shirley, *Royal Letters*, no. xxxiii, 40–1; *CPL* i. 110, 126, 195; *Reg. Hon. III*, ii. no. 5921; *Les registres de Grégoire IX*, ed. L. Auvray, S. Clémencet, and L. Carolus Barré, 4 vols (Paris, 1890–1995), i. no. 612, iii. no. 5407.
[50] *CPL* i. 93, 97, 101, 104; *Reg. Hon. III*, ii. nos 4446, 4975, 5390, 5747.
[51] British Library, Cotton MS Faustina A III fo. 233.
[52] *CPL* i.105; *Reg. Hon. III*, ii. no. 5810.

The diocese: the duties of a bishop

Within his diocese, the bishop was shepherd of a large flock, consisting of all the clergy and laity. The clergy meant all those in his chapter, in secular colleges, hospitals, schools and parishes, and all those in religious orders, monks and nuns. His episcopal order meant that it was he who carried out the ordinations of the different grades of clergy and blessed the heads of religious houses.[53] Prior to the ordinations, there were no doubt detailed examinations of the candidates as to their knowledge and suitability, of which we can only now get a glimpse from chance references, as in the papal mandate to Jocelin, referred to above. Later on, by the fourteenth century, ordinations and blessings were recorded in the bishops' registers, but at this date we have no such lists. For ordinations, as for the bishop's consecration and dedication of churches and altars, his confirmation of children and the blessing of the chrism and holy oils, we have only chance references in surviving charters and chronicles.[54] Somewhat bizarrely, the only reference to ordination for Jocelin is in the episcopal rolls of his brother, Hugh of Lincoln.[55]

Registers

Did Jocelin have a register or rolls on which were recorded his administrative acts like his brother, whose records are the earliest of their kind to have survived?[56] Hugh had rolls dating from 1214 on which institutions to livings and the setting up of vicarages were recorded, and a survey volume of vicarage endowments and appropriation deeds, known as the *Liber Antiquus*, and he may have had visitation rolls.[57] Another contemporary, Archbishop Walter de Grey of York, had rolls kept of his administration of the diocese, which from 1225 onwards record institutions, collations, licences,

---

[53] For his blessing of three abbots of Glastonbury, Abbot William in 1219, probably at Glastonbury, Abbot Robert in 1223 at Bath and Abbot Michael in 1235 at London, see *The Chronicle of Glastonbury Abbey*, ed. J.P. Carley, trans. D. Townsend (Woodbridge, 1985), 206–11.

[54] There is reference to the bishop's dedication of the church of Compton Bishop in 1236: *Wells MSS* i. 27–8, no. lxxxiii.

[55] *Rotuli Hugonis de Welles*, ii. 106.

[56] The earliest extant register for Bath and Wells is a fragment for Bishop Walter Giffard, covering the period from August 1264 to November 1266; it is printed in *The Registers of Walter Giffard, Bishop of Bath and Wells, 1265–6, and of Henry Bowett, Bishop of Bath and Wells, 1401–7*, ed. T.S. Holmes, Somerset Record Society 13 (1899), 1–11.

[57] See D. Smith, 'The Rolls of Hugh of Wells, Bishop of Lincoln 1209–35', *Bulletin of the Institute of Historical Research*, 45 (1972), 155–95, at 170.

indulgences, provisions of papal clerks and confirmations of tithes.[58] Similar documents were drawn up by Jocelin's chancery, and as he, like Bishop Hugh of Lincoln and Archbishop Walter de Grey, had detailed knowledge and first-hand experience of the royal chancery, I think it very likely that Jocelin did have rolls recording some of his administrative acts. Indeed, it would be curiously ironic if Jocelin, who formally witnessed some of his brother's administrative acts, on one occasion at Grantham actually admitting and instituting a clerk on the bishop's behalf, did not keep records.[59]

What do we know of the men who issued his documents? The household was the hub of the bishop's administration and within the Wells brothers circle, which remained extremely close, there were plenty of skilled clerks. The clerks of Jocelin's household are revealed in the charters, and from 1208 at least there were dataries, who supervised the bishop's chancery and checked the accuracy of documents before adding the date. The datary's office was very familiar to Hugh and Jocelin since both had served the king in that capacity. Peter of Chichester, Bishop Jocelin's datary in 1208, had been in exile with the Wells brothers. Three of the other dataries are entitled master, Master Gilbert of Taunton, Master Philip de Gildeford, and Master Walter of Maidstone. The one non-master, John de Templo (presumably from the Temple in London), occurs also as the bishop's and the dean and chapter's attorney in the *curia regis* (royal court); the office of attorney required some legal expertise.[60]

Synods

It was an episcopal duty to hold synods, which were usually celebrated annually.[61] We have reference to one synod held by Bishop Jocelin at Bath abbey in April 1220, but we know nothing about who was present or what was discussed. The only records remaining concern the challenges by the abbot of Glastonbury and the dean of Wells to the prior of Bath sitting on the bishop's right![62]

58 *The Register or Rolls of Walter Gray*, ed. J. Raine, Surtees Society 56 (1872); Smith has argued that the large size of these two dioceses account for enrolment ('Rolls of Hugh of Wells', 157).
59 *Rotuli Hugonis de Welles*, iii. 149.
60 See *Fasti 1066–1300* vii. 10, 73, 94 (Peter of Chichester); 83 (Gilbert of Taunton); 94 (Philip de Gildeford); 107 (Walter of Maidstone); and 91 (John de Templo). All the dataries were given canonries and some advanced to higher office.
61 See *Councils and Synods* II. i 175, 723.
62 *Glast. Chart.* i. 8–9; *Wells MSS* i. 52.

Diocesan statutes

The synod was the place where diocesan statutes were made known. Of Jocelin's contemporaries, the archbishop of Canterbury and several of the bishops are known to have issued statutes for their dioceses.[63] The Statutes of Richard Poore of Salisbury, which drew on various sources, including the Fourth Lateran decrees, must have been known to Jocelin.[64] They covered the seven sacraments; confession was to be made three times a year, and communion taken at Easter, Christmas and Whitsun. The major sins – homicide, sacrilege, incest, rape of nuns and virgins, violence against parents, broken vows, some of which could only be absolved by the pope – are specified. Two or three men were to be appointed in each rural deanery charged with revealing to the bishop any gross misconduct by the clergy, such as fornication and the keeping of concubines. There were clauses about residence, the appointment of vicars, and the care and use of the parish church. Church vessels and books were to be properly looked after; non-ecclesiastical objects were not to be left in churches; and the playing of bawdy games in the church and graveyard was forbidden. Doctors were to be made aware of their duty to send patients to a priest. Originally issued for the diocese of Salisbury, the Statutes were updated between 1219 and 1228, and then reissued by Poore when he became bishop of Durham. Did Jocelin ever issue such statutes? It is likely, and it may be that they were promulgated at the synod of 1220.

The bishop had jurisdiction over the clergy and lay people of the diocese. The information gained at visitations and reports of malpractices might lead to action before the bishop in his consistory court, to which miscreant clergy and laity could be summoned.[65] The bishop's court had jurisdiction over all marriage cases, and cases concerning sexual crimes, legitimacy, wills, libel, breach of contract, heresy, witchcraft, church offences, and clergy discipline. English ecclesiastical court records for most dioceses do not predate the fourteenth century (and the records for the bishop's consistory at Wells do not survive from before the mid-fifteenth century);[66] nevertheless, there is absolutely no doubt that Bishop Jocelin or his legal officer, called the official,[67] would have dealt with such cases in his court. And we

---

63 For a list, see Appendix B in M. Gibbs and J. Lang, *Bishops and Reform 1215–1272* (Oxford, 1934), 183–4; and for the printed texts, *Councils and Synods* II. i. *passim*.

64 *Councils and Synods* II. i. 57–96.

65 The visitation of the parishes was carried out by the archdeacons.

66 See *Dean Cosyn and Wells Cathedral Miscellanea*, ed. A. Watkin, Somerset Record Society 56 (1941), xxxi; and R.W. Dunning, 'The Wells Consistory Court in the Fifteenth Century', *Proceedings of the Somersetshire Archaeological Society* 106 (1962), 46–61.

67 Three bishop's officials are known under Jocelin: Richard 1209×13, Master John de Ickford 1217×18, and Master William of Bitton I (who later became archdeacon and bishop) in 1231. There is also mention of an official of the archdeacon of Wells, Master

have one reference to his dealing with criminous clerks. Clergy who had been apprehended by the civil authorities for crimes of violence, murder and the like, termed criminous clerks, were referred to their bishop for trial if they claimed 'benefit of clergy', as did three clerks held in the gaol at Ilchester in 1234.[68] Unfortunately we do not know how Jocelin dealt with them.

The bishop settled cases between parties usually in his consistory court. Frequently disputes were brought there by religious houses and concerned their properties and rights: often ownership of churches and the allotment of tithes. We have record of them simply because religious houses kept cartularies in which they recorded such matters. The bishop heard cases about advowson, for example, over the church of Talland (Cornwall) between the Hospitallers of Buckland and Master Geoffrey de Lidiard;[69] and about the possession of churches, for example, between the priory of Bruton and Master Adam, archdeacon of Oxford, over the church of Shepton Montague.[70]

The bishop might make ordinances (sometimes called ordinations, meaning decisions or decrees) on any matters that concerned him within his diocese, not acting as a judge in court. He issued ordinances that provided wax for the light of St Andrew, ordered that on the death of the present incumbents of Chew and Wellington 10 marks should be paid yearly to the service of the Blessed Virgin Mary;[71] decreed that the canons of Canonsleigh should receive 20 shillings yearly from the church of Sampford Arundel, and made arrangements about the tithes of Williton and the church of Over Stowey,[72] and the church of Chewton and its chapels.[73] And he made many provisions for his chapter and canons in ordinances.

The bishop was also often asked to confirm awards, settlements and judge-delegate decisions, because he had the necessary powers of enforcement through his officers, and to inspect or confirm charters, providing a word-for-word copy. He confirmed a composition made in 1239 between the prior of Stogursey and the rector of Sampford Brett over the tithes of Aller eighteen months later at Wells; and similarly a judge-delegate award

---

Robert de Mariscis in April 1242, who later became official of the achdeacon of Lincoln. See *Fasti 1066–1300* vii. 21, 54, 89, 97, and the references cited there.

68 *CCR 1231–34*, 429.

69 *Letters of Pope Innocent III*, no. 1162; *A Cartulary of Buckland Priory*, ed. F.W. Weaver, Somerset Record Society 25 (1909); 106; this however was appealed to the pope.

70 *Wells MSS* i. 473–4 and R III fo. 346v, and *Cart. Bruton and Montacute*, Bruton no. 109.

71 *Wells MSS* i. 48 no. clxv, and 253.

72 *The Cartulary of Canonsleigh Abbey*, ed. Vera C.M. London, Devon and Cornwall Record Society new series 32 (Torquay, 1965), 41–2, and *Wells MSS* i. 83–4; *Cartulary of St Mark's Hospital, Bristol*, ed. C.D. Ross, Bristol Records Society 21 (Bristol, 1959), no. 241.

73 British Library, Cotton MS Otho B xiv fo. 64 and *Wells MSS* i. 398.

some five years after the original judgment.[74] Such confirmations usually rehearsed the text of the original document and were necessary in case of further legal action. Similarly grants by previous bishops would be brought for confirmation by the new bishop and the bishop could be asked to inspect a whole range of early charters, ratify gifts, and confirm a grant of advowson and an award, as he did for Bruton priory.[75] As an added protection, the bishop's archives might well be used by laymen and clergy alike as a safe place of deposit.

Administration

Scattered through the records in the Wells cathedral archives and recorded in the cartularies of the Somerset religious houses are numerous references to Jocelin's administration. We can look at a sample of these acts. When a living became vacant through the death or resignation of the incumbent, the patron of the benefice (often a religious institution) appointed a new man and sent him with his letters of presentation to the bishop for approval. Only when the bishop was satisfied with the candidate's suitability, age, orders and literacy would he institute and order the induction into the benefice. The bishop also had to be sure that if the church was served by a vicar, the vicar was provided with an adequate and defined income. When Jocelin instituted Thomas of Pilton, chaplain, to the vicarage of Pilton, very detailed arrangements were made. The vicar was to have the altarage, a house, two acres of meadow, the first mortuary and specified small tithes, not including those of lambswool, cheese, mills, geese and eggs, money from the guild and 'churchsete', and tithes of a mill and of warrens.[76] The usual arrangement was for the vicar to have the small tithes (basically the tithe of everything except corn) and the rector the greater tithes, and for the rector to be responsible for the repair of the chancel, books and vestments, and for paying the archdeacon's procurations (expenses).[77] On occasion, when a perpetual vicarage was established, a money payment, a pension, might be paid by the vicar to the rector, as mentioned when Jocelin collated (where

---

[74] *Stogursey Charters*, ed. T.D. Tremlett and N. Blakiston, Somerset Record Society 61 (1949), no. 41; *Chart. Glast.* i. 29–31.

[75] *Calendar of Documents preserved in France*, ed. J.H. Round, i (London, 1890), 172–4 no. 486; *Cart. Bruton and Montacute*, Bruton nos 65, 107, 108, 109.

[76] *The Registers of Oliver King Bishop of Bath and Wells 1496–1503 and Hadrian de Castello Bishop of Bath and Wells 1503–1510*, ed. H. Maxwell-Lyte, Somerset Record Society 54 (1939), 97 no. 570.

[77] *Two Cartularies of the Benedictine Abbeys of Muchelney and Athelney*, ed. E.H. Bates, Somerset Record Society 14 (1899), 49.

the bishop had the presentation) and instituted Richard de Attebere in the church of Charlton Mackrell.[78] The bishop's power to license and to issue indulgences can be seen from Jocelin's records. He licensed Henry son of Richard's chapel in the parish of Charlton,[79] and allowed remission of thirty days' penance to all from his diocese visiting the hospital near the church of St Ethelbert, Hereford.[80] This would not have constituted the sole issue of such documents. Licences for private chapels (usually granted to manorial lords who claimed impassable roads, preventing their attendance at the parish church) and indulgences to those visiting religious houses were not uncommon.

Religious houses

Within his diocese the bishop was responsible for four Benedictine houses, Glastonbury, Bath, Athelney and Muchelney, and a small cell at Stogursey dependent on the mother house of Lonlay in France; and five Augustinian houses, at Keynsham, following the Victorine rule, Bruton, Taunton, Barlinch and Woodspring. At Buckland, all the sisters of the order of St John of Jerusalem (the Hospitallers) were settled in the late twelfth century;[81] and there were Benedictine nuns at Barrow Gurney and Cannington, to whom his brother Hugh had left bequests in his first testament.[82] There were eight hospitals in the diocese at this time – two at Bath, two at Ilchester, one in the suburbs of Bristol, one at Bridgwater, one at Taunton and Hugh and Jocelin's foundation at Wells[83] – an alien priory of the great abbey of Cluny at Montacute, a recently founded Cistercian house at Cleeve, and two Charterhouses at Witham and Hinton.

What were the rights and duties of the bishop in relation to these communities? Besides his sacramental duties, the bishop had a general duty to approve new foundations and act as their patron and protector. Jocelin approved the foundation of the hospital at Bridgwater in 1219,[84] and the Augustinian priory of Woodspring, at the request of William de Courtenay. The reasons for William's generosity in seeking to turn a chapel dedicated

---

[78] *Wells MSS* i. 404 (R III fo.192v).

[79] *Cart. Bruton and Montacute*, Bruton no. 206.

[80] Dean and Chapter of Hereford muniments no. 2042, dated 18 October 1226 at the Old Temple, 'by the hand of the bishop'.

[81] D. Knowles and R.N. Hadcock, *Medieval Religious Houses*, 2nd edn (Harlow, 1971), 278–9, 284.

[82] *Acta of Hugh of Wells*, no. 2.

[83] Hugh's bequests to the hospital survived his later revision of his testament; see *ibid.*, no. 408. The hospital of St John at Wells had been founded in accordance with the wishes of their father; see *CChR 1226–57*, 128.

[84] *Bath Charts.* ii. 22 no. 105.

to St Thomas of Canterbury into a full-scale religious house was one of expiation, for his grandfather Reginald FitzUrse had been one of Becket's murderers.[85]

Appropriation

Religious houses having patronage could by appropriation keep the rectorial income for themselves, allotting a smaller amount to an appointed vicar. Often this was a means of diverting funds to a cause such as providing more money for the sacristy or the almonry, that is for building and repairs and for poor relief. Jocelin allowed the appropriation of Norton sub Hamdon to the abbey of Grestein on conditions that protected the vicar, who was to have 12 marks a year from which he had to pay procurations and synodals to the archdeacon; the abbey was to pay 40 shillings yearly to the common fund of the cathedral.[86] Glastonbury was permitted to appropriate the church of Shapwick and a vicarage was confirmed by Jocelin on 30 September 1230.[87] The bishop gave the church of Evercreech to his hospital at Wells for the maintenance of the poor there and those ministering to them, saving provision for a vicar at Evercreech, and he allowed the hospital at Ilchester to appropriate the local parish church of St Mary the Less.[88]

The bishop might visit the Benedictine and Augustinian houses and the hospitals in the diocese. There is one reference to a visitation of Keynsham abbey, following a dispute between the abbot and the convent; Jocelin held enquiries in person, and later sent his clerks.[89] His activities were more restricted in his dealings with the Cistercians, Cluniacs and Carthusians in the diocese. Jocelin's relations with Cleeve, a house established under his predecessor, have left no trace in the archives. Cistercian houses were exempt from most aspects of episcopal supervision and the same was true of the Cluniac priory at Montacute. But the religious communities were answerable to the bishop if they had any parishes, and in this respect the Montacute cartulary shows Jocelin as a caring bishop. He granted Montacute exemption from the tithes of the demesne in the parish of Mudford (the church was in his patronage); made a ruling on tithes of the demesne of Carlingcott; and permitted the use of the income of Montacute and

---

85 Mon. Angl. VI. i. 415, prints William's letter; for Jocelin's confirmation, Bath Charts. ii. 58–9 no. 260.
86 Wells MSS i. 399 (R III fo. 185).
87 Chart. Glast. i. 35–6.
88 Wells MSS i. 390 (R III fo. 159); Reg. Drokensford, 68.
89 Annales Monastici, i. 96 (Annals of Tewkesbury). He had custody of the Benedictine house of Athelney during a vacancy in 1227: Cart. Muchelney and Athelney, 199–200, and CPR 1225–32, 112.

Chinnock churches for extending charity and hospitality in the house 'in reverence for St Peter and the Order of Cluny'.[90] The sources are silent on the two Charterhouses at Hinton and Witham, except for a document of Jocelin's dated at Witham Charterhouse.[91]

The great Benedictine house at Glastonbury received Jocelin as its abbot in 1206, following his predecessor Savaric's acquisition of the abbey, and Jocelin remained abbot until 1219. Jocelin's relations with Glastonbury were not markedly different from those with other monastic houses in his diocese. There is evidence that he carried out the normal business of a diocesan: confirming arrangements, instituting clerks in benefices, arranging for vicarages and pensions, settling disputes over tithes and so on, and allowing appropriations.[92] There is no evidence of a formal visitation of the monastery after he ceased to be its abbot in 1219, but in 1235 he was responsible for the removal of Abbot Robert of Bath. The reason for the removal (or resignation) was Abbot Robert's appointment of a lay steward against the wishes of the convent.[93] The abbey's chroniclers, who would normally have favoured such an action, not wishing to endow the bishop with the power of dismissal, preferred to say that Abbot Robert had retired of his own free will and returned to Bath where he enjoyed an annual pension for life.[94] Even before his election as bishop, Jocelin had been seen by the monks of Glastonbury as a Wells clerk, hostile to Glastonbury and jealous of its wealth, who had gone with a party from Wells to seize some of the monks who were refusing to obey Savaric. The story may well be apocryphal, but it certainly illustrates the monks' dislike of episcopal authority.[95]

Jocelin's relations with Bath cannot have been entirely cordial either. Although he was in no way responsible for Savaric's annexation of the abbey of Glastonbury, he did not hasten to end this arrangement. Before his election, to which the convent unanimously agreed, Jocelin had been in the service of this very prior, Robert, whom he later removed from Glastonbury, and had received his first benefice from him. The ancient abbey of St Peter and St Paul at Bath was the site of the bishop's chair and it was here that Jocelin was enthroned; his gifts of vestments and ornaments on that occasion were generous, and later his anniversary was celebrated in albs, 100 poor people were fed, and the table of the brothers was well provided.[96] There is no record of visitation, but the bishop carried out the

---

90   *Cart. Bruton and Montacute*, Montacute nos 182, 185, 187.
91   *Ibid.*, Bruton no. 206.
92   *Chart. Glast.* i. (v), (viii), 21, 35–6, 39, 67.
93   The Annals of Tewkesbury say that he was removed: *Annales Monastici* i. 95.
94   *Domerham* ii. 502; and *The Chronicle of Glastonbury Abbey*, ed. J.P. Carley (Woodbridge, 1985), 210–11.
95   *Domerham*, ii. 387–8; *Chronicle of Glastonbury*, 194–5.
96   *Bath Charts.* ii. 155 no. 808.

usual duties. The separation of the church of Bath from Glastonbury in 1219 – Jocelin had used the joint title from 1213 – meant that Jocelin's title now became bishop of Bath only, and in 1220 he wrote to the pope petitioning for licence to use the title of bishop of Bath and Wells, lest, as he put it, there might seem to be some diminution in his status. The pope, unable to find evidence that the church of Wells had ever been a cathedral, commissioned his legate Pandulf to look into the matter.[97] It is not clear whether the licence was ever granted; certainly Jocelin did not use the title, and the union of Bath and Wells had to wait until after his death.

So how do we evaluate Jocelin today? The medieval obituaries of Jocelin date from considerably after his death. Produced within the community at Wells, they concentrate particularly on his constitutional arrangements for the cathedral, praising his building-works, the dedication of the church of Wells, the foundation of the hospital and his institution of the daily Ladymass. This view of Jocelin as a man whose 'fame rests on the work which he did at Wells' (that is the building and the constitution)[98] and as 'the see's restorer'[99] has not much altered over the course of time. The role of a bishop in the thirteenth century was complex and onerous. It is not difficult to form a very favourable judgment on Jocelin's activities on behalf of the king's government, as an experienced administrator, 'devoid of political ambition',[100] at a time when stability was imperative for the survival of the Crown. The judgement of the Glastonbury chroniclers is a harsh one: 'a man versed in temporal affairs and ambition'.[101] It can, of course, be explained by the fact that no active bishop could expect to be popular with the monks of a prestigious Benedictine abbey, such as Glastonbury, put under his control by his predecessor. As a diocesan, Jocelin emerges as an efficient administrator, not in the vanguard of reform, but certainly assiduous in his day-to-day duties within the diocese. As a judge, he probably knew more of the royal courts and the exchequer[102] than of the papal court, and of the common law than the canon law, but he in no way shirked his duties in the ecclesiastical courts. He was probably never a

---

[97] *CPL* i. 70; *Reg. Hon. III*, i. no. 2364.

[98] C.L. Kingsford, 'Jocelin of Wells' in *Dictionary of National Biography* x (1908), 835–6, at 836; and for the revision see R.W. Dunning, *ODNB* lviii. 63–4.

[99] A. Gransden, 'The History of Wells Cathedral *c*.1090–1547', in *Wells Cathedral: a History*, ed. L.S. Colchester (Shepton Mallet, 1982), 34.

[100] West, *Justiciarship*, 249.

[101] *Domerham*, ii. 441, 445; *Chronicle of Glastonbury*, 198–9.

[102] A contemporary lampoon ran: 'If the question were perchance asked of the bishop of Bath, "How many marks come in to the king's purse in the Exchequer?" he would answer readily, "A thousand, a hundred, and so on, I collect in to the king's purse", learned as he is in this decalogue, blind in the form of the canon'; T. Wright, *The Political Songs of England*, Camden Society 6 (London, 1839), 10.

scholar, nor an extensive patron. Intent on fostering the secular community at Wells, his patronage was confined, almost exclusively, to the building of a very 'English' cathedral. Jocelin filled the role of the bishop as a builder with singular distinction. This is the most obvious part of his legacy, but he had, as I have shown, other episcopal qualities that should not be overlooked.

3

Jocelin of Wells and His Cathedral Chapter

DIANA GREENWAY

When I was invited to speak on Jocelin of Wells and his cathedral chapter at the 2006 conference on the bishop and his career, I accepted readily and with great pleasure. But later it occurred to me that it would have been more accurate to have entitled my lecture 'Jocelin of Wells and his *quasi*-cathedral chapter'. For in Jocelin's time the church of Wells was technically no longer, and not yet, a cathedral. It was existing in an interim, *quasi*, phase.

Historically the ancient minster of St Andrew at Wells had been made the mother church of the newly created see of Somerset in 909. But after a flowering of chapter life under Bishop Giso (who ruled from 1061 to 1088),[1] Wells lost its cathedral status when Bishop John of Tours removed the epis-copal throne to the abbey of Bath in c.1090. John demolished the cloister, refectory and dormitory which Giso had built for the canons of Wells. The canons were forced to return to the unreformed practice of living in houses in the town. Further, John impoverished the chapter by alienating a portion of its revenues to a layman, Hildebert, who was probably his brother.[2] From 1090 until 1245, the sole cathedral of the see was not the church of Wells but the abbey church of Bath, and the monks of Bath, not the canons of Wells, formed the cathedral chapter.

As we know, eventually Wells did recover its cathedral status. In the process of recovery, the accession of Bishop Robert in 1136 was a turning-point. From that time further decline was halted, and the church and its chapter began to be nurtured under active episcopal patronage. The consti-tution was developed in line with the customs of the greater Anglo-Norman cathedrals, such as Salisbury, Lincoln and York, and landed endowments and income were recovered, expanded and secured so as to support a growing and well-ordered community. As a result, the chapter's sense of identity

---

[1] For Giso, see S. Keynes, 'Giso, Bishop of Wells (1061–1088)' *Anglo-Norman Studies*, 19 (1997), 203–71.

[2] See 'Historiola' and 'Historia Major' in *Collectanea I*, 61.

developed to the point where the canons were able to assert their right to participate, with the monks of Bath, in the episcopal election of 1173, when Bishop Reginald was elected,[3] and again in 1206, at the election of Jocelin. But in 1206 Wells was still, technically, not a cathedral, and Jocelin was enthroned at Bath only. As a collegiate church, however, the scale of Wells was quite anomalous: in 1206 there were fifty-eight canons,[4] showing the chapter to be larger than even the largest contemporary English cathedral chapter, Lincoln, which had fifty-six canons, and Salisbury, which had fifty-two. These three were considerably larger than all the other cathedrals and collegiate churches in England.

Jocelin was himself a canon of Wells when elected. The dean and canons, when they petitioned the pope to confirm the election in April 1206, described him, in a well-known phrase, as having been brought up in the bosom of the church of Wells from infancy – a primo lacte – literally from his first milk.[5] This was not mere hyperbole. As the son of a local landowner, Edward of Wells, Jocelin, with his older brother Hugh, was associated with the church from an early age, and some time before 1191 both Jocelin and Hugh are found acting as clerks to Bishop Reginald.[6] Under Reginald's successor, Savaric, both brothers became canons of Wells, and Hugh was made archdeacon.[7] When elected bishop in 1206, therefore, Jocelin was already intimately acquainted with the individual members of the chapter as well as with the leading citizens of Wells, and had nearly twenty years' experience of the customs, affairs and problems of the church.

The most obvious physical feature of the church in 1206 was that it was an unfinished construction, a massive building-site. Bishop Reginald had begun the work in 1175, in accordance with his vision of a church and cloister on a truly grand scale to replace the complex of crumbling and inadequate Anglo-Saxon and Norman buildings. As a boy and teenager, Jocelin would have watched the first stages of this great project. By the time he first played a part in the church's affairs, as a young man in the late 1180s, the foundations of the nave had been laid. During the 1190s, when he was promoted to a canonry, the old church, which until then had still stood to the south of the new one, was demolished. In the early 1200s, the

---

3   EEA x. xxxi–xxxii.
4   The election documents of 1206 name fifty-seven canons, including Jocelin (see *Fasti 1066–1300* vii. 120–1). A fifty-eighth prebend, held by the abbot of Athelney, had been created before 1205 (*ibid.*, 62–3).
5   *Wells MSS* i. 63.
6   See, e.g., EEA x. nos 68–9 (Hugh of Wells), 72 and 80 (both Hugh and Jocelin of Wells). It is important to note that Jocelin of Wells is not to be identified with Jocelin the chaplain of Bishop Reginald: the latter was a different individual, who attested forty of Reginald's charters, right through the episcopate (1174–91), and was senior to Jocelin of Wells; see *Fasti 1066–1300* vii. 86.
7   For Jocelin, see *ibid.*, 87, and for Hugh *ibid.*, 33, 58.

central tower was begun and work proceeded on the nave.[8] In this great enterprise, there seems not to have been any disharmony within the chapter or between bishop and chapter, such as is documented at Salisbury when the new cathedral was under construction there. Bishops Reginald and Savaric made careful provision for the financing of the work so as to minimise the canons' obligations,[9] and it is safe to assume that the canons were enthusiastic supporters of the project.

The first part of the new church to be brought into use, by c.1180, was an eastern Lady Chapel.[10] Before the quire was ready, about three years later, it was here, in the Lady Chapel, that the canons or their vicars fulfilled their primary obligation, the regular liturgy of the seven daily offices or 'hours' (Lauds/Matins, Prime, Terce, Sext, None, Vespers, Compline). But a Lady Chapel's true function was to serve as the space for a service additional to these seven offices – the daily mass of the Blessed Virgin Mary, the Ladymass. Devotion to the Blessed Virgin had greatly intensified in England in the twelfth century, and by the last years of the century the practice of celebrating the daily Ladymass was nearly universal in the greater churches in England. It was a special, solemn, early morning mass, sung rather than spoken, and included elaborate antiphons and sequences that could be set to polyphonic music. As soon as the quire at Wells was ready for use, in c.1183, the regular liturgy was transferred there, and the Lady Chapel could be used exclusively for the Ladymass. In the late 1190s Bishop Savaric assigned money for the payment of the priests who celebrated this mass.[11]

We know that Jocelin shared contemporary devotion to the Blessed Virgin Mary. The representation on his counter-seal, which was impressed on the reverse of his official episcopal seal, was of the Virgin and Child enthroned. The Virgin is feeding the infant Christ (*virgo lactans*), and below, within a trefoiled canopy, is a bishop, kneeling in adoration, doubtless Jocelin himself.[12]

This is the context in which we should see Jocelin's first precisely dated act, a statute issued on Ash Wednesday, 7 March, 1207, less than ten months after his consecration as bishop, in which he made detailed stipulations about the Ladymass and the other services devoted to the Virgin which were to be sung before her altar in the Lady Chapel. The Ladymass was to be celebrated by thirteen vicars of the church of Wells, of whom three were

---

[8]   See Rodwell, *Wells Cathedral*; for a summary of the chronology, see *ibid.*, i. 145–6.
[9]   See *EEA* x. nos 150, 259; and also below, p. 111.
[10] The evidence for the early use of the Lady Chapel, and subsequently of the quire, is provided by the temporary doors, discussed in Rodwell, *Wells Cathedral* i. 136–9, and by Jerry Sampson, below p. 111.
[11] *EEA* x. no. 246.
[12] See P. Binski, *Becket's Crown* (New Haven, and London, 2004), 113–14; and Church, *Chapters*, plate I, facing 36.

to be priests acting in turn week by week. The thirteen clerks were to be paid 1d. a day out of the bishop's own purse, and in addition the chapter agreed to grant full commons to the three who were priests.[13] Thus bishop and canons were bound together in an arrangement that survived until the sixteenth century.[14] Later, in the 1220s and 1230s, the sculptures above the central portal of the west front, the Virgin and Child and the Coronation of the Virgin, proclaimed to the world that, although the church was dedicated to St Andrew, this was a place where the Virgin Mary was held in special honour.

What kind of men were the canons of this great church? It has to be admitted that not all of them made much of a mark. Of the fifty-eight who were members of the chapter in 1206, seventeen, a third, are otherwise unknown.[15] But of the rest, the majority were quite active and some of them very distinguished.

Fifteen, or just over a quarter of the canons, were called masters, that is to say they were university-educated, mostly, we are to imagine, at Paris, though some may have studied at Oxford. Of the graduates, two at least were authors: Master Peter of Blois, archdeacon of Bath, a Frenchman, and canon of three French cathedrals as well as archdeacon of London, was a prolific theological writer of intellectual distinction; and the dean of Wells, Master Alexander Medicus, a physician, was also a moral theologian. Most of the senior positions in the church were filled by members of this graduate group: Master Alexander Medicus the dean, Master William de Sancta Fide the precentor, Master Roger of Winsham the chancellor, Master Peter of Blois the archdeacon of Bath and Master William of Wrotham the archdeacon of Taunton. A smaller group among the canons of 1206, consisting of seven individuals, were royal administrators; of these the most notable were Walter de Grey, the king's chancellor, who was to become bishop of Worcester in 1214, and from 1215 for the next forty years was archbishop of York, and Hugh of Wells, Jocelin's brother, who was a chancery clerk and became bishop of Lincoln in 1209. Ten of the known canons in 1206, who were neither graduates nor royal officers, came from local families, either from Wells itself or from villages in Somerset; of these, at least two, and probably more, owed their canonries to the fact that they were kinsmen of the donors of prebends. Five more, who do not fall into any of the above categories, were clerks in Bishop Savaric's administration. Finally, three were abbots of Benedictine monasteries, one in Normandy, at

---

[13] *Wells MSS* i. 377.

[14] *Ibid.*, ii. 703. In 1215 Jocelin gave a further endowment to the Ladymass: 10 marks each from two parish churches (Chew Magna and Wellington) to support the 'service of the glorious Virgin', *Wells MSS* i. 48; cf. *ibid.*, 150.

[15] For the list, see *Fasti 1066–1300* vii. 120–1. The biographical details that follow are drawn from the same volume.

Le Bec-Hellouin, and two in Somerset, at Muchelney and Athelney: Bishop Savaric had made settlements with these three abbeys to admit their abbots to prebends in the church of Wells.

Having looked at the kind of men who comprised the chapter when Jocelin became bishop in 1206, we must now consider the character of the appointments he made himself. All the positions in the chapter were in the bishop's gift, with the exceptions of the deanery (discussed below) and the three monastic prebends. The first feature to note is an increase under Jocelin in the proportion of canons called master: of his sixty-five appointments, thirty-three, a good half, were of masters. We should not think of this as exceptional, however, for it is in line with the trend in English cathedrals in the early thirteenth century.

But there is an unexpected change under Jocelin, a decline in the proportion of royal officials. I have found only two appointed by Jocelin, and only one of the two was at all distinguished. He was William de Ralegh, the judge, later to be bishop of Norwich until translated to the see of Winchester.

Although it is surprising that Jocelin's appointments to the chapter do not reflect his connections to the royal court and his own service to the crown, they do reveal some of his other personal networks. One such network was built up during his exile in the period of the Interdict. For just over three years, between the end of 1209 and the spring of 1213, Jocelin was in France, accompanied by a small group from Wells, six of whose names are known to us. Of these six, two, Master Ralph of Lechlade[16] and Master Elias of Dereham,[17] were already members of the chapter. The other four known companions of Jocelin's exile were simple clerks or chaplains, but all of them gained canonries as rewards for their loyalty after the return to Wells in 1213.[18] These four appointments by Jocelin belong to the broader category of clerical administrators within the chapter. In 1206 there were only five canons in this group. In addition to the four exiles, Jocelin made a further ten such appointments: of the ten, seven were masters, and the jobs they performed for the bishop included duties as clerks, chaplains, attorneys, dataries and legal officers.

Two further circles can be detected in Jocelin's appointments to the chapter: networks connected with the two cathedrals with which Jocelin had personal links, Lincoln and Salisbury. At least seven of his canons were either members of the household of his brother, Bishop Hugh of Lincoln, or

---

[16] He had been a clerk in Bishop Reginald's household by c.1174, had become archdeacon of Taunton in the mid-1180s, was made precentor by Jocelin in 1208, and by the time of the exile, in 1209, he was dean; he died before the return to England in 1213.

[17] One of Jocelin's first appointments as canon, between May 1206 and December 1209.

[18] Elias the chaplain, Peter of Chichester, Roger the chaplain of Chewton and William de Hammes.

canons of Lincoln Minster. And another seven were members of the chapter of Salisbury, where Jocelin's close political associate, Richard Poore, was bishop.

How were the individual canons organised into a 'chapter'? What were their duties and management structure? By 1206 the chapter of Wells was organised along similar lines to the chapters of the greater English cathedrals.[19] The hierarchy consisted of dean (and sub-dean), precentor (and succentor), chancellor, treasurer, and three archdeacons (Bath, Wells and Taunton). This structure had been established largely between 1136 and 1191 by Bishops Robert and Reginald. Both had drawn heavily on the model of Salisbury: under Robert, advice on various points had been sought directly from the dean and chapter of Salisbury, and Reginald, who had been the archdeacon of Salisbury and was also the bishop of Salisbury's son, had doubtless drawn on his own experience.

It was Salisbury that led the field in the compilation of cathedral constitutions. Its first written code, called the constitution of St Osmund, has traditionally been assigned to the year 1090, but was in fact first compiled in the 1150s, revised in the 1160s, and expanded after 1197. The Wells version of this post-1197 constitution, known as the 'Antiqua Statuta',[20] was probably introduced at Wells by Bishop Jocelin in the early years of his pontificate, before 1209,[21] perhaps encouraged by the dean of Wells, Master Alexander Medicus, who had been a canon of Salisbury, and by the chancellor, Master Roger of Winsham, who had been a familiar of the bishop of Salisbury, Herbert Poore.

The 'Antiqua Statuta' sets out the basic structure of the chapter and outlines the duties and rights of the dignitaries, archdeacons and canons. The dean has the prime position and general oversight of everything that goes on in the church; the precentor is second only to the dean and has responsibility for the conduct of the services; the chancellor is in charge of education and books; the treasurer looks after the ornaments, vestments

19 For an overview, see Kathleen Edwards, *The English Secular Cathedrals in the Middle Ages*, 2nd edn (Manchester, 1967).
20 The 'Antiqua Statuta' is printed in H.E. Reynolds, ed., *Wells Cathedral: Its Foundation, History and Statutes* (Leeds, 1881), 55–7. The text repeats clauses 1, 7–8, and 9–39 of the so-called 'Institutio' of Saint Osmund, with additions chiefly drawn from the 'Consuetudinarium' of Richard Poore (see my study of the composition of the 'Institutio': D. Greenway, 'The False *Institutio* of St Osmund', in *Tradition and Change*, ed. D. Greenway, C. Holdsworth and J. Sayers (Cambridge, 1985), 77–101, text at 94–6).
21 If my dating of the 'Institutio' of St Osmund is correct (see article cited in previous note), the 'Antiqua Statuta' most probably belongs to the period after 1206. A document dated 3 June 1209, annexing the church of Wedmore to the deanery (*Wells MSS* i. 66), looks like fine-tuning after the promulgation of the 'Antiqua Statuta'. And see below, pp. 60–1, for the reforms of 1208 and 1209.

and lighting;[22] the sub-dean acts as deputy for the dean and the succentor for the precentor; the archdeacons have the care of religion in the parishes; and all those members of the chapter who are resident, and fulfil their prime duty of attending the seven services of canonical hours in quire, are to receive commons, in addition to the income of their individual prebends. This constitution remained in force at Wells throughout the Middle Ages.[23]

The 'Antiqua Statuta' was a short document, without much detail. One addition to the legislation, to fill out a gap, was made soon after Jocelin's return from exile. On 14 June 1216 he issued a statute which laid down the procedure to be followed on the death of a dean.[24] Jocelin states in this document that in his experience at least two previous deans had been elected by the chapter,[25] and he believed also that election had been the canonical norm before the time of his own memory.[26] Therefore he confirmed the chapter's right to elect, provided they speedily inform the bishop of the death of a dean and request from him licence to elect, and having elected the most suitable man without delay they present him to the bishop for confirmation. Thus what had been an unwritten custom was regularised and enshrined in statute. Why did Jocelin feel it necessary to commit it to writing? It is very likely that 1213 had seen the appointment by Pope Innocent III of an unelected dean, Master Leonius.[27] Immediately after the death of Leonius, which occurred in late 1215 or early 1216, Jocelin acted to ensure that for the future the chapter's right to elect was formally recognised and confirmed. But in doing so he safeguarded the bishop's overall authority by insisting on the chapter's duty to seek licence to elect. It is significant that even in this addition to the constitutional code at Wells, Jocelin was following Salisbury custom: at that time, every English cathedral chapter had the right to elect their dean, but only at Salisbury, and from 1216 also at Wells, was it necessary to have the bishop's licence.

No church can function properly without adequate funding. The members of the chapter had two main sources of revenue. One was the income that came from their individual prebends. The other was their share of the commons, which came from the profit of the common property of the chapter, the common fund.

---

[22] See also the detailed list of the treasurer's duties in Jocelin's ordinance of 1226, *Wells MSS* i. 36–7.

[23] In 1313 it was consulted in 'an ancient book of customs'; *ibid.*, 154.

[24] *Ibid.*, 65, 151.

[25] These were probably Master Alexander Medicus (late 1180s) and Master Ralph of Lechlade (1208 or 1209); see *Fasti 1066–1300* vii. 9.

[26] There were only two deans at Wells before Master Alexander: Ivo, who occurs from the early 1140s, and Richard, from 1164 or 1165; *ibid.*, 8–9.

[27] Cf. *ibid.*, 9–10.

By 1206 the prebendal system at Wells was well established, having been set up by Bishop Robert and enlarged by his two successors, Reginald and Savaric. The canons enjoyed immunity from archidiaconal and other charges in their prebends.[28] Around thirty (more than half the total) of the prebends consisted of parish churches, from each of which the canon would take the tithes, offerings, fees, profits of the glebe, etc. During his pontificate Jocelin confirmed the properties of various of these parish-church prebends, adjudicated in disputes relating to some of them, and founded another six of this type.

However, Jocelin conducted a complete overhaul of the remaining prebends. These consisted of cash payments out of the profits of some large estates, which were managed by provosts. While he was in exile in France, between 1209 and 1213, Jocelin issued an ordinance that Combe St Nicholas, which hitherto had at most supported the precentor and three canons, was in future to support ten prebends of 10 marks each, the provost being appointed by the bishop from one of the ten.[29] Later, in 1234, the five similar prebends of Winsham, which had been established by Bishop Robert, were added by Jocelin to the provostship of Combe.[30] And by 1242, another large estate, that of Wedmore, was reorganised in a rather similar way, to provide for the deanery and four other prebends, each valued at £4.[31]

At the end of Jocelin's pontificate the total number of prebends was fifty-two. This represented a slight reduction on the figure of fifty-eight in 1206, when some of the canons had insecure or meagre financial support, a few even depending on handouts from the bishop's purse. By contrast, in 1242, each of the fifty-two had a securely established annual income, a basic prerequisite for the carrying out of the church's main function of worship.

Jocelin dealt with the resources of the dignitaries in a similar practical manner. Very early in his career, before his exile, he accomplished a complete rearrangement of the endowments of the dignities. On 4 March 1208, he made sweeping changes to the precentory (which lost Combe and gained the church of Pilton), the chancellery (which lost Winsham and gained the church of Kingsbury), the treasury (which lost St Cuthbert, Wells, and gained the church of Evercreech),[32] and the succentory (which gained land in Wells).[33] Just over a year later, on 3 June 1209, he completed

---

[28] See the charter of Hugh of Wells as archdeacon, 29 May 1205, *Wells MSS* i. 30, confirming Savaric's decree of 6 October 1203, *EEA* x. no. 244.
[29] *Wells MSS* i. 58; see *Fasti 1066–1300* vii. 43–4.
[30] *Wells MSS* i. 243–5; *Fasti 1066–1300* vii. 44.
[31] *Wells MSS* i. 60; *Fasti 1066–1300* vii. 72–5.
[32] Later, between 1219 and 1236, Evercreech was exchanged by Jocelin for Martock: *Wells MSS* i. 51.
[33] *CChR 1341–1417*, 25–6; and see *Fasti 1066–1300* vii. 12, 15, 18, 23.

his rearrangements for the deanery and the sub-deanery (the church of Wedmore was assigned to the deanery in exchange for that of Wookey, now assigned to the sub-deanery).[34] The archdeaconries of Bath and Wells both had satisfactory endowments already, and it was not until towards the end of his pontificate, in April 1241, that he made formal provision for the third archdeaconry, that of Taunton, by granting it a newly founded prebend (Milverton).[35]

Having seen Jocelin's thorough-going reform of the prebends and dignities, we must now consider the other source of remuneration of members of the chapter, the commons. This was a resident canon's share of the profits of the chapter's common property, the *communa* or common fund. In most cathedrals the commons was issued in two forms: first, a distribution ('quotidians') for those resident on any one day, and second, a share of the surplus of the fund, paid either quarterly or yearly to those who passed a residence qualification. At Wells the latter share-out was made at the end of the year and the residence qualification was laid down in the chapter statutes made in Jocelin's presence on 27 May 1241: residence for a simple canon was defined as half a year, either continuous or intermitted, and for a dignitary two thirds of a year, either continuous or intermitted.[36] An ordinance issued by Jocelin on 17 October 1242, only a month before his death, gives valuable details about the distributions (Figure 2). It shows that down to that date the daily commons had been paid partly in cash and partly in bread. The new rates were more generous: the bishop was to receive 8d. instead of 6d. and another 5d. instead of four white loaves; the five senior dignitaries (known as the *persone*) – dean, precentor, archdeacon of Wells, chancellor and treasurer – were to receive 8d. instead of 6d. and another 4d. instead of two white and two black loaves; all the other canons were to receive 4d. instead of 3d. and another 2d. instead of one white and one black loaf.[37] The residue in the fund at the end of the year was to be distributed equally among the five senior dignitaries and the canons resident, according to the same residence qualification as that laid down in 1241.

The common fund, from which the distributions were made, had been considerably enlarged by Jocelin so as to produce the extra yields that he was able to grant in his ordinance of 1242. He had augmented the fund in the late 1230s and early 1240s in a series of grants of churches and

---

34 *Wells MSS* i. 66, 3 June 1209, referring also to earlier provisions for the precentor, chancellor, treasurer and succentor.
35 *Wells MSS* i. 469, and see *Fasti 1066–1300* vii. 35.
36 *Wells MSS* i. 531; *Wells Cathedral*, ed. Reynolds, 57; Church, *Chapters*, 233.
37 *Wells MSS* i. 60, ii. 555; Church, *Chapters*, 235–7.

Figure 2. Ordinance of Bishop Jocelin, changing the common payments of the canons and vicars of Wells from bread to money; 17 October 1242. Wells Cathedral Charter 41a. Reproduced with permission of the Dean and Chapter of Wells.

manors (Plate 5).[38] He stipulated in 1241 that accounts and inventories of the contents of the barns and everything that belonged to the common fund were to be rendered annually for audit every October. As he stated in the preamble to his ordinance of 1242, his augmentation of the common fund was designed to bring about an improvement in provision for the clergy ministering in the fine new church, whose nave, west front and towers had been largely completed in the 1220s and 1230s, and the whole of which had been dedicated on 23 October 1239.

Consideration of funding naturally raises the question of the financing of the great rebuilding at Wells. Although the bishops – Reginald, Savaric and Jocelin – doubtless made contributions out of episcopal income towards the costs of the project, a large responsibility fell on the dean and chapter. There was a specially endowed and ring-fenced fabric fund, to which donors were encouraged to add their gifts,[39] but this was intended for building maintenance, rather then construction. In addition, in 1215 Jocelin followed Bishop Reginald's example of granting the fruits of vacant churches in the diocese specifically for the fabric until the building-work be finished.[40] But further extraordinary levies were necessary in the form of charges on the canons' prebends. Such charges seem to have been levied first in Reginald's time.[41] We do not know the details of this system, nor how long it was in force. But it seems that it had been discontinued by the time of the dedication in 1239, when there were large debts outstanding. Acting on the advice of Jocelin, who was following a precedent drawn from Salisbury, the chapter levied a tax of one fifth on every prebend for seven years, or longer if necessary.[42]

---

[38] Church of Congresbury, 1 May 1237: *Wells MSS* i. 49. Manor and church of North Curry, 30 September 1239: *ibid.*, 31–2. Manor of Winscombe at the dedication of the church of Wells, 23 October 1239: *ibid.*, 59. Churches of Cheddar, 29 December 1239: *ibid.*, 32. Church of Mudford, 14 January 1240: *ibid.*, 32. Church of Norton sub Hamdon, 14 February 1242: *ibid.*, 399. Church of Chewton, 17 February 1242: *ibid.*, 398. Annual payments from churches of Stawley and Nunney, n.d.: *ibid.*, 149. Moiety of church of Whitchurch Canonicorum, n.d.: *ibid.*, 149, cf. 522ff.

[39] The land of Biddisham was set aside for the fabric by Bishop Robert: *EEA* x. no. 46; and see *Fasti 1066–1300* vii. 112; for date, see *Fasti 1066–1300* vii. 117–19.

[40] Reginald's grant is *EEA* x. no. 150: 'in usus operationis ... donec per dei miserationis auxilium consummetur.' Jocelin's order, granting two thirds of the fruits that customarily came to the bishop (the archdeacon took the other third), is *Wells MSS* i. 67. In 1249 the dean and chapter successfully claimed the fruits from Bishop William de Bitton I on the grounds that they had enjoyed possession for more than forty years: *Wells MSS* i. 5.

[41] See Master Alexander's gift, 1176 x 89, *Wells MSS* i. 490, and for the date and identity of Master Alexander, see *Fasti 1066–1300* vii. 55.

[42] *Wells MSS* i. 82. For Salisbury, see *Vetus Registrum Sarisberiense, alias dictum Registrum S. Osmundi*, ed. W.H. Rich Jones, 2 vols, Rolls Series 78 (London, 1883–84) ii. 8, 41.

The major purpose of much of Jocelin's legislative activity vis-à-vis the chapter was to achieve the highest possible standard of worship in the church of Wells. Canonical residence was central. We have seen how Jocelin not only stipulated the basic residential requirements – half a year for simple canons and two thirds of a year for dignitaries – but also actively promoted residence by establishing adequate incomes for residents. There was another very practical way in which he encouraged canons to reside: this was the acquisition by purchase and gift of a number of houses for canons, close to the church, in an area which was to become known as the Liberty. One of the earliest acquisitions by Jocelin was an area, with houses, to the north of the church, described as 'before the great gate of the canons', which was granted to the church and bishop by Master Nicholas of Wells, possibly a member of Jocelin's family, between May 1206 and December 1209; one of the houses subsequently assigned by Jocelin as a canonical house is now the Music School.[43] Several other houses near the church were added to the stock of canonical dwellings under Jocelin's supervision. Perhaps the most important was the one he granted in 1236 to the dean, Master William de Merton, and his successor deans in perpetuity:[44] it was to be held by all the deans of Wells until the 1950s and is now known as the Old Deanery.[45]

But dignitaries and canons were not required to be in residence all the time, and even when resident, and present in church, they were not necessarily capable of achieving high musical standards. Therefore by the second half of the twelfth century many canons had made arrangements for their quire duties (principally performing the liturgy, the canonical hours) to be carried out vicariously, that is by vicars, later called vicars choral.[46] As with vicarages in parish churches, without episcopal regulation there was some possibility of exploitation and abuse. Jocelin acted to ensure that both kinds of vicars were properly appointed and remunerated. When he issued his ordinance on the deanery and sub-deanery, for example, in 1209, he specified that the dean was to have a vicar in the quire of Wells who was to be in priest's orders and to receive 4 marks yearly, and the sub-dean's vicar was to have a minimum stipend of 2 marks yearly.[47] During his pontificate he laid down similar regulations for the quire vicarages of almost all the prebends:

---

43 *Wells MSS* i. 18; Church, *Chapters*, 177–8; D. Sherwin Bailey, *The Canonical Houses of Wells* (Gloucester, 1982), 123–7.
44 *Wells MSS* i. 49; Church, *Chapters*, 225.
45 Bailey, *Canonical Houses*, 102–9.
46 Cf. *EEA* x. nos 46, 240, 249, 259. On vicars choral in general, see R. Hall and D. Stocker, eds, *Vicars Choral at English Cathedrals* (Oxford, 2005). The letter from the chapter of Salisbury to the bishop of Bath, *Wells MSS* i. 31, cited by J. Barrow, 'Vicars Choral and Chaplains in Northern European Cathedrals 1100–1250', *Studies in Church History* 26 (1989), 87–97, at 90, probably belongs to the mid-thirteenth century rather than the mid-twelfth.
47 *Wells MSS* i. 66.

at his death only three prebends lacked formally constituted vicars choral.[48] The ordinance given at the end of his life, in October 1242, concerning the distribution of commons, already mentioned in relation to dignitaries and canons, stipulated that vicars choral were to receive 1d. a day instead of a loaf every other day.[49] In addition to this allowance, a vicar would receive a fixed stipend, as laid down by the bishop when the vicarage was formally constituted. An alternative to receiving the stipend was for the vicar to be accommodated and fed in the house of his canon. Before the completion of the vicars' hall, in 1348, some vicars certainly did live in their canons' houses: there is a clear reference to this practice in the statutes of Dean Godley, dated 1331.[50] Other vicars, however, lived semi-independently: I say 'semi', because a chapter statute drawn up in 1243, the year after Jocelin's death, laid down that 'no vicar should live alone, but two at least together',[51] a provision aimed at maintaining some discipline in a notoriously badly behaved group.

That the great changes and upheavals of Jocelin's episcopate produced no obvious strains or conflicts between bishop and chapter is a tribute to the good sense of both. In fact, numerous documents show them working harmoniously together in a long series of policy decisions that were formally approved and sealed by both bishop and chapter in chapter-meetings at Wells. The statutes issued on 27 May 1241 included provision for a bell to be assigned to call the canons to chapter.[52] At this period, the only suitable space for the chapter to conduct its meetings was the chapel of St Mary by the cloister, which stood off the cloister's east walk, in roughly the position where monastic chapter houses were normally situated.[53] It was conveniently close to Jocelin's new palace, but at some distance from the canonical houses to the north of the church – hence the utility of the bell.

At the beginning of this chapter I described Wells in 1206 as a 'quasi-cathedral. During his thirty-six years as bishop, Jocelin carried out a programme of reform designed to develop the chapter and its institutions so as to eliminate the 'quasi'. When he died in November 1242 he was buried in the quire of a newly dedicated church that was indistinguishable from a cathedral, with a chapter of disciplined and well-educated canons. They and their hierarchy of dean and dignitaries had all the attributes of a cathedral chapter – an articulated constitution and sufficient individual and shared endowments to support the worship and pastoral activities of

[48] See *Collectanea I*, 65.
[49] See above n. 37.
[50] Reynolds, *Wells Cathedral*, 76.
[51] *Wells MSS* i. 254 embedded in statutes of 1298–99.
[52] *Wells MSS* i. 531; Reynolds, *Wells Cathedral*, 57; Church, *Chapters*, 233.
[53] See Rodwell, *Wells Cathedral* i. 343ff., esp. 345.

a cathedral. On 3 January 1245, less than three years after Jocelin's death, the church of Wells regained its rightful status. After proper investigation the pope granted that in future the bishop's throne should be in each of the churches of Bath and Wells and that henceforth the occupant of the see should be styled 'bishop of Bath and Wells'.[54] This happy and long-lasting outcome is a testament to the effectiveness of Jocelin's policies for the church and chapter in whose service he spent most of his life.

[54] Church, *Chapters*, 253; *CPL* i. 212; brief note only in *Wells MSS* i. 364.

4

The Bishop and His Cathedral Cities

SETHINA WATSON

Jocelin of Wells was a local man whose family networks and rapid career rise were both firmly rooted in the Somerset diocese, and most particularly in the up-and-coming borough of Wells. His life spanned the very decades when English provincial towns were experiencing their most rapid growth and when so many were emerging onto the national map as centres of wealth and power. Across the country communities like Wells were undergoing a dramatic demographic and commercial expansion, securing their most decisive political liberties and creating new forms of civic government.[1] Jocelin and his brother Hugh are distinctive examples of the many ways in which a bishop's career and identity might be forged by these rapidly growing towns of post-Conquest England. They were from a local landholding family, but they took their names, as did their father, from the borough. The swift rise of father and, especially, his sons owed much to the emerging ecclesiastical and urban communities in Wells: the borough had fostered their father's fortune and influence, while the church nurtured the brothers' careers as episcopal and soon royal clerics.[2] Both were promoted to sees, their titles of bishop of Bath and bishop of Lincoln drawn respectively, as was customary, from the urban seat which gave the diocese its name. Yet whereas Hugh's civic affiliations as native son (of Wells) and bishop (of Lincoln) remained discrete and stable, Jocelin's were intertwined and shifting, complicated both by the diverging fortunes of Wells and Bath as towns and by controversy over the location of his episcopal seat. The Somerset see had failed to

---

[1] J. Tait, *The Medieval English Borough: Studies on its Origins and Constitutional History* (Manchester, 1936), 240; S. Reynolds, *An Introduction to the History of English Medieval Towns* (Oxford, 1977), 102–10. A recent discussion and bibliography can be found in R. Britnell, *Britain and Ireland 1050–1530: Economy and Society* (Oxford, 2004), 71–2, 140–9.

[2] Hugh's career and his family are discussed in *Acta of Hugh of Wells*, xxviii–xxxi. For the activities of Edward in Wells, see *EEA* x. nos 152 and 177 and below. He is one of a number of local witnesses, apparently leading men of the town, to an early confirmation of borough trading rights (*ibid.*, no. 177).

settle in one city, and the situation had reached crisis point by his accession, with Bath, Wells and Glastonbury each having a claim. The ties between a bishop and city were perhaps never so complex, nor so laid bare, as during the episcopate of Jocelin of Wells, bishop of Bath.

The problem of bishop and city

Of course, the relationship of a bishop to his cathedral city was in fact mediated through a web of ties to place and community. This was particularly true for the Somerset diocese, where the bishops' shifting, sometimes controversial, uses of Bath, Wells and Glastonbury were often more concerned with the major churches of each place than with the towns themselves. As the Glastonbury controversy illustrates, the role and rights of the chapters were crucial in defining the location of the episcopal seat. Similarly, the bishops expressed their political or administrative attachments most vividly through building campaigns or enriching the financing for palace, cathedral or chapter. Since these questions have been examined elsewhere in this volume, and by others more qualified, I have chosen to examine the bishop's relationship to his cities in more limited terms in hopes of shedding a different light on Jocelin's career. This essay will consequently confine itself to a consideration of 'city' in two senses: as site (both geographic and symbolic) and as a centre (of economy and population). Identifying a bishop with a metropolis is problematic for England in the twelfth and early thirteenth centuries (and certainly for the relatively minor Bath and Wells), but the issue was peculiarly relevant because of its difficulties. Indeed, the importance of this ideal in the face of its impoverished reality was very much a topic of contemporary concern. The ancient affiliation of bishop with city had developed from the remnants of the Roman Empire, when the bishop's urban seat became the centre of administration, provisioning and defence. During the early Middle Ages, the terms *civitas* (cathedral city) and *metropolitanus* (metropolitan, archbishop) embodied ideas of both episcopal jurisdiction and of urban space.[3] It was an association that continued into Jocelin's day, when a late twelfth-century chronicler complained that 'Rochester and Chichester are mere hamlets [*viculi*] and there is no reason why they should be called cities [*civitates*] except for the bishops' seats.'[4] By

---

[3]   For a recent description, D. Nicholas, *The Growth of the Medieval City: from Late Antiquity to the Early Fourteenth Century* (London, 1997), 25.

[4]   *Chronicle of Richard of Devizes of the Time of King Richard the First*, ed. J.T. Appleby (London, 1963), 66–7.

Jocelin's time the idea of 'city' was commonly associated with wealth, power and population, but the label was attached to a bishop's seat.

The ideal of a bishop in his city was thus both ancient and entirely modern in twelfth-century England. When reformers from the continent arrived in England in the middle of the eleventh century, they were unimpressed to find a native church whose dioceses were impoverished and whose suffragan bishops often had their seats in small towns and hamlets. The problem was compounded by the fame, power and income of many monastic houses that far outshone the minor cathedral churches in wealth, prestige and influence, fortified by rich endowments, renowned saint cults and monks able and willing to defend their possessions.[5] In contrast to many cities on the continent, the boroughs of Anglo-Saxon England, with their markets and mints, had often flourished away from episcopal seats, in fortified settlements that were closely connected to royal administration.[6] Lotharingian and Norman reformers found the poverty of cathedral churches and their remote locations to be both inconvenient and ignoble. Work to remove the sees was given impetus and justification in Archbishop Lanfranc's great reforming council in London in 1075, which declared that it went against both papal and conciliar decree to have episcopal seats in villages. The council therefore authorised the translation of three bishoprics 'from villages to cities' and promised to address others who still remained 'in villages and hamlets' when the king returned from his foreign wars.[7] Between 1050 and 1100 there was a thorough reorganisation of bishoprics, as diocesan seats were moved to urban centres and often to the more important monastic houses which were sited there: thus the see at Crediton moved to Exeter (1050), Dorchester to Lincoln (1072), North Elmham to Thetford (1072) then Norwich (1094–5), Sherborne to Salisbury (1075–78), Selsey to Chichester (1075), Lichfield to Chester (1075) then Coventry (1102), and Wells to Bath (1088–90).[8]

Reorganisation on this scale was peculiar to England, permanently transforming the diocesan map. In his major study, Christopher Brooke ties this upheaval directly to Lanfranc's 1075 council, noting that the archbishop turned in desperation for conciliar authority to little-cited canons of the

---

5   D.J.A. Matthew, *The Norman Conquest* (London, 1966), 85–9.
6   Reynolds, *An Introduction*, 24–37, 92–6; J. Campbell, 'Power and Authority 600–1300', in *The Cambridge Urban History of Britain I: 600–1540*, ed. D.M. Palliser (Cambridge, 2000), 51–78, esp. 53–60.
7   'Ex decretis summorum pontificum, Damasi videlicet et Leonis, necnon ex conciliis Sardicensi atque Laodicensi, in quibus prohibetur episcopales sedes in villis existere, concessum est regia munificentia et sinodali auctoritate prefatis tribus episcopis de villis ad civitates transire': *Councils and Synods*, i. ii, 613.
8   E.U. Crosby, *Bishop and Chapter in Twelfth-Century England* (Cambridge, 1994), 32–3.

distant councils of Sardicia and Laodicea; in so doing he was using them as pretext rather than motive for his decree.[9] With city walls and, soon, nearby Norman castles these new sites had better defences, a pressing concern with the looming civil war of that year. 'It is ironical to observe', Brooke notes, 'how permanent were the plans made under the emergency conditions of the 1070s for the future of these sees.'[10] Although centred in the 1070s, the reorganisation spanned the second half of the eleventh century and into the twelfth, and included the foundation of new dioceses with seats in Ely (1108) and Carlisle (1133). Many of the moves were motivated, too, by a desire to claim the fame and wealth of some of the more substantial monastic houses located in these towns;[11] but it is notable that the argument was framed in terms of an ecclesiastical ideal that a bishop belonged in a city.

The better defences offered by cities were clearly an incentive, as the 1050 confirmation of the transfer of Exeter explicitly noted;[12] but at a time when many places offered defensive capabilities in the form of ancient borough walls or castles, the new sites had other, less noted, features in common. The cities were on major Roman roads: Lincoln was only slightly more central within its huge diocese than Dorchester had been, but it was at the intersection of Ermine Street (the major route north from London) and the Fosse Way (east–west to Exeter); remote Sherborne removed to Salisbury, from which five Roman roads departed; Selsey was on a southern promontory jutting into the Channel, while the new seat at Chichester was at the intersection of roads north-east to London, west to Winchester and north to Watling Street. In common with the diocesan seats that were not removed (Canterbury, York, Winchester, London, Worcester, Hereford and Rochester), most of the new sees were now located at major Roman centres, ancient sites near roads and ports which were better for transport, communication, population and profit. Secular royal administration after the Conquest essentially adopted the Anglo-Saxon administrative map, with its shires, shire-towns and hundreds, supplemented by a pragmatic geography of castle-building and defence.[13] In contrast, the pattern of reorganised dioceses reveals a programme of systematic reform. This reform sought to improve the fame, wealth and defence of cathedral churches, but it was shaped by, and in turn helped promote, an older ideal of the bishop

---

9   He notes that 'I know of no contemporary parallel for the citation of these authorities to justify such a move'. C.N.L. Brooke, 'Archbishop Lanfranc, the English Bishops, and the Council of London of 1075', *Studia Gratiana* 12 (1967), 41–59 (53 and n.).

10 *Ibid.*, 53–5 (55).

11 Matthew, *Norman Conquest*, 186–7.

12 *Councils and Synods*, i. i, 525–8. Here also the transfer stressed the move 'a Credionensi villula ad civitatem Exoniam' (from the hamlet of Crediton to the city of Exeter).

13 J.A. Green, *The Government of England under Henry I* (Cambridge, 1986), 106–13.

in his city and, in the new *civitates*, a more Romanised diocesan map of England.

In all cases except one the moves were linear and largely complete by the early twelfth century. This does not mean, of course, that they were simple. In two cases, robust protests by local abbeys foiled episcopal designs, forcing the sees to settle elsewhere: the East Anglian see arrived at Norwich by 1095 via Thetford and after an aborted foray on Bury St Edmunds, and the Lichfield see failed to intrude on a resistant Chester and eventually resettled at Coventry in 1102.[14] One diocese, however, failed to settle until the mid-thirteenth century. The see of Somerset or Wells became the see of Bath in 1090, of Bath with Wells, of Bath and Glastonbury (in 1197 and 1213–19), and of Bath (1219–44), before being confirmed, finally, in 1245, as Bath and Wells.[15] It was immediately before and during Jocelin's episcopate that the claims of all three were most contested and, ultimately, resolved, and when the claims of Wells were formally delineated; shortly after his death, they were fully confirmed.

At a time when reform ideals so clearly tied a bishop to his urban seat, and despite removing to its very own *civitas* in 1090, the bishopric of Somerset failed to settle decisively in one geographical location. The bishop maintained an official seat in Bath, but for over 150 years his identity was the most rootless of any English bishop. At no time was this more obvious than during the episcopate of Jocelin of Wells. When his neighbour Richard Poore, bishop of Salisbury, was commencing his new cathedral (of Salisbury) with its ambitious new city (of Salisbury), Jocelin of Wells, bishop of Bath and Glastonbury, who had been elected by the chapters of Bath and Wells, had recently become bishop of Bath (his claim to Glastonbury finally terminated), and held his synods at Bath but devoted his building energies on the church, palace and cloister at Wells.[16] This fragmented relationship between bishop and place in Somerset presents an opportunity to ask wider questions about the connection between bishop and city during a time of transition, when ideals of diocesan administration, urban community and wealth were all changing so quickly. It is in this light that we shall consider Jocelin's complex inheritance and his role in creating the diocese of Bath and Wells.

---

[14] V.H. Galbraith, 'The East Anglian See and the Abbey of Bury St Edmunds', *English Historical Review*, 40 (1925), 222–8.

[15] These refer to changes in the bishop's title during these years, with the exception of 'Bath with Wells' which recognises the influence of Wells as a secondary episcopal church from the last quarter of the twelfth century, notably the chapter's right to jointly elect the bishop and provide assent (and objection) to certain episcopal actions, *EEA* x. xxxii-xxxvi, lxxxvii, and no. 192.

[16] For the synod, *Glast. Chart.* i. 8–9.

The cathedral cities of Bath and Wells

There was supposed to have been only one cathedral city. When John of Tours became bishop of Somerset, he secured licence from King William II to remove the see from Wells to Bath and, in a separate deed of 1091, procured the city of Bath from the king at a purported cost of 500 marks. The deed of transfer noted that Lanfranc's work had aided in the removal, which included the grant of Bath priory 'for the augmentation of the bishopric of Somerset, and especially so that from now on [the bishop] should have his seat in that place'; the gift of the city was similarly to augment his episcopal seat.[17] Henry I confirmed the grant of the city of Bath (*de civitate Bathon'*) in 1101 'in order that in that place from this time forward shall be the head and mother church of the whole bishopric of Somerset'.[18] The importance of Bath as a city was further underscored by William of Malmesbury who explained that John of Tours had removed the see to Bath because he thought it 'insufficiently glorious' to dwell dishonourably in such a village as Wells.[19] John clearly intended the removal to be permanent. He destroyed the domestic buildings of the canons at Wells and evicted the chapter, seizing much of their income and turning it over to his steward.[20] At the same time, he developed Bath priory, enhancing its endowment, gathering learned monks and providing rich bequests of books and ornaments.[21] The diocese in turn became associated with the city: the sometime bishop of Somerset or Wells was now the bishop of Bath. As John himself decreed in 1106, 'I, John, by the grace of God bishop of Bath ... have laboured and finally brought about, with proper authority, that the seat and mother church of the whole bishopric of Somerset shall be in the city of Bath in the church of St Peter'.[22] Henceforth, the diocese of Somerset was to be the diocese of Bath.[23]

---

17 'ad Sumersetensis episcopatus augmentationem, eatenus praesertim ut inibi instituat praesuleam sedem': *Mon. Angl.* ii. 266; R.A.L. Smith, 'John of Tours, Bishop of Bath 1088–1122' in his *Collected Papers* (London, 1947), 74–82 (76–7). For a recent discussion of the movements of the see, highlighting the development of the episcopal estate, see *EEA* x. xxiv–xxxvi.

18 '[donum de civitate Bathoniae] constitui et concessi ut ibi deinceps sit caput et mater ecclesia totius episcopatus de Somersete': *Mon. Angl.* ii. 267.

19 'minoris gloriae putans si in uilla resideret inglorius, transferre thronum in Bathoniam animo intendit': *Gesta Pontificum*, 304.

20 'Historiola', 9–41 (at 22); *Collectanea I*, 61.

21 *EEA* x. no. 3; *Bath Charts.* nos 53 and 808; *Gesta Pontificum*, 306.

22 'Ego Iohannes gratia dei Bathoniensis episcopus ... allaboravi et ad effectum perduxi cum decenti auctoritate ut caput et mater ecclesia totius episcopatus de Sumerseta sit in urbe Bathonia in ecclesia sancti Petri': *EEA* x. no. 3.

23 For the older terminology of the diocese of Somerset, see *The Anglo-Saxon Chronicle*, trans. and ed. M.J. Swanton (London, 1966), 189.

Bath was certainly a more distinguished choice for an episcopal seat. It was an ancient city, with ancient ruins, near the intersection of the Roman roads from Bristol to London and from Exeter to the north (the Fosse Way). In a prosperous valley, it was a larger settlement than Wells, and an Anglo-Saxon borough with town walls. The Domesday Survey, which was made four years before John removed to Bath, records Wells as a productive backwater: a sprawling, populous manor of scattered hamlets with pastoral and arable farming.[24] Under the ecclesiastical lordship of bishop and canons, it produced an income of £42 from six mills, ploughed land, pasture, woodland and moor.[25] Bath, by contrast, was a royal borough with over 150 burgesses, a royal mint and the lordship of nearby Batheaston; it paid incomes to royal, ecclesiastical and secular lords, including £65 to the king and another £11 to his sheriff.[26] John may have found the monks of Bath 'dullards' and 'uncultivated' when he arrived, as William of Malmesbury reported, but the abbey was identified with a great Anglo-Saxon saint, Alphege, through whom it could boast connections to the monastic reform movement under Dunstan and before that to Anglo-Saxon kings.[27] Nor was the move contested, as were those to Chester or, successfully, to Bury St Edmunds. Indeed, John rode into Bath without the jurisdictional controversies that had beset other such relocations. Since he purchased the town wholesale from the king, he had no resident secular power to contend with, and his acquisition of the more moderate priory, itself clearly in need of political protection, went smoothly in comparison to the fierce battles waged by powerful abbeys like Bury and, later, Glastonbury. In fact both city and priory had recently been razed during the 1088 rebellion of Robert de Mowbray, perhaps facilitating their transfer by the king to the bishop a year later.[28]

With so much seemingly in its favour, why did the city become such a compromised seat for the bishop, and so swiftly? Perhaps because it offered many reasons to remove there but no overwhelming reason to remain. Bath had indeed been an important Roman town, but this was originally for therapeutic rather than military or economic reasons. Its ancient wonders, the ruins of the baths, were signs of a fabulous past, but one that recorded pagan endeavour rather than Anglo-Saxon miracle. Bath continued to draw

[24] Shaw, *Community*, 15–16.
[25] *DB* 240.
[26] *Ibid.*, 233–4, 240, 242.
[27] 'quod essent hebetes et eius estimatione barbari': *Gesta Pontificum*, 306–7. Bath was the site of King Edgar's impressive coronation in 973. Alphege was a national figure, a renowned holy man and reformer, once abbot of Bath and chosen by Dunstan to be bishop of Winchester; he was martyred by the Danes while archbishop of Canterbury, and his tomb was at Canterbury.
[28] *The Chronicle of John of Worcester*, ed. R.R. Darlington and P. McGurk (Oxford, 1998), iii. 52–3; *EEA* x. xxiv.

the wretched to its baths but not to its shrines; it was one of the few cathedral churches never to acquire its own great saint.[29] These ancient honours
belonged to Glastonbury. The episcopal holdings, even including the city,
were worth £170, only half the value of the larger, if more pastoral, estates
at Wells.[30] Although defended by city walls, Bath and its priory lacked
the commanding strongholds of the churches at Durham and Lincoln. A
late twelfth-century commentator mocked its location, alleging that Bath,
'placed or rather dumped down in the midst of the valleys, in an exceed-
ingly heavy air and sulphurous vapour, is at the gates of hell'.[31] Unlike
Norwich, it was neither a great port city nor the economic power-house of
its region. Indeed, and most catastrophically for John's city, these honours
belonged to its neighbour, nearby Bristol. Just thirteen miles along the road
and at the mouth of the river Avon, which also served Bath, Bristol was
swiftly becoming the major port and city of the south-west. Bristol was not
itself a candidate for an episcopal seat: it was a border town, straddling
ancient Mercia and Wessex, contemporary Gloucester and Somerset, and
the dioceses of Worcester and Somerset. However, its border status probably
encouraged its dramatic growth after the Conquest, and certainly aided the
city's tendency to act as a base for rebellion. The rapid rise of this border
town in the twelfth century increasingly threatened Bath, commercially,
politically and even physically. Even though Bath was at the intersection of
two major roads, it was really, and increasingly, *en route* to Bristol.

These deficits might have been overcome by a determined bishop, and
had Bath possessed any one of these religious, defensive or economic features
it might well have retained its status as Somerset's sole cathedral city. But
the nearby location of towns with stronger claims to wealth, miracle and
power made Bath vulnerable, and under Bishop Robert of Lewes (1136–66)
its primacy was first challenged. His motives may have been captured in
the *Gesta Stephani*, a chronicle of the civil wars during the reign of King
Stephen, whose anonymous author has since been identified as Bishop
Robert.[32] In *Gesta Stephani* he worries often about the threat created by
the proximity and ambition of Bristol. This 'stepmother of all England', as
the author witheringly terms it, was 'almost the richest city of all in the
country', with impregnable defences, a harbour to accommodate 1,000 ships,
and a greedy, aggressive populace. Bath, he notes by contrast, had strong

---

29 The others were Carlisle, Exeter, Coventry and Wells. B. Nilson, *Cathedral Shrines of
Medieval England* (Woodbridge, 1998), 6.
30 Crosby, *Bishop and Chapter*, 53–4. The limited inducements of Bath prompt Crosby to
'wonder why John thought to move his see there in the first place', *ibid.*, 53.
31 'Batonia in imis uallium in crasso nimis aere et uapore sulphereo posita, immo deposita,
est ad portas inferi', in *Chron. Richard of Devizes*, 66–7. The author was bemoaning the
backward state of urban life in England more generally.
32 *Gesta Stephani*, ed. K.R. Potter and R.H.C. Davis (London, 1976), xxxiv–xxxviii.

defences that protected not wealth, greed and trade, but rather little springs 'of agreeable warmth, wholesome and pleasant to look upon'. Whereas the sick of all England flocked into Bath 'to wash away their infirmities in the health-giving waters', the people of Bristol carried their rapacity and 'most foul brigandage' outward, and 'to almost every part of England'.[33] If Bath gathered the weak and healed them, Bristol sent its own power outward, to destroy. And Robert had good reason for his fears. Just two years after he had become bishop, in 1138, the threat of Bristol was vividly brought home when forces from Bristol attacked Bath, kidnapping the bishop (Robert himself) and, once again, burning the church and city.[34] That was twice in fifty years that Bath had been devastated by rebels from Bristol.

The depth of the fear and dismay expressed in the *Gesta* suggests that this incident may have prompted Robert to look outside Bath for a level of administrative, and personal, security, and therefore inspired his rejuvenation of Wells. Robert did not abandon Bath as his episcopal seat: he rebuilt the priory, secured papal recognition both of the church as cathedral and of the transfer of the see to Bath, and granted an indulgence to those who visited the priory on the anniversary of his dedication of a cross there.[35] But he also turned again to Wells, beginning to rebuild the abandoned church and community.[36] This work was continued by his successor, Reginald FitzJocelin (1174–91), whose episcopate coincided with a widespread and dramatic expansion in diocesan government. New administrative structures, courts and systems of oversight demanded men with greater training in the law and expertise in administration. These officials had to be supported, and Reginald turned to the chapter at Wells to facilitate his growing administration.[37] As a secular chapter it offered distinct advantages over Bath's community of monks. The bishop could appoint men of proven ability to its prebends, which in turn attracted ambitious, educated scholars who wished to serve the church without submitting to monastic

---

[33] 'turpissimi huius latrocinii': *Gesta Stephani*, 57–65 (esp. 57, 59, 63). The great wealth of Bristol can be seen in the pipe rolls of the twelfth century. At the end of Robert's episcopate, Bristol accounted for 500 marks (£333) per year to the exchequer: *Pipe Roll*, 12 Henry II, 97.

[34] *Chronicle of John of Worcester*, iii. 228, 230.

[35] *Collectanea I*. 62; *EEA* x. no. 17; *Papsturkunden in England*, ed. Walther Holtzmann, 3 vols (Göttingen, 1952), ii. no. 90, and for context, *EEA* x. xxvi.

[36] *EEA* x. nos 46–53. Robert's rebuilding of Wells is detailed in Frances Ramsey, 'Robert of Lewes, Bishop of Bath, 1136–66: a Cluniac Bishop in his Diocese', in *Belief and Culture in the Middle Ages: Studies Presented to Henry Mayr-Harting*, ed. Richard Gameson and Henrietta Leyser (Oxford, 2001), 251–63; and the prebends and estates in Crosby, *Bishop and Chapter*, 56–60. Both conclude that Robert was not trying to create a cathedral in Wells but rather to recreate Giso's destroyed church; and see *EEA* x. xxv–vi.

[37] *EEA* x. xxviii and nos 149–74. The bishop had greater influence in the appointments to secular chapters, both in prebends and offices, than he did in monastic chapters, Edwards, *Eng. Secular Cathedrals*, 119–23.

obedience. The secular church's more limited residential requirements and lighter liturgical duties permitted greater freedom of movement in service of both diocese and household. It is therefore no coincidence that the secular church of Wells was emerging when an expanding diocesan government most needed the services of its canons; by the early 1170s, this diocesan role began to foster ambitions among the chapter. It produced the 'Historiola', a history exploring both Wells's claims to the see and why the seat had been moved to Bath. In addition, Bishop Reginald may have been elected by the chapters at both Bath and Wells. Copies exist of a c.1174 papal confirmation that the churches of Wells and Bath share the right to elect and consecrate the bishop, and another recording the Wells chapter's role in the election.[38]

This resurrection of the church of Wells under Bishops Robert and Reginald was paralleled by their cultivation of the local town.[39] Robert transformed the village of Wells into a borough. His first charter had established fairs on the festivals of the Invention of the Holy Cross, St Calixtus and St Andrew; granted freedom from disturbance and tolls for those conducting business on the eve and day of each feast; and, importantly, designated a space on the streets for a market. This he did, he said, because the disorderly commotion of commercial exchange, especially on these feast days, was spilling into the church and its vestibule, disrupting its ministers and the prayers of the faithful, and bringing shame to the church. He could not 'suffer the house of prayer to become a den of trade'.[40] Robert was responding to a level of organic commercial development within the village, and acting primarily to protect the religious observance in the church, but

---

[38] *Papsturkunden in England*, ii. nos 133, 167. Frances Ramsey finds in the 'Historiola' 'ample evidence of the increasing self-consciousness of the chapter', *EEA* x. xxxiii. For the view that neither the canons nor their bishops sought cathedral status for the Wells church, see Crosby, *Bishop and Chapter*, 60–1. Reginald did much to foster Wells, but his gifts of books, relics, and ornaments to Bath priory display a commitment to developing the existing cathedral church, *Bath Charts*. ii. no. 808. For the 'Historiola', see n. 20 above.

[39] The major study of the town of Wells is Shaw, *Community*. It explores the development of the urban community from the mid-thirteenth century and includes an examination of the economic and topographical development of the borough in the twelfth century (11–17, 26–31). The early political development is considered in Sethina Watson, 'City as Charter: Charity and the Lordship of English Towns, 1170–1250', in *Cities, Texts and Social Networks, 400–1500: Experiences and Perceptions of Medieval Urban Space*, ed. A. Lester, C. Symes and C. Goodson (Aldershot, 2010), 235–62, esp. 242–7.

[40] 'Non nullorum autem constat experientie quod tumultus nundinarum, quae in eadem ecclesia et in atrio eius hactenus esse consueverunt, ad dedecus et incommodum eiusdem ecclesie accedit, cum in ea ministrantibus quam maxime sit inportunus quia et eorum devotionem inpedit et orationum quietem perturbat verum, ne contra vocem dominicam domum orationis [sp]eluncam patiamur fieri negotiationis': *EEA* x. no. 55. The phrase is from John 2:16, 'nolite facere domum Patris me domum negotiationis.' The feasts were 3 May, 14 October and 30 November.

he nonetheless deserves credit for the urban foundations of Wells. This commercial growth would have been stimulated by his building of the church and provisioning of its community and given focus and encouragement by the new church's festivals and the crowds that they drew. By establishing customary places for trading on the streets, this first charter began to formalise a market; his second charter constituted Wells as a borough and delineated its boundaries. The latter deed does not survive, but it is noted in a confirmation by Reginald, who did much to uphold and develop Robert's work, notably guaranteeing the freedoms of those in the borough to hold and sell property, and to come and go.[41] The 'Historia Major' states that Reginald 'more than anyone made the village of Wells into a free borough and freed its burgesses in perpetuity from the villein services with which they had previously been so greatly oppressed'.[42] There is no explicit evidence that either Robert or Reginald aimed to return the see to Wells, but their resurrection of the church and cultivation of its town do seem to have been part of a concerted programme to develop a secondary diocesan church and settlement. Events at the close of the century would accelerate this reorientation of the diocese back towards Wells.

The status of Bath and Wells in the early thirteenth century

By the beginning of Jocelin's episcopate, Wells was a thriving borough town. Its economy was based on the local pastoral farming, relying heavily on hides, leathers and tanning, glove-making and, as the following century advanced, increasingly on wool and cloth production.[43] By the early thirteenth century, charters mention mills (including a fulling mill), a bridge, and a stone quarry to the east.[44] Credit for its transformation cannot be given to the town's first native bishop, however, since the key steps in its development had all been during the second half of the twelfth century. To accommodate vigorous growth and new building, Robert's original boundaries for the borough had been enlarged by Reginald and confirmed by Savaric.[45] By the time of Jocelin's accession, the limits of the borough were fixed at the boundaries that would define the town for the rest of the Middle Ages. Robert's six days of fairs had been increased to nine, then twelve, by Reginald, who expanded the festival's fair from two to three

---

[41] *EEA* x. nos 175–6.
[42] 'Reginaldus primus omnium fecit villam Wellie liberum burgum, et burgenses ejusdem exoneravit pro perpetuo ab operibus servilibus, quibus ipsi prius fuerunt multum oppressi': *Collectanea I*, 63; and see Shaw, *Community*, 28 n.
[43] Shaw, *Community*, 33.
[44] *EEA* x. no. 263; *Bath Charts.* ii. no. 232.
[45] *EEA* x. nos 176, 263.

days and added another three-day fair on the anniversary of the dedication of the chapel of St Thomas the Martyr.[46] The final major borough charter, issued by King John in 1201, added an eight-day fair on the translation of St Andrew (bringing the total to twenty days of fairs) and granted Wells the status of royal borough with a weekly Sunday market.[47] At about this time, Bishop Savaric issued his charter, confirming the status of the borough, its final boundaries, liberties and commercial rights. Although the community itself continued to grow as a social, commercial and political body, this final episcopal charter of liberties marked the conclusion of the formal process of borough development.[48] The rush of episcopal charters suddenly ceased in the early thirteenth century, and Jocelin, the native son, was now the first bishop not to issue a charter to the new borough. Wells had emerged rapidly from backwater to thriving borough in half a century and by 1206 was an ambitious commercial community in the ascendant. However, its rights and freedoms had all been settled before Jocelin became bishop.

Meanwhile, the cathedral city of Bath had fallen out of episcopal custody entirely. In 1189, during the episcopate of Reginald, the citizens of Bath obtained a charter from King Richard which granted those who belonged to its merchant guild their own market and the same liberties that were held by the guild of Winchester.[49] These included the rights to hold land and property within the city according to their own customs and to adjudicate their own disputes, and the freedoms for markets and other customs, including from toll and payments at fairs or to use bridges. Unlike the succession of borough charters to Wells, these privileges were a consequence of national rather than local demands. Richard I's accession had marked a change in royal policy, and the Crown, desperate to raise money, was now eager to sell many of the rights it had so closely guarded. Urban communities across England, and most particularly those of the older and more developed towns, took advantage of this opportunity to secure substantial new privileges.[50] The citizens of Bath may have been acting in such a way, but it is also possible that Bishop Reginald assisted in the acquisition of Bath's privileges since he was in Dover on the day that the king issued the Bath

---

46 *Ibid.*, nos 176–7. Charter no. 177 provides for only three fairs, suggesting that this deed pre-dates Reginald's grant of the fourth three-day fair in no. 176. All four three-day fairs were confirmed by Savaric, *ibid.*, no. 263.

47 In C.M. Church, 'Some Account of Savaric, Bishop of Bath and Glastonbury 1192–1205', *Archaeologia*, 51 (1888): 73–107 at 105. Shaw, *Community*, 30, cites slightly different figures.

48 *EEA* x. no. 263; *Wells City Charters*, ed. D.O. Shilton and R. Holworthy, Somerset Record Society 46 (1932), 1–16. The subsequent development of Wells, especially through the fourteenth and fifteenth centuries, is detailed in Shaw, *Community*, 64–285.

49 *CChR 1226–57*, 311.

50 Tait, *Medieval English Borough*, 177–9; Reynolds, *English Medieval Towns*, 107–8.

city charter there.[51] We cannot know whether this was at the behest of the citizens or from Reginald's own desire to develop the city. If Reginald had an attachment to Bath, however, it was not shared by his successor. A few years later, in 1193, the city was back in royal hands, sold by Bishop Savaric to the king in exchange for Glastonbury abbey, in the transaction which marked the beginning of his attempts to relocate the see there.[52] The city would not be wholly under episcopal jurisdiction again until 1275, when Bishop Robert Burnell surrendered patronage of Glastonbury abbey to the king and in return regained full possession of city and suburbs.[53]

It is therefore difficult to talk about Bishop Jocelin in relation to 'cathedral cities' at Wells and Bath. The former owed its development to his predecessors; the latter was in his time, and once again, a royal city. Furthermore, the episcopate of Savaric (1192–1205) had even challenged the intrinsic relationship between seat and city. Savaric had neglected the chapters of Bath and Wells, and even sold the city of Bath, in his pursuit of an episcopal seat in Glastonbury. The lure of this remote place – never becoming what can be termed a cathedral city – was its ancient abbey. With its considerable endowment of manorial estates and churches, the abbey offered the diocese great wealth.[54] And perhaps just as importantly, for a diocese whose seat seemed neither settled nor distinguished, Glastonbury offered roots and prestige. It was not only an ancient centre of worship, but now also the home of a legendary English past, for the popular Arthurian legends of the late twelfth century had been tied to the abbey by the recent discovery of King Arthur's bones.[55] Savaric's quest to make Glastonbury the new episcopal seat severed the relationship between diocese and city: the wealth and prestige of Glastonbury were both decidedly *uncivic* in form and display. And, like the abbey at Bury St Edmunds, this powerful house was prepared to fight the bishop's designs. As a canon at Wells Jocelin had been part of Savaric's assault on Glastonbury; as bishop he 'vigorously defended himself' against the litigation brought by the abbey in a desperate bid to preserve its

---

51 The charter was dated 7 December 1189; Reginald was in Dover certainly from 6 to 8 December (*EEA* x. 209, from the *CChR 1341–1417*, 21–2), as was the bishop of Winchester (*EEA* viii. 222). Winchester's liberties were confirmed in March 1190: *Foedera, Conventiones, Litterae et cujuscunque generis acta publica*, ed. T. Rymer and R. Sanderson (London, 1816), i. i, 50–1 where Reginald is a witness.

52 Church, *Chapters*, 94–7; *Glast. Chart.* i. 80–1. Savaric's efforts and their response are detailed in C.R. Cheney, *Pope Innocent III and England* (Stuttgart, 1976), 220–5, and *EEA* x. xxviii–xxix.

53 The king retained the Barton, which the priory continued to hold at fee-farm: *CCR 1272–79*, 245–6; *CChR 1257–1300*, 192.

54 For Glastonbury's ancient wealth see, L. Abrams, *Anglo-Saxon Glastonbury: Church and Endowment* (Woodbridge, 1996). The abbey and its tenants held estates worth almost £1,000 at the conquest (*ibid.*, 316–17).

55 A. Gransden, 'The Growth of the Glastonbury Traditions and Legends in the Twelfth Century', *Journal of Ecclesiastical History*, 27 (1976), 337–58.

autonomy.[56] The abbey was victorious, but the settlement was not finalised until thirteen years into Jocelin's episcopate. By the time of Jocelin's accession to the see, then, the bishop of Somerset, and indeed Jocelin himself, found his loyalty compromised both to the idea of a single episcopal seat and to the ideal of an urban seat.

Yet the pursuit of Glastonbury was unexpectedly decisive in the formation of the diocese, and it is perhaps the second reason why we talk of cathedral cities rather than one cathedral city. An interest in its history as a cathedral chapter, and evidence of its acting in the election of the bishop, can be seen among the chapter at Wells as early as the 1170s, but its emerging claims were frustrated by the manoeuvres first of Bath priory in the election of Savaric, and then of Savaric himself.[57] However, the bishop's designs on Glastonbury united the abbey and the chapters of Bath and Wells in opposition. After Savaric's death a public meeting of king, nobles and representatives of the three chapters concluded that the bishop's ambitions had seriously damaged the see and the untenable situation must be remedied. The seat should be resettled: Glastonbury abbey should be separated from Bath priory, removed from the bishop's hand and restored to its original state; meanwhile the city of Bath should be placed once again in the hands of the church, this time held at farm by the priory from the king.[58] Although he assumed the title bishop of Bath and Glastonbury, Jocelin was the first bishop whose election and consecration were carried out after this agreement, and after another settlement that Bath and Wells should be dual cathedral chapters, each with delineated rights in the election procedure.[59]

In addition, the failure of the bid to remove to Glastonbury prompted the bishop to look again at the prosperous town of Wells. With the settlement of 1219, Jocelin was forced to renounce his claims to both abbey and title.[60] This prompted an almost immediate petition to Pope Honorius III in which Jocelin worried that the change in title from 'Bishop of Bath and Glastonbury' to 'Bishop of Bath' might appear to signal a loss of status for the bishop. He thus sought permission to assume the title of 'Bishop of Bath and Wells'. In response, the papal legate Pandulf was charged in early 1220 to

---

[56] 'In qua lite idem episcopus ad tempus viriliter se defendit:' *Collectanea I*, 64–5; *Glast. Chart*. i. xl–xlvi, 73–95. For his early role, Church, *Chapters*, 106, 131–2.

[57] *EEA* x. xxi–xxv.

[58] The petitions and their response are copied in *Glast. Chart*. i. 80–7. For the abbey's successful petition to prosecute their case to sever Bath and Glastonbury, *CPL* i. 25. In 1204 the king granted the Barton at farm to Bath priory, *Rot. Chart.*, 19.

[59] Expenses were paid for the representatives from both the Bath and Wells chapters when they were summoned to the royal court to elect the bishop: *Rot. Litt. Claus*. i. 63b. For the agreement and the statement of Jocelin's joint election see J.A.C. Vincent, *The First Bishop of Bath and Wells* (Exeter, 1899), app. nos 72–3, and *EEA* x. xxxvi. The circumstances of Jocelin's election are outlined in Crosby, *Bishop and Chapter*, 64–5.

[60] For the complex negotiations, *Glast. Chart*. i. 87–94.

investigate whether Wells had anciently been a cathedral and, if so, to allow Jocelin his desired title.[61] In the diocesan synod of 1220 the claims of both the dean of Wells and the prior of Bath to sit at the right hand of the bishop were decided in favour of the prior, although the authority of the dean was not to be prejudiced by this.[62] The pursuit of Glastonbury had encouraged the bishop to look beyond Bath for seat and title, and the vacuum created by its loss was permanently filled by Wells. Jocelin never did use the title Bishop of Bath and Wells, but it was assumed almost immediately by his successor, Roger of Salisbury. Roger may have been the first bishop of Bath and Wells, but the reforging of the bishop's identity – even if in response to the failed designs of Savaric – had clearly taken place a generation earlier, under Jocelin. It may be in this light that we might understand his energetic building of the church and palace in Wells.

Jocelin's episcopate spanned a period of pivotal, if development for the town communities of Bath and Wells. In the second half of the twelfth century, especially its last decade, there had been the rush of charters of incorporation of the episcopal, then royal, borough of Wells and of the guild in Bath. For the following half century, the records are frustratingly silent but, suddenly, in the mid-thirteenth century, a variety of sources reveal ambitious civic communities, each with a range of administrative and political institutions. With its own guild, Bath was the most powerful. In 1247 Henry III confirmed the 1189 charter of the citizens of Bath and, shortly thereafter in 1256, added privileges 'for the improvement of our city of Bath'. Significantly, this included freedom from intrusion by the king's officers, which permitted the citizens' own bailiffs to answer the king's writs, to appoint their own coroners and to redirect goods to a citizen's heirs when he had died without a will.[63] There is also evidence of a variety of corporate activities and organisation in Bath. From 1242 survives the first statement that the 'whole guild of Bath' witnessed a charter and attached their common seal; and by 1249 the commonalty maintained a chapel to St Catherine at St Mary de Stalls Church.[64] From the third quarter of the thir-

---

[61] 'ut cum hactenus Bathonien' et Glastonien' Episcopus fuerit noncupatus, ne videatur quasi capite diminutus, nuncupandi se Bathonien' et Wellen' Episcopum sibi licentiam concedere dignaremur, presertim quia sicut asserit ecclesia Wellen' ab antiquo extitit Cathedralis .... si rem inveneris ita esse, predicto Episcopo se nominandi Bathonien' Episcopum et Wellen' auctoritate nostra concedas liberam facultatem': Vincent, *First Bishop of Bath and Wells*, app. no. 90; CPL i. 70.

[62] *Wells MSS* i. 52.

[63] *Rotuli Hundredorum temp. Hen. III et Edw. I*, 2 vols (London, 1812–18), ii. 119, 132; CChR 1300–26, 212; King, *Municipal Records of Bath*, 6–7.

[64] 'et omnibus gillanis Bathon' quorum commune sigillum ad huius robur et testimonium presenti carte est appensum': *Medieval Deeds of Bath and District*, ed. B.R. Kemp and D.M.M. Shorrocks, Somerset Record Society 73 (1974), ii. no. 301/16; King, *Municipal Records of Bath*, 10.

teenth century, names and dates of a succession of mayors become identifiable, as do a number of affiliated civic officials, such as provosts.[65] In Wells, too, the emerging borough is hidden from the records. The noisy traders who prompted Bishop Robert's first charter had become, in Savaric's deeds, 'our burgesses' and the recipients of specific privileges and freedoms. Since 1174 these had included the freedom to adjudicate on civil and criminal matters in their own court, provided that those involving mortal wounds, bodily injury or petitioners requesting episcopal ruling would still be heard in the bishop's court.[66] After soliciting a copy and confirmation of Robert's first market charter, the burgesses of Wells cannot be seen acting as a body until 1242–43, when their bailiffs proffered John's 1201 charter to the royal justices of the Somerset eyre, to assert that the eyre had no jurisdiction over borough property.[67] They won the argument but lost the case: the property was found to lie outside the town and thus under the jurisdiction of the justices.

The activities and officers of the urban communities remain largely hidden between c.1200 and the 1240s. It is clear that a community of burgesses (in Wells) and of citizens (in Bath), with a legal and limited political form existed in both towns at this time, but our insights are restricted to scattered deeds that grant, sell or rent property.[68] This is a common pattern for urban communities in England, and one of the main reasons why studies of urban communities typically begin in the mid-thirteenth century.[69] There are glimpses of organised action by the citizens of Bath before this time. In 1227 'our citizens of Bath' came before the royal justices in eyre at Ilchester asserting their right to be impleaded in Bath.[70] In that same year the king's charter of liberties to the new church and city of Salisbury was dispatched, with instructions for its public reading to his local sheriffs and to the 'good men' of a handful of local towns, including Bath.[71] Wells was not included

[65] *Ancient Deeds belonging to the Corporation of Bath, xiii–xvi cent.*, ed. C.W. Shickle (Bath, 1921), 3–10, 47–9, 71–7. The commonalty also acted as a body to effect agreements with the prior and convent: ibid., 61–2, 142–3.
[66] *EEA* x. no. 176.
[67] *The Somersetshire Pleas (Civil and Criminal) from the Rolls of the Itinerant Justices*, ed. C.E.H. Chadwyck Healey, Somerset Record Society11 (1897), no. 422; Shaw, *Community*, 107.
[68] Patterns of such grants, especially to hospitals, do suggest evidence of an emerging civic polity in towns across England in these decades, see Watson, 'City as Charter', 256–62. For the more limited pattern in Bath, see the urban properties granted to the hospital of St John the Baptist, calendared in *Medieval Deeds of Bath*, i. nos 23–55.
[69] For the case for pursuing the richer later materials, and the limits of what can be gleaned from charters of liberties, see G. Rosser, 'The Essence of Medieval Urban Communities', *Transactions of the Royal Historical Soc*, 5th ser. 34 (1984), 91–112, and Shaw, *Community*, 104–13.
[70] 'cives nostri Bathon": *Rot. Lit. Claus.* ii. 174b.
[71] 'probis hominibus Bathon": *ibid.*, ii. 177b.

in this list, despite its nearer proximity to Salisbury, perhaps because it had a more limited political status and, in addition, was directly in the bishop's hand and thus not a royal town. Shortly thereafter, in 1229, the 'men of Bath' appealed against recent fines levied against them by the sheriff for the escape of thieves, and gained a stay until their case might be heard by the justices in eyre.[72] Both urban communities had gained their main political and legal rights at the end of the previous century, and both emerge onto the historical record as organised, and active, political bodies from c.1245. The intervening period, which coincides almost precisely with Jocelin's tenure as bishop, was clearly crucial but remains frustratingly veiled.

Early deeds display an active property market and emerging civic government in Bath. Although no explicit mention is made of a court of the city or commonalty, a number of deeds were probably made in such a court. They were witnessed not by local knights and royal or ecclesiastical officials, but by the bailiff of the city and a group of men, perhaps civic officers, notably, John de Porta, David Parvus of Bath, Andrew the cleric, John Cook and Gerard 'from outside the northgate'.[73] It was clearly a city court in which the 1242 deed was ratified and witnessed by several of these men and their successors along with 'the whole guild of Bath'.[74] Nevertheless, the majority of property transactions at this time, even of property within the city wall, were recorded in the hundred court, which was under the supervision of the bishop and, later, the priory. A group of 'citizens of Bath' witnessed a hundred deed dated from the early thirteenth century.[75] In addition, the names of some citizens, such as John de Porta, become more prominent in the hundred court witness lists as the first half of the thirteenth century progressed. This may reflect a rise in the local standing of the civic polity, or at least of its key representatives. John de Porta was the earliest recorded mayor, but his use of this title cannot be dated before the middle of the century.[76] Indeed, there is no clear evidence of civic officials until the 1240s, around the time of Henry III's charter of liberties. Other communities, such as Exeter, Cambridge and Nottingham, have left greater evidence of early civic organisation, but the pattern seen in Bath is not unlike that found in provincial towns across the county, where the identities of civic officials

---

[72] CR 1227–31, 219.
[73] Medieval Deeds of Bath, i. nos 26–8, 58 and 122; ii. 301/8.
[74] Ibid., ii. 301/16.
[75] SRO, DD/TB/20/2, 4; for the similarity between the witnesses here and that of a deed witnessed by 'toto hundredo Bathonie' see ibid., 13. Both are calendared in Medieval Deeds of Bath, i. nos 14 and 32.
[76] King, Municipal Records of Bath, app. A ii, no. 49. King suggests a date of c.1230, but most of those named in the charter were active c.1240 or even, in the case of Thomas Swein, later: Medieval Deeds of Bath, ii. nos 5/248 and 301/16.

begin to emerge more securely in the years approaching the mid-thirteenth century.

However, there are several reasons to suggest that Bath was not thriving, commercially or politically, as much as many comparable English provincial towns. Bath was still dominated by crown, bishop and priory. In the early thirteenth century, the city had been under the administration of a royal bailiff and the king maintained a royal residence there (which had once been the bishop's) where he accommodated servants such as William Crasso in 1208 and William Parvus in 1205.[77] From 1218 the city was held at farm by the priory from the king and his bailiff, until the bishop regained full possession from the king in 1275.[78] Officials who are mentioned in early deeds of Bath and its hundred can be more easily tied to priory, crown or bishop than to the citizens.[79] Property transactions were witnessed by leading local men, and several have names that suggest trades: goldsmith, robe-maker, skinner, painter and, perhaps, winemaker.[80] Yet the picture they paint is of a relatively subdued commercial economy: there are few such names and these are, at times, countered by many less commercial professions, such as archer, forester, keeper of the bridge, cook or falconer.[81] From the middle of the thirteenth century, when more deeds survive, there are more names suggesting trades – including dyer, mason, 'gold', 'cornmanger' and several tailors and smiths – but even these are relatively limited compared to the many trades seen in comparable deeds in towns such as Bury St Edmunds and Oxford.[82] Even the few deeds from Wells at this time reveal merchants

---

[77] Vincent, *First Bishop of Bath and Wells*, app. no. 79; *Rot. Lit. Claus.* i. 53b and 106b.

[78] The final disputes with royal officials, including Hugh de Vivon, as to who should answer for the actions and payments relating to the city were settled in 1218, *PR 1216–25*, 138, 147–8.

[79] They include Richard of Ford, bailiff of the hundred, and master Alan of Creeton, official of Bath (both the bishop's men in the late twelfth century), and Master John of Ickford, the bishop's official from 1207 to c.1230; a marshal of the prior of Bath in 1205–6; Geoffrey of Bath, king's servant, in 1229; Kaskill of Weston and Robert de Reigny, bailiffs of Bath, apparently for the priory: *EEA* x. lvi and nos 76 and 203–4; *Medieval Deeds of Bath*, i. nos 12, 26 n, 59, 168 n. and ii. nos 1/245, 2/257301/8; *CR 1227–31*, 267.

[80] 'Reinero aurifabro, Serlone par(a)mentario, Serlone pelliparie, Humfrido pictore, Ernaldo vignur': SRO, DD/TB/20/2, 4, 11, 13–14, and 26, cal. in *Medieval Deeds of Bath*, i. nos 14, 27, 32, and 54.

[81] *Ibid.*, i. nos 14, 27, 28, and 37; ii. nos 3/246 and 4/247; and see King, *Municipal Records of Bath*, app. A ii, nos 47–51.

[82] For example, 'Henrico tailor, Rogero tincture, Walteri le taillur, Willelmo fabro, Hugo cementario, Radulpho scissore, Nicholao Scurmer, Johnnne Gold, Rodberto le Cornmanger and Silvestro Fabro': SRO, DD/TB/20/2, 12 and 16, cal. *Medieval Deeds of Bath*, i. nos 30 and 37; and *ibid.*, ii. nos 4/247 and 31/300. In comparison, deeds in Bury St Edmunds before c.1250 reveal the names of mayors, aldermen and bailiffs, as well as a number of goldsmiths, merchants, moneyers, wool-workers and spicers, and others identified as dyer, potter, tailor, cheese-smoker (?smeresmoker), carter, butler and transporter (?treiettarius): *Charters of the Medieval Hospitals of Bury St Edmunds*, ed. C. Harper-Bill (Woodbridge, 1994), nos 3, 5, 7, 8, 11, 16–17, 21, 107, 125, 128–9 and 184.

and a painter, carpenter, spicer, baker, miller and fuller.[83] This may simply reflect the limited nature of the evidence, but it is possible that Bishop Robert's early fears about Bristol's destructive influence were being realised. The great port city continued to boom through the thirteenth century, while Bath, one of the major towns in England at the time of the Domesday Survey, floundered. By 1334 it had fallen low in the rankings of English town wealth. In the lay subsidy of that year it was assessed at £133.33, a relatively paltry amount in comparison to mighty Bristol (£2,200), nearby Gloucester (at £540.75 ranked eighteenth in the country) and even Wells (at £190).[84] The general picture suggested of Bath in the late twelfth and early thirteenth centuries, then, is of a city that was politically proud and inventive but economically stagnating.

Jocelin and the cities of Bath and Wells

The evidence for Bishop Jocelin's intervention in the cities of Bath and Wells is limited at best. Bath may have been a royal city between 1192 and 1275, but Jocelin had gained the farm of the city and the Barton (that is, the hundred of Bath) early in his episcopate, for an annual rent of £50 paid to the royal exchequer.[85] The Barton had been held by the priory since 1204 and was retained by them again from 1217; it was gained, they claimed *in quo warranto*, from King John 'during his time of tribulation'.[86] The city of Bath was granted to Queen Eleanor as part of her dower in 1236, but the prior continued to return the £50 for its farm via the constable of Bristol castle.[87] During the time when he held the Barton and city at farm from the king, Jocelin's most significant action had been a minor reallocation of its rents. Of the £50 farm, the Barton had anciently paid £30 and the city £20. Jocelin reversed this, taking £30 from the city and £20 from the Barton 'to the confusion of the said city', as the citizens later complained.[88] It is possible that this is evidence of a rising urban prosperity that is less evident in charters and later taxation, but it is more likely to have been to accommodate the creation or expansion of Claverton park, 'a great park without Bath' on land which Jocelin had removed from the Barton and merged with the manor of Hampton as part of Hampton hundred.[89]

[83] *Wells City Charters*, 18–20.
[84] R. Britnell, 'The Economy of British Towns 600–1300', in *Cambridge Urban History of Britain*, 122; *The Lay Subsidy of 1334*, ed. Robin E. Glasscock, Records of Social and Economic History n.s. 11 (Oxford, 1975), 90–1, 273.
[85] He took possession in 1215: *Rot. Lit. Claus.* i. 184, 187 and 454b.
[86] 'tempore tribulacionis sue': *Rot. Hund.* ii. 123a; *Rot. Lit. Claus.* i. 338, 340; *Pipe Roll 7 John*, Pipe Roll Society n.s.19 (1941), 137.
[87] *CChR 1226–57*, 218; *Pipe Roll 1241–42*, ed. H.L. Cannon (New Haven, 1918), 333–4.
[88] 'ad confusionem dicte civitatis': *Rot. Hund.* ii. 123, 132.
[89] *Medieval Deeds Bath*, ii. no. 302/13.

In Wells Jocelin resolved a minor controversy in 1237 between the dean and sub-dean as to their jurisdiction of borough and suburbs, and his ruling provides an insight into the administrative workings of the court. The dean should preside over the court, and the sub-dean only in the dean's absence, but if both were to be away then the dean could appoint another judge. The fines of anyone from town or suburbs who was subject to the bishop should be applied to the fabric of the church of Wells, and both the dean and sub-dean should keep a common roll of acts, or register of deeds (*communem rotulum actorum*).[90] There is another, intriguing, snapshot of Jocelin in the bishop's court, but this time as subject to its jurisdiction. In the archive of the dean and chapter are three charters, drawn up in that court during the episcopate of Bishop Reginald (1174–91). Two concern the purchase of lands at Wells and Launcherley (a village to the south of Wells) by Jocelin's father, Edward of Wells, together with Edward's heirs, the latter referring certainly to Hugh and almost certainly also to Jocelin.[91] Among the witnesses of the third grant, of a messuage and croft in Wells to Walter son of Harvey, a cleric, can be found 'Hugh son of Edward, [and] Gosceline his brother'.[92] The first deed explicitly states that the sale was executed in the bishop's court under Master Ralph de Lechlade, the bishop's steward; the other two were witnessed by the dean or the dean and sub-dean. The unusual preservation among the chapter muniments, of at least the first two of these deeds, may be due to Bishop Jocelin depositing them among the chapter muniments during his later work with his brother for the hospital of St John the Baptist. The court deeds therefore reveal little of Jocelin the bishop but more of Jocelin the private man, acting in concert with, and for, his family. A few charters survive whereby the bishop confirms properties in Wells as gifts to the church or holdings for servants.[93] With the exception of the hospital at Wells, to which we shall return, Jocelin the bishop has left few records of actions in or pertaining to the towns of Bath and Wells.[94]

In marked contrast to his limited apparent interest in his cities, Bishop Jocelin was an enthusiastic developer of his regional estate and its resources.

90   Wells cathedral Register I (*Liber Albus I*), fos 43v–44r, cal. in *Wells MSS* i. 49.
91   They are cathedral charters nos 9 and 10, both cal. *Wells MSS* ii. 547, and no. 9 now printed *EEA* x. no. 152. In the first Hugh is named as Edward's heir; the second makes a more general reference to 'Edward and his heirs by hereditary right'. Both are witnessed by a 'Jocelin the chaplain', but this is probably the episcopal chaplain who witnessed so many of Reginald's deeds, *EEA* x. li.
92   Wells cathedral charter no. 13, *Wells MSS* ii. 549.
93   *Wells City Charters*, 17–18; *Bath Charts.* no. 232; *Wells MSS* i. 18, 49, 477, 491–2. Some of this was property of Hugh of Wells.
94   Even the 'Historia Major', which celebrates Reginald's work in the town, only mentions Jocelin's efforts in aid of the church and hospital, *Collectanea I*, 64–5.

Work started near Wells almost immediately after his accession when, in 1207, he gained permission from the king to enclose the wood within his manor of Wells, to the south of the town, in order to make a park; in the same year he gained royal consent to make a fishpond on his manor of Radstock.[95] Preoccupied by national affairs and the resolution of the contro-versy with Glastonbury abbey, Jocelin's economic work was interrupted for the decade after John's death.[96] However, 1227 to 1236 were years of active estate development, when Jocelin obtained royal grants, confirmations and licences to develop his lands. Much of this work involved the creation and extension of parks. In addition to the parks at Wells and Claverton outside Bath, Jocelin secured royal approval in 1227 and 1228 to disafforest the manors of North Curry, Kingsbury and Pucklechurch (Glos.) and, free from the intrusion of royal officials, to enclose the land, make parks, clear land for agriculture and take wood for his own use or sale; he was granted permission to enclose his wood in Periwood to make a park, and to create a deer-leap in and expand to the south by seven acres his park of Dogmersfield.[97] Between 1234 and 1235, he asserted sixty acres of woodland in Cheddar, in incre-ments of twenty acres.[98] Jocelin's position in the centre of royal government had facilitated access to a stream of royal grants and licences, permitting this active development of his estate.

He also worked to expand industrial and commercial revenues. His predecessors had recognised the value of mining and industrial production: Robert had retained the saltworks at Keyhaven (valued at almost £3 per year) even after he had granted them to Bath priory, and Reginald had obtained a royal grant to mine lead on his land and to create a borough at Rackley, whose port he may have hoped to develop.[99] Jocelin, however, was peculiarly industrious. He secured permission to search the king's forest on the Mendip hills for iron, lead or any other type of mineral, and to open mines wherever he might find anything.[100] He may have established boroughs at Chard and Wellington, and certainly provided Chard with its borough customs in 1234.[101] In 1227 he purchased the ancient borough of Axbridge from Maurice de Gaunt and it is probably this acquisition that

[95] *Rot. Chart.*, 169, 171.
[96] D.A. Carpenter, *The Minority of Henry III* (London, 1990), 322–3, 343–9, 379–80. For the final statement of the bishop's rights regarding the abbey in 1227: CChR 1226–57, 6–7; *Glast. Chart.* i. 188.
[97] CChR 1226–57, 4, 16, 43, 44, 75–6; CR 1227–31, 23 58.
[98] CR 1231–34, 530, 532; CR 1234–37, 11, 149.
[99] EEA x. xxvii; CChR 1300–26, 473–4; Church, *Chapters*, 66–7.
[100] CR 1234–37, 86, 92–3.
[101] M. Aston and R. Leech, *Historic Towns in Somerset: Archaeology and Planning*, Western Archaeological Trust Surveys 2 (Bristol, 1977), 31, 143; CPR 1281–92, 216, printed in translation in E. Green, 'On the History of Chard', *Proceedings of the Somerset Archaeolog-ical and Natural History Society*, 28 (1882), 28–78 (48–9); and see discussion of Somerset

precipitated his dramatic clearing and developing of nearby land at Ched-dar.[102] From King John he gained exemption throughout his own lands for the bishop and his men and freedom from payment of royal market tolls for the chapters of Bath and Wells.[103] His most significant licence was acquired in 1227: a royal charter, permitting Jocelin and his successors to establish in any of their manors a market on one day of the week and fairs for two or three days of the year, as long as any were not to the detriment of nearby markets.[104]

Jocelin's episcopate coincided with a period of intensive commercial expansion. Even in the twelfth century, Somerset had been rich in boroughs and markets. In addition to its thirteen pre-Conquest boroughs,[105] it had seen boroughs created at Montacute, Downend Wells and Rackley before 1189, the latter two by the bishop. The sixteen years between 1189 and 1205 had seen the addition of boroughs with markets at Dunster and Bridg-water, and the dean and chapter's market at North Curry. But even this activity paled in comparison to the rapid creation of local markets and fairs in the twenty years after 1213. By 1225 boroughs with markets were estab-lished in Stogursey, followed shortly by Crowcombe (in 1227) and Chard (in 1234). Markets were also granted to South Petherton (1213), Weare (1218), Shepton Mallet (1219), Nether Stowey (by 1222), Watchet (1222), Churchstanton (1223), Somerton (1226), Beercrocombe (1231), Barwick (1231), Staple Fitzpaine (1233) and Wincanton (1235).[106] To the many existing fairs were added new fairs at South Petherton, Somerton, Crow-combe, Barwick, Beercrocombe, Glastonbury, Thorne St Margaret, Merriott and Staple Fitzpaine. Jocelin acted against this emerging patchwork of local commercial centres when any threatened the profits of his own markets. Shepton Mallet was just five miles from Wells and its lord, Hugh de Vivon, had lately been granted a second market there, allowing markets now on Wednesday and Thursday. In 1235 Jocelin obtained a royal injunction instructing the sheriff of Somerset to terminate this second market that was to the detriment of the bishop's markets.[107] This was swiftly augmented by

boroughs in W. Savage, 'Somerset Towns', *Proceedings of the Somerset Archaeological and Natural History Society*, 99 (1956), 49–74.
102   *Wells MSS* i. 471; Vincent, *First Bishop of Bath and Wells*, app. no. 97.
103   *Wells MSS* i. 7, 309.
104   *CChR 1226–57*, 16.
105   Bath, Axbridge, Bruton, Crewkerne, Frome, Ilchester, Ilminster, Langport, Lyng, Milborne Port, Milverton, Taunton and Watchet.
106   M.W. Beresford and H.P.R. Finberg, *English Medieval Boroughs: a Hand-list* (Newton Abbot, 1973), 154–60; M. Beresford, *New Towns of the Middle Ages: Town Plantation in England, Wales and Gascony* (London, 1967), 483–6; *The Gazetteer of Markets and Fairs in England and Wales to 1516* (Centre for Metropolitan History), online at http://www.history.ac.uk/cmh/gaz/gazweb2.html (updated July 2007).
107   *CR 1234–37*, 152; Shaw, *Community*, 32.

another royal charter, broadcast to the sheriff of Somerset and Dorset, which decreed that no market that had been created after 1217 outside the royal demesne could remain if it damaged any of the bishop's existing markets.[108] It is interesting to note that after 1235 the rush of new Somerset markets abruptly slowed. Boroughs at Badgworth and Nether Weare are both first recorded in 1243, but clearly existed earlier. In the ten years following 1235 only two new grants for markets can be identified: at Buckland Dinham in 1239 and Midsomer Norton in 1242. The latter was secured by the same Hugh de Vivon whom Jocelin had caused the sheriff to move against at Shepton Mallet in 1235; by 1242, however, Hugh de Vivon was sheriff of Somerset.[109]

As the pattern of boroughs and markets in Somerset reveals, urban growth was often tied to seigneurial self-interest, and particularly so for a bishop and his city. In his charter to 'our burgesses in Wells' Bishop Savaric had observed that his predecessors had made similar grants in order 'to augment the honour, dignity and rents of themselves and their successors'.[110] A thriving local borough or city was both financially profitable and convenient. Its occupants were eager to govern themselves while generating considerable incomes: with land worth up to ten times that of farmland, urban properties produced good rents (in Wells 12d. for each holding), the fairs and markets generated stallage (rents for stalls), tolls (for attending fairs and transporting wares into town), and fines for contravening regulations on hours of trading, standards, weights and measures.[111] Residents and visitors were taxed for their use of any facilities owned and administered by the lord, which might include his mill, oven, bake-house, bridges and court. A town increased income and reduced expenses. The local markets and traders eased the job of provisioning a growing chapter and episcopal household, bringing foods, wares and more exotic goods to the cathedral's doorstep. The wider trading networks facilitated communications while also providing access to merchants who could undertake more significant commissions, such as the two merchants paid £261 6s. in 1315 to provide warm winter material to clothe the bishop's household.[112] It also supplied

---

[108] 'cartam nostram in qua continetur quod nullum mercatum quod post primam coronationem nostram levatum sit vel decetero levabitur extra dominica nostra ad nocumentum alicujus mercatorum suorum que idem episcopus habuit ante coronationem illam stet vel teneatur aliquo tempore. Ed ideo tibi precipimus quod predictam cartam nostram in predictis comitatibus legi et teneri facias': CR 1234–37, 234; CChR 1226–57, 216.

[109] Pipe Roll 1241–42, 325.

[110] 'in augmentum honoris, dignitatis et reddituum suorum et omnium sibi succedentium': EEA x. no. 263.

[111] For the cultivation of towns and their benefits see Beresford, New Towns, 57–77.

[112] Reg. Drokensford, 103. Similarly, the prior of Bath procured 600 sacks of wool from a merchant: Bath Charts. no. 783.

specialised workers on whose talents the clerical community could draw. The growing borough of Wells would have supplied many of these practical conveniences, and profits, for the bishop and his church.

In contrast to his predecessors, however, Jocelin looked more to his region than to his cities to secure episcopal wealth and prestige. There are no surviving charters issued by him concerning the urban communities of Bath or Wells, and no evidence that he interfered to foster either the stagnating city or the burgeoning town. Nevertheless, Jocelin was an active economic administrator, energetically exploiting the regional landscape, its many settlements and commercial networks. He developed parkland, mining, trade and local markets, which he in turn protected from competition. Although the question of a seat for his see was peculiarly pressing throughout his episcopacy, it is oddly difficult to see Jocelin acting, or thinking, in terms of a civic seat. In contrast to his early predecessor John of Tours or even to his neighbours the bishops of Salisbury, he was not fostering a single urban seat, but developing instead a second church and a regional network of parks, resources and commercial rights. When John of Tours had moved the see to Bath, he allocated the profits of the city of Bath to the necessary building-works for his new cathedral and its chapter.[113] For his buildings at Wells, Jocelin, by contrast, relied on regional incomes and, as Diana Greenway has noted (in chapter 3 of this volume), on the proceeds from vacant churches across the diocese and taxes from prebends.[114] Two of his earliest acts as bishop were to surrender the bishop's house at Bath and to secure the right to expand the park at Wells.[115] This suggests an early desire to develop Wells as a diocesan residence, and his subsequent building there clearly propelled the search for materials through mining and woodland. Yet even in his development of Wells as church and residence, Jocelin was a bishop who thought regionally in terms of resources and profit.

The hospital of St John the Baptist

One final ambiguity in Bishop Jocelin's relationship to his cities can be found, paradoxically, in what has always been seen as his greatest gift to the town of Wells itself: the hospital of St John the Baptist. The closer we examine this hospital, the less we can attribute it to Jocelin as bishop, or even primarily to Jocelin. The *Historia Major* asserts that Jocelin and his brother Hugh founded the hospital together, and certainly the two

---

[113] 'De urbe ... hoc constitui ut omnes redditus ponantur ad perficiendum novum opus quod incepi': *EEA* x. no. 3.

[114] Reginald had also used the incomes of vacant churches 'in usus operationis ex toto cedant donec per dei miserationis auxilium consummetur': *ibid.*, no. 150.

[115] *Rot. Chart.*, 169; *Rot. Litt. Claus.* i. 106b.

worked closely to establish the house.[116] Nevertheless, Jocelin's own charter regarding its foundation called it 'the hospital which my brother Hugh II bishop of Lincoln built'.[117] The project first took form during the Inter- dict, when the two brothers, Jocelin and Hugh, were in exile in France, the latter having recently been consecrated bishop of Lincoln.[118] There, in November of 1212 at St-Martin-de-Garenne, a stop between Rouen and Paris, Hugh wrote his first will, clearly with the assistance of Jocelin, who was named executor and acted as its first witness. Hugh's will set aside two separate and significant sums: 300 marks (£200) to create a hospital or to perform other alms for the soul of Jordan de Turri, and 500 marks (£333) to build a hospital at Wells.[119] The idea for a hospital at Wells may have been inspired by Bishop Reginald's foundation of St John the Baptist, Bath, built and endowed during years when both brothers were episcopal clerics. Hugh had witnessed grants to this hospital, and both Hugh and Jocelin are included in the witness-list of Reginald's own, and most important, charter to the hospital.[120] Hugh's first will was in many ways an exercise in imagi- nation, with the bishop in exile disposing of property that was not in his possession but which, as the will's title stated hopefully, 'should be restored to me in England'.[121] The Liber Albus II preserves a copy of a charter of a different Hugh of Wells, granting to Bishop Jocelin and the church of Wells his 'whole place with houses in Wells' to arrange as the bishop should wish, as other houses of the canons.[122] The charter can be dated 1209–12 by its notation that one of its witnesses, Ralph de Lechlade, was dean of Wells, a position Ralph held briefly, and largely in exile with Jocelin.[123] Many of the other witnesses (who include Bishop Hugh) also witnessed Hugh's will, suggesting the charter was of a similar date and occasion. Hugh of Wells

[116] Collectanea I, 65.

[117] 'quod dominus frater meus … ibi construxit', TNA, C53/25, mem. 11, cal. CChR 1226– 57, 128.

[118] Acta of Hugh of Wells, xxix.

[119] Ibid., no. 2. This is probably the Jordan de Turri, or 'Jordan cleric of the Tower', who was a member of the household of Richard de Ilchester, following him from the exchequer to the diocese of Winchester, then returning to the exchequer after that bishop's death in 1188. Still active in 1204–5, it may have been here that he met Hugh or Jocelin during their years in royal service in London. He probably died in 1205, when proper- ties he had owned in London were confirmed to Thomas Luvell of Evercreech: EEA viii. 105–48 (esp. no. 186); Charles Duggan, 'Richard of Ilchester, Royal Servant and Bishop', Transactions of the Royal Historical Society, 5th series 16 (1966), 1–21 (4 n); Acta of Hugh of Wells, xxviii–xxix; Pipe Roll 1 Richard, 136, 149, 301; Cur. Reg. R. iii. 215 and 275; Rot. Chart., 155.

[120] EEA x. no. 80; SRO DD/TB/20/2, 71, 81–2, cal. Medieval Deeds of Bath, nos 110 and 121. There is an additional, later grant of income to the hospital payable by Bishop Hugh from land that was quitclaimed to Bishop Jocelin (SRO DD/TB/20/2, 113).

[121] 'testamentum meum de bonis meis que michi restituenda sunt in Anglia.'

[122] Wells cathedral Register III, fo. 385v.

[123] Fasti 1066–1300 vii. 9.

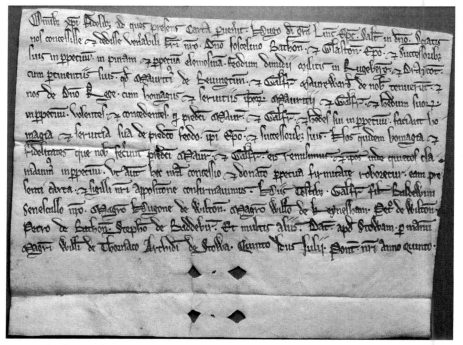

Figure 3. The Wells brothers. Hugh, bishop of Lincoln, grants to Jocelin, bishop of Bath and Glastonbury, half a knight's fee in Rowberrow and Draycott; 11 July 1214. Wells Cathedral Charter 22. Reproduced with permission of the Dean and Chapter of Wells.

later became archdeacon of Bath in 1214 under Jocelin and held a prebend in Lincoln cathedral under Hugh, and has been thought to be related to the brothers. Witnesses William, Roger and Herbert were all also 'of Wells'.[124] Of course, this does not mean the six men 'of Wells' who were involved in this charter were relatives of the brothers, but it does stress the local and personal bonds behind this occasion and its possible connections to the brothers' wider ambitions in Wells.[125]

124 *Ibid.*, 29. David Smith is more cautious in presuming family ties, but still highlights the important role of Hugh son of Osbert of Wells in the administration of Bishop Hugh (*Acta of Hugh of Wells*, xxviii). 'Hugh, Roger and Jocelin of Wells' occur together on an 1195–1204 deed of Bishop Savaric and on Bishop Reginald's charter to the hospital at Bath, EEA x. nos 80 and 234. Hugh's place with houses was beside property belonging to Nicholas of Wells, who in 1207 had granted land before the priory's great gate in a the deed witnessed by Jocelin's brother Hugh, when archdeacon of Wells; the land has been associated with the creation of the canons' close (*Wells MSS* i. 18; Church, *Chapters*, 179). See below for evidence that Jocelin used personal or family incomes to procure holdings for the chapter in exchange for properties which constituted a more convenient endowment for the hospital.
125 Among the number of local men who witnessed an early charter (1174–88) secured by

Bishop Hugh's own provision for his hospital began shortly after his return from exile. On 11 and 12 July 1214, he transferred a series of his personal properties to Bishop Jocelin. These included the patronage of the church of Axbridge, half a knight's fee both in Norton and in Rowberrow and Draycott (Som.), and quittance of suit in his courts in the hundreds of Cheddar and Winterstoke for Jocelin and his men.[126] None of these deeds mentions the proposed hospital, but a number have been copied into the *Liber Albus II* along with a group of deeds that relate to Hugh and Jocelin's work to create the early hospital endowment.[127] Curiously, the same register preserves a copy of Hugh's will.[128] There is limited evidence, too, of the brothers acting to secure lands in Wells at this time, perhaps for the hospital: Jocelin secured the quitclaim of half a hide in Wells which Hugh had held, and also procured ten acres of land to the west of the borough which included two acres of meadow beside the watercourse, to the north of the fulling mill.[129] However, no reference can be found to the hospital until 1215, when a more concrete plan began to emerge. In September of that year, en route to the Fourth Lateran Council, Hugh enacted a charter which granted, with Jocelin's assent, all his property in Wells, both within and without the borough, 'to make a hospital at Wells'.[130] This almost certainly included the properties in and around Wells that his father, Edward of Wells, had worked to acquire during the twelfth century. Hugh was Edward's heir, and this transfer of the properties to Jocelin would account for the unusual survival of these original deeds among the Wells cathedral muniments, some of the earliest of the church's surviving charters.[131] The hospital itself may still not yet have been constructed and the 1215 deed contains no further details as to its proposed endowment, form or oversight. In fact, it was not until almost twenty years later when Hugh finalised his plans for the hospital, this time in his second and final will. Aged and infirm, he had retired to his residence at Stowe Park in March 1233 where, perhaps already on his deathbed, he made preparations for his will, and for the hospital, in May of 1233. His early ideal of two hospitals had now become one: the hospital at Wells would also be for the soul of Jordan de Turri.[132] The will noted that he had 'long ago' (*pridem*) supplied his brother with 200 marks

the burgesses from Bishop Reginald, only two men are designated 'of Wells': Edward and Jocelin: *EEA* x. no. 177.
126 *Acta of Hugh of Wells*, nos 8–11. These constitute some of our earliest known deeds of Hugh as bishop.
127 Wells cathedral Register III, fos 341v–351v, cal. *Wells MSS* i. 471–2, 474–6.
128 Wells cathedral Register III, fos. 248v–249v.
129 SRO DD/TB/20/2, 113, cal. *Medieval Deeds of Bath*, no. 163; *Wells MSS* i. 477.
130 'ad faciendum unum hospitale apud Welles': *Acta of Hugh of Wells*, no. 42.
131 See above, and *EEA* x. no. 152.
132 *Acta of Hugh of Wells*, no. 408.

for the work of the hospital, and it added lands and incomes from Hugh's own fee. These included his custody of lands and heirs in Thurning and Cromwell: the former of one of his knights, the latter explicitly 'in my fee'.[133] Some of it was, or had become, family land: he had provided his own land at Dornford as the marriage portion of his niece, Agatha, but this was to revert to the hospital if Agatha had no children. The plans for the hospital were therefore both begun and brought to conclusion by Hugh's two wills.

If the initiative and endowment for the hospital had been supplied by Hugh, the work of creating the hospital fell to Jocelin, the more local brother. Jocelin secured from the Wells chapter the right of the hospital to a chantry and bells, and to burial for those brothers who were *conversi*, under the sign of the hospital (1220–36).[134] And it was his charter of 1230 for the hospital 'which my brother Hugh II bishop of Lincoln built' that comprised the hospital's foundation charter, securing an endowment of the nearby manor of Cranmore and entrusting patronage of the hospital to the bishop of Bath.[135] The following year Jocelin added a grant of Evercreech church (1231).[136] In so doing, however, Jocelin was executing Hugh's vision and, indeed, his last will. Between 1227, when Hugh had been granted permission to draft a new will, and 1233, when its final form was drafted on his deathbed at Stowe Park, the brothers scrambled to consolidate the hospital.[137] Hugh's original (1215) grant was enrolled on the charter roll at Westminster in 1231, as was his last 1231 grant to Jocelin for the hospital.[138] Hugh's death must have seemed imminent, since in 1231 the brothers gained dual royal grants that should either die that year the king would not immediately seize their estates but allow executors to retain their property until the following Michaelmas.[139] And his role in providing both the vision and inheritance made the deadline pressing. Jocelin worked rapidly to endow and arrange the hospital, but even his benefactions may have been engineered and paid for by Hugh. Jocelin's endowment of the manor of Cranmore was worth £16 per year and had been purchased from the

133 *Ibid.*, no. 407 and n.
134 Wells cathedral Register I, fo. 43r–v; Register II, fo. 16v, cal. *Wells MSS* i. 49 and 531. The agreement was made with the consent of Peter, dean of Wells, whose dates provide the agreement's limits. *Fasti 1066–1300* vii. 10. Church, citing Archer's 18th-century manuscript *Chronicon Wellense* dates the deed to 1221 (Church, *Chapters*, 201).
135 TNA C53/25 mem. 11, cal. *CChR 1226–57*, 128.
136 Wells cathedral Register III, fo. 159r–v, cal. *Wells MSS* i. 390.
137 Present at Stowe Park, Jocelin was the first witness to the will. For the royal grants of permission, *Acta of Hugh of Wells*, no. 408 n.
138 *CChR 1226–57*, 131, 185; *Acta of Hugh of Wells*, no. 407.
139 *CChR 1226–57*, 137; *Wells MSS* i. 471. After Hugh's death, Jocelin acted as both his personal executor and keeper of the temporalities of the diocese during the vacancy: *CR 1234–37*, 64–5, 76–7.

episcopal estate. At roughly ten times annual income, the manor's purchase price would probably have been just over 200 marks, a sum oddly similar to Hugh's earlier monetary bequest which may have been used to procure this nearby manor at least, as the charter states, until alternative regular provision could be secured for the hospital. Cranmore may have been indirectly purchased through the securing of Axbridge borough. Originally sold by Hugh in 1204, the borough of Axbridge was repurchased for 100 marks in 1227 for the bishop of Bath, after much effort by the brothers.[140] It is possible that this was offered in part exchange to the episcopal estate in return for the manor of Cranmore. In these pivotal years between 1227 and 1233, Jocelin's foundation charter was both drafted (in June 1230) and enrolled on the royal charter roll (in January 1231). The process of drafting the will, and finalising the legacy of Hugh's estate was intricately intertwined with the creation of the Wells hospital. In the weeks before his will was drawn up, there is only one other known deed issued by Bishop Hugh. A grant, witnessed by seven of the eleven named executors of his will, was issued two days before his will to Jocelin of custody of the heirs and lands which were to form the substance of his final, contribution 'to the use and improvement of the hospital'.[141] Hugh's provisions for the hospital not only begin his will, but also constitute its most detailed arrangements.

Nevertheless, Jocelin's contribution, as brother and bishop, was to have a significant effect on the hospital. He worked closely with his brother throughout: Jocelin was present at the hospital's first formulation, in Hugh's will of 1212; he received into his own hands the properties and monies that were intended to create the house; and he laboured industriously during Hugh's final years to realise his vision. His status as local bishop made the establishment grander and more secure than it might otherwise have been, allowing Jocelin to secure a reliable endowment, a powerful and consistent patron in the bishop, and extensive rights to services and burial which were often hard to wrest from the local parish. His work set the hospital on a steady course which saw it through the rest of the Middle Ages: even in 1500 the priests, deacon and brethren of the hospital were taking an oath 'according to the ordinance of lord Jocelin'.[142] However, the house itself was a peculiarly familial foundation, founded by the brothers from Hugh's own estates and for the souls of the family.[143] Jocelin's foundation charter is explicit. It states that,

---

140 CChR 1226–57, 75. The purchase of Axbridge is copied into the Wells register beside the royal licence for executors to retain property in case of the bishop's death: Wells MSS i. 471.

141 Acta of Hugh of Wells, no. 407.

142 Wells MSS ii. 161.

143 In his last will, Hugh notes that the hospital was for his own soul and those of his father, mother, ancesters and heirs, as well as Jordan de Turri: Acta of Hugh of Wells, no. 408.

for the maintenance of the poor of the hospital of Wells and their ministers which, my own brother [*frater meus*] Hugh the second, bishop of Lincoln, with my assent built there in honour of God and the Glorious Virgin and St John the Baptist, for the souls of our father and mother and our own souls, and in accordance with the desire of our father.[144]

The hospital was created by the brothers in obedience to their father's dying wish: it therefore owes its genesis not to Jocelin, or even Hugh, but to Edward of Wells.

A comparison with Bishop Reginald's foundation of St John the Baptist, Bath, highlights how unusually personal was the brothers' hospital in Wells. Reginald built his hospital using episcopal funds and influence. He purchased properties to form the hospital site, in the south-west corner of the city, beside two of its most popular baths. The early deeds note that 'the hospital of the baths in Bath' was founded for the poor resorting there,[145] an image that recalls the words of his predecessor, Robert, that Bath was the city where the sick flock to seek healing in its baths. In its very establishment, then, Reginald's hospital connected episcopal charity with the identity of the city. He found other ways to tie together bishop, diocese and city in his hospital through the endowment that he gathered. The hospital was to be sustained by episcopal profits: a sheaf of corn annually from every acre of the episcopal demesne, regular wood from the bishop's park, and the right to graze their horses, cows and sheep in his pastures; it would also receive 4 marks of silver annually from the 'pennies of charity' in the archdeaconries of both Bath and Wells.[146] Finally, he entrusted St John's to the local supervision of the cathedral chapter, Bath priory, who in turn granted a sheaf of corn annually from each of its demesnes and one tenth of all the bread, cheese and salted meat produced for the convent.[147] Reginald's hospital was a civic symbol of episcopal power, drawing publicly upon the incomes of bishop, convent and diocesan government to maintain the sick poor who sought the healing of the baths that gave his city its reputation. His was clearly an episcopal charity; Hugh and Jocelin's hospital was far more personal.

Only a generation separated the foundation of these two hospitals, but their characters and circumstances demonstrate how far the relationship between

---

144 'secutus desiderium bone memorie patris nostri': TNA C53/25, mem. 11.
145 'hospitali sancti Johannis Baptiste de balneis in Bathon": EEA x. nos 77–8; *Medieval Deeds of Bath*, i. no. 121.
146 EEA x. nos 80–1, 190. It has been suggested that the 'pennies of charity' were drawn from a charge on priests at synod in support of the building of the cathedral (*Medieval Deeds of Bath*, i. no. 6 n.). If this is so, then Reginald was also affiliating the upkeep of the hospital with the grandest and most public pastoral duty of the diocesan.
147 EEA x. no. 80.

bishop and city had changed in Somerset in that time. The early ideal of John of Tours, of the dignified unity of bishop and city, can still be witnessed in Reginald's actions in Bath, where the identity of city was clearly still tied into the power, wealth and pastoral role of the bishop. In contrast to his episcopal hospital was the more personal hospital of St John the Baptist, Wells, created by two brothers who were carrying out the wishes of their late father, endowed in their hometown with private incomes and local, even apparently family, lands, for their own souls and those of their parents. This was Jocelin not as bishop but as brother and loyal son. The more ambiguous relationship between bishop and city that was apparent in the early thirteenth century was not of Jocelin's own making, but it does characterise his tenure as bishop, perhaps more than any of his predecessors and successors. The bishops of Somerset retained an uncertain relationship to their cities as symbolic sites and economic centres. Unlike other reformed sees, this was a diocese whose new seat at Bath never quite took hold. The resulting search for security and prestige led Jocelin's predecessors to pursue ties to both Wells and Glastonbury.

When Jocelin became bishop, Bath was a well-established city with political vision but lacking economic vigour. In the shadow of nearby Bristol, it had once been the victim of its wealthy neighbour's aggression and remained a victim of the port city's success. Wells, on the other hand, was moving from strength to strength, a legally formed borough that was growing rapidly alongside its local church and chapter. Wells had been the making of Jocelin, and Jocelin, in his own way, was the making of Wells, but not as might have been expected. Through his substantial building projects, in church, palace and cloister, and through his efforts to protect its markets from the threat of nearby Shepton Mallet, Jocelin fostered the town which was to become the largest in Somerset, after the border town of Bristol, by the fourteenth century.[148] Conclusively rebuffed by Glastonbury abbey, Jocelin turned to Wells as the second town of the diocese, developing the chapter and residence there. His affection for Wells may have helped foster the geographical realignment of the diocese, first toward Wells, then away from Bath. He was the first bishop to be buried at Wells since the see had been moved to Bath 150 years earlier, and his successors followed suit. Besides his immediate successor Roger (the last bishop to be elected solely by the Bath chapter), the next bishop certainly known to be buried in Bath was James Mountagu in 1608. Curiously, however, Jocelin's own interest in the town of Wells itself appears to have been less episcopal than personal. He has left no evidence of an intention to create a civic seat at Wells, and his great project, the hospital, was distinctively familial in

148 Shaw, *Community*, 62.

both its inspiration and endowment. Jocelin finally abandoned the ideal of a single, symbolic diocesan centre that had been begun by John of Tours and continued by his successors in favour of a regional identity and wider networks of profits, rights and administration. For a man so closely affiliated with – and so clearly attached to – his city, as a bishop he might oddly be seen as less civic and more broadly diocesan in his actions.

BISHOP JOCELIN THE BUILDER

5

Jocelin of Wells as a Palace Builder

TIM TATTON-BROWN

When Jocelin became bishop of Wells in 1206, cathedral building-work on a huge scale had been taking place in England for a century or so. Starting with Canterbury in 1071, some extraordinary new buildings were erected which evolved rapidly from the fairly crude but often massive Romanesque buildings of the later eleventh century to the wonderful early Gothic rib-vaulted structures of the later twelfth century.[1] At Wells itself a magnificent new cathedral (started in c.1175) was nearing completion, with its eastern arm, if not its nave, ready for use.[2] Alongside this work, but less well known because most of the buildings are now much less well preserved, the bishops were putting up fine official residences for themselves, which by the late twelfth century can often be called 'palaces'. These episcopal palaces, which could often be as grand as contemporary royal palaces in England, were almost always situated close to their cathedrals, though most of the bishops also had a series of other, lesser residences at some of the major manors that they owned.[3]

In the early thirteenth century most bishops put up, for the first time, fine new residences in London as well, so that they could be near the developing royal court at Westminster. Many of their London houses were situated on the Thames littoral, still known as the Strand, between the royal palace at Westminster and the city. Two of the most important, the residences of the archbishop of Canterbury and the bishop of Winchester, were, however, already well established on the south bank of the Thames before

---

[1] See E. Fernie, *The Architecture of Norman England* (Oxford, 2000), though the rebuilding process had got under way before 1066, notably at Edward the Confessor's Westminster Abbey.

[2] Rodwell, *Wells Cathedral*.

[3] In Wells diocese, for example, there were residences at places like Banwell, Cheddar, Evercreech and Wookey. At the last-named site, only 2½ miles west of Wells, building-work started in 1224.

1200 at Lambeth[4] and Southwark.[5] By the later Middle Ages all bishops spent much of their time travelling around their dioceses and between their cathedral palaces and their London 'inns', as they were often later called, via a series of other manorial residences. The later medieval and early Tudor bishops of Bath and Wells lived at Bath Inn until 1545 (later it became Arundel House) on the Strand, when they were in London. This site had been granted to Bishop Jocelin by the bishop of London between 1221 and 1228, and in 1232 Jocelin gave it to his successors in the see of Bath and Wells 'together with all houses and buildings there on'.[6] Almost nothing is known of these buildings, but it is probable that Bishop Jocelin erected a fine residence there, as well as his magnificent 'palace' at Wells.[7] Across the river, and a little downstream, at Southwark, Bishop Peter des Roches of Winchester had, by the 1220s, already built himself a very fine and very large new great hall and chamber block, both at first-floor level, to dominate the city. A large fragment of the building still survives.[8] It is also very likely that Archbishop Stephen Langton completely rebuilt his residence at Lambeth in the years immediately after the death of King John in 1216.[9] Once again, a large fragment of this, the shell of the chapel (on an earlier vaulted undercroft), still survives and this too once dominated the waterfront opposite the royal palace at Westminster.[10] Other bishops, like Jocelin, probably erected lesser residences along the Strand waterfront in the 1220s (Salisbury, Norwich, Carlisle and Durham), but nothing now remains of these buildings, which were taken away from the bishops in the mid-sixteenth century.[11]

By far the largest, and most important, episcopal residence of the early thirteen century, however, was the enormous aisled hall and chamber block erected at Canterbury. This was probably started soon after 1200 by Archbishop Hubert Walter, and completed by Stephen Langton in time for the

[4]   T. Tatton-Brown, 'The Beginnings of Lambeth Palace', *Anglo-Norman Studies*, 24 (2002), 203–14.
[5]   M. Carlin, *Medieval Southwark* (London, 1996), 32–44.
[6]   C.L. Kingsford, 'Bath Inn or Arundel House', *Archaeologia*, 72 (1922), 243–77.
[7]   For the few remains, found on the site in September 1972, see M.J. Hammerson, 'Excavations on the Site of Arundel House in the Strand, WC2 in 1972', *Transactions of the London and Middlesex Archaeological Society*, 26 (1975), 209–51.
[8]   D. Seeley, C. Phillips and M. Samuel, *Winchester Palace: Excavations at the Southwark Residence of the Bishops of Winchester*, MOLAS Monograph 31 (London, 2006), 36–54.
[9]   Tatton-Brown, 'The Beginnings of Lambeth Palace', 214.
[10] The chapel was burnt out in 1944 and reroofed and refurbished in 1955. See T. Tatton-Brown, *Lambeth Palace: a History of the Archbishops of Canterbury and their Houses* (London, 2000), 99–101.
[11] For a brief general survey of these houses, see J. Schofield, *Medieval London Houses* (New Haven and London, 1995), 210–12. The grandest of these, and the nearest to Westminster, was the Archbishop of York's house in Whitehall.

great translation ceremonies for St Thomas Becket in July 1220.[12] It is within this broader context of episcopal building-work that we should set Bishop Jocelin's palace building-work at Wells. Before looking at the early thirteenth-century work in more detail, however, we should perhaps briefly survey the building of episcopal residences between the later eleventh and late twelfth centuries in England.

Probably the earliest reference to a major new episcopal residence in England is Domesday Book's entry on Archbishop Lanfranc, which tells us that twenty-seven houses (*mansurae*) had to be destroyed for the archbishop's *nova hospitatione* in Canterbury.[13] Excavation work has shown that this new *hospitatio* was situated[14] immediately to the north-west of the north-west tower of the cathedral. By 1086 Lanfranc had divided up all the cathedral's large estates between himself and the monks, and created an approximately three-acre enclave for his own residence immediately to the west of the monastic precinct. To do this twenty-seven houses in the town had to be demolished and rebuilt to the west of the diverted main street to the Northgate. A large dogleg in the street survives to this day. The new archiepiscopal enclave was surrounded by a thick masonry wall (some fragments of which still survive), and in its south-east corner, and attached to the cathedral as we have seen, a chamber block, chapel and first-floor hall were probably soon constructed. This complex of buildings, which had direct access to the cathedral's north-west tower, were to be mentioned in the many accounts of the events that took place in and around them in the hours before the murder of Archbishop Thomas Becket on the afternoon of 29 December 1170.[15] The huge new early thirteenth-century great hall and chamber, mentioned above, were added to the existing late eleventh- and twelfth-century complex on its north side.

Other monastic bishops, like Gundulf at Rochester (1077–1108), Walkelin at Winchester (1070–98), John of Tours at Bath (1088–1122) and Herbert de Losinga at Norwich (1096–1119) probably followed Lanfranc's lead, and constructed similar residences next to their new cathedrals, but only at Norwich does a large fragment survive of a massive early Norman first-floor episcopal residence.[16] This adjoined the north side of the cathedral nave, and gave direct access to the gallery over the north aisle. At the core of this building was a small keep-like structure, and it is clear that in this first phase of episcopal building, defence and direct private access to the

[12] J. Rady, T. Tatton-Brown and J.A. Bowen, 'The Archbishop's Palace, Canterbury', *Journal of the British Archaeological Assocation*, 144 (1991), 1–60.

[13] *Domesday Book*, ed. J. Morris, i. *Kent* (Chichester, 1983), 2. 16.

[14] For details of this see Rady *et al.*, The Archbishop's Palace'.

[15] F. Barlow, *Thomas Becket* (London, 1986).

[16] I. Atherton, E. Fernie, C. Harper-Bill and H. Smith, eds, *Norwich Cathedral, Church, City and Diocese, 1096–1996* (London, 1996), 109–11.

cathedral were important considerations. At Durham (which also became a monastic cathedral in 1083), the episcopal residence from the 1070s was in the castle bailey west of the motte and immediately north of the cathedral. Here too was constructed a sequence of massive masonry structures, with all the principal rooms at first-floor level.[17]

At the secular cathedrals there was a similar situation, and perhaps the most remarkable of all the early fortified episcopal residences was Bishop Remi's group of first-floor chambers (built c.1075–92) in the strongly fortified block that formed the western end of the nave at Lincoln minster.[18] Much of the lower part of this structure which incorporated a monumental entrance into the west end of the cathedral is still preserved within its great thirteenth-century western facade. At Salisbury, the old Iron Age hillfort at what is now called Old Sarum was turned into a large new castle by William the Conqueror. At its centre, a very large new ring-ditch was cut to form the inner bailey of the castle. Uniquely a new Romanesque cathedral was built in the north-west quarter of the surrounding outer bailey, after the *cathedra* was moved to this site from Sherborne in 1075.[19] This first relatively modest cathedral was completed in 1092 under Bishop Osmund (1078–99), who was also the royal chancellor; it is possible that his main residence was in the late eleventh-century keep or 'Great Tower' as it was called, on the western side of the inner bailey.[20] Immediately to the north-east of the great tower in the inner bailey are the remains of a large courtyard house, which must have been built in the early twelfth century by Osmund's successor as bishop, Roger (1102–39). This bishop, who dominated the reign of Henry I, acted at various times as the king's 'viceroy'[21] and he is recorded as having built other splendid palatial residences at his castles at Sherborne, Malmesbury and Devizes.[22] The surviving residence in the castle at Salisbury was probably both a royal and episcopal residence, and was the finest palace of its date in England. It was, however, soon to be eclipsed by an even more splendid residence, built at Wolvesey in Winchester for Bishop Henry of Blois (1129–71), brother of King Stephen. Much of the ruins of this

---

17 M. Leyland, 'The Origins and Development of Durham Castle', in *Anglo-Norman Durham, 1093–1193*, ed. D. Rollason, M. Harvey and M. Prestwich (Woodbridge, 1994), 407–24.

18 R. Gem, 'Lincoln Minster: *Ecclesia Pulchra, Ecclesia Fortis*', in *Medieval Art and Architecture at Lincoln Cathedral*, British Archaeological Association Conference Transactions 8 (Leeds, 1986), 9–28.

19 For the best general survey of Old Sarum, see Royal Commission on Historical Monuments, *Ancient and Historical Monuments in the City of Salisbury I* (London, 1980), 1–24.

20 For Osmund, see *EEA* xviii.

21 E.J. Kealey, *Roger of Salisbury, Viceroy of England* (London, 1972), and *EEA* xviii.

22 Henry of Huntingdon, *Historia Anglorum*, ed. D. Greenway (Oxford, 1996), 720–1. The great keep of Rochester castle, built for Henry I in 1127 by Archbishop William de Corbeil, also appears to have been a residence for the king and the archbishop.

magnificent structure have been excavated,[23] and it is clear that Bishop Henry took over the large first-floor hall building of his predecessor, William Giffard (1107–29), on a new site to the south-east of the cathedral, and turned it into a vast fortified courtyard palace surrounded by a moat.

By the mid- to later twelfth century many of the other English bishops were putting up new residences on new sites, or were enlarging still further their existing houses. In Durham castle, for example, Bishop Hugh le Puiset (1153–95) had added a large new north range by c.1160,[24] while at Lincoln, Bishop Robert de Chesney, in c.1155, started a completely new residence on the steep hillside immediately to the south of the cathedral.[25] Another apparently new feature of this period was the creation of large ground-floor aisled halls. Remarkably there are still surviving the remains of a later twelfth-century timber aisled hall at the 'poor' episcopal residence at Hereford.[26] This, now well-known four-bay structure, which was probably built by Bishop William de Vere (1186–98), once had a three-storey stone chamber block beside it, at its southern end. To the north, but separate from it, was the remarkable two-storey freestanding chapel, built by Bishop Robert of Lorraine (1079–95) in the late eleventh century.[27]

In Salisbury the relatively small (only 185 ft long) cathedral in the castle at Old Sarum was greatly enlarged on the east (with a new choir and presbytery) by Bishop Roger in the early twelfth century. This enlargement was perhaps taking place in the 1120s at the same time as the construction of the bishop's (and the king's) great courtyard residence in the inner bailey, already mentioned. In 1139, however, Bishop Roger fell from grace and died, and all his castles were taken from him by King Stephen. When the new bishop, Jocelin de Bohun,[28] was elected in 1142, he had no residence there, and had to construct a completely new palace to the north-east of the cathedral. This residence lies between the cloister, which must have been constructed contemporaneously, and the north curtain wall. The whole building was probably demolished only about seventy years after it was built (when the cathedral was moved down the hill, to New Salisbury, in the early thirteenth century), but its complete plan was uncovered by excava-

---

[23] M. Biddle, *Wolvesey: The Old Bishop's Palace, Winchester, Hants.* (London, 1986).

[24] Leyland, 'The Origins and Development of Durham Castle'.

[25] Though it is possible that Bishop Alexander (1123–48) started the building-work after being granted the land in the 1140s by King Stephen. See H. Chapman, G. Coppack and P. Drewett, *Excavations at the Bishop's Palace, Lincoln, 1968–72* (London, 1975), 5.

[26] J. Blair, 'The Twelfth Century Bishop's Palace at Hereford', *Medieval Archaeology*, 31 (1987), 59–72.

[27] N. Drinkwater, 'Hereford Cathedral: the Bishop's Chapel of St Katherine and St Mary Magdalene', *Archaeological Journal*, 111 (1954), 129–137. This chapel was demolished in the 1730s, but part of its north wall still survives within the later cloister south wall.

[28] *EEA* xviii. xlii–xlvii, and *ODNB*.

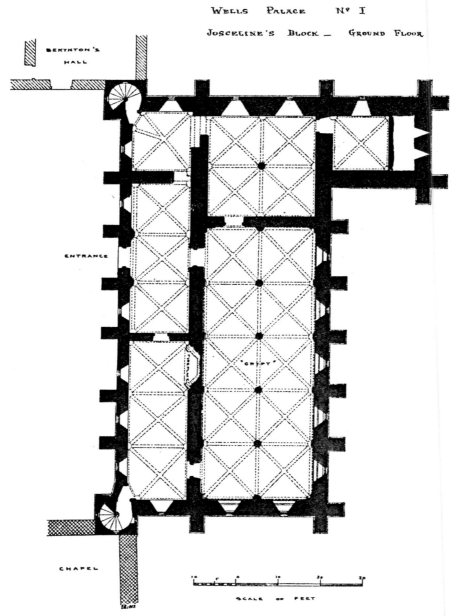

Figure 4. Bishop Jocelin's range; plans of ground and first floors. *Proceedings of the Somersetshire Archaeological and Natural History Society,* 35 (1888), between pp. 53 and 55.

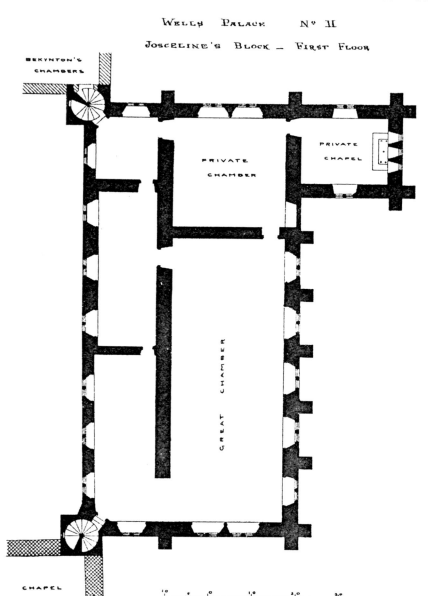

tion in 1914.[29] This residence was also built around a courtyard, with the principal building, an aisled hall 100 ft long by 60 ft wide, on the east. To the west of the courtyard were the bishop's private lodgings (the principal chambers were probably at first-floor level), with beyond it a walled garden. The excavators found that the aisled hall was probably of six bays with a large porch on the east, and a dais at the southern end. In size the hall was almost comparable to the 1230s great hall built at Winchester for Henry III by Bishop Peter des Roches (1206–38).[30] Of similar size, and perhaps first built for Henry II,[31] is the fine four-bay aisled hall, incorporating a buttery and pantry at its west end at Clarendon Palace, which lies only three miles south-east of Old Sarum.

By the later twelfth century, therefore, we can show that the principal episcopal residences of the major bishops were comparable in scale to the majority of the royal residences, and that the centre of the residence was an aisled great hall. The one exception, however, was at Westminster where the king's principal residence had the colossal Westminster Hall at its heart. By the early thirteenth century, Westminster was also becoming the centralised place of government and, as we have seen, this required the bishops to build themselves large new town houses nearby.

It is against that background that Bishop Jocelin (1206–42) erected his own magnificent palatial residence at Wells, perhaps starting the work in 1207–8, and completing it in the 1220s. This is not the place to discuss the building in great detail,[32] but it seems likely that Jocelin's surviving building was an exceptionally large chamber block that perhaps lay alongside an earlier (perhaps late twelfth-century) aisled hall on the east. This hall would have been replaced when Bishop Robert Burnell (1275–92) erected his much grander aisled hall to the south-west in the 1280s. Perhaps the best indicator of the position of the earlier hall is the original lack of buttresses on the west side of Jocelin's building, in contrast to the major buttresses supporting the vaults on the north, east and south sides.[33] The original aisled hall may have been built in Bishop Reginald's time (1174–94), once the building of the new cathedral had got under way. Reginald was the son of Bishop Jocelin de Bohun of Salisbury, and had served for a time as his father's archdeacon in Wiltshire.[34] When he too became a bishop, it would

---

[29] See W. Hawley's interim report on the excavations in 1914 in *Proceedings of the Society of Antiquaries*, 2nd series, 27 (November 1914–June 1915), 230–8.

[30] M. Biddle and B. Clayre, *Winchester Castle and the Great Hall* (Winchester, 1983), 25.

[31] *Pace* T.B. James and C. Gerrard, *Clarendon, Landscape of Kings* (Macclesfield, 2007).

[32] See Sampson's chapter in this volume, pp. 119–22.

[33] The present buttresses on the west, as well as on the porch, were not added until a new top storey was put on the building in the nineteenth century.

[34] *EEA* xviii.

have been natural for him to want a fine residence like his father's palace at Old Sarum.

After the chaos at the end of John's reign and in the first years of Henry III's, a very large amount of new building-work got under way on the English cathedrals. This was the period when, most famously, the completely new cathedral at Salisbury was erected (c.1217–66), when the new eastern arm at Worcester was put up (c.1224–60),[35] and when the magnificent west front of Wells was built (c.1219–50).[36] Much less well known, however, was the building alongside these works of even more splendid palaces, as well as the London inns, for many of the bishops. The most splendid of them all was the previously mentioned great hall, chamber block and detached kitchen at Canterbury, but we also know that Bishop Richard Poore was rapidly erecting a palace for himself right beside the construction site for his new cathedral, which may have been partially complete by 1225.[37] Only the vaulted undercroft of the great chamber and a few other fragments of this building now survive,[38] very similar in style to Bishop Jocelin's building at Wells and to Archbishop Stephen Langton's great palace at Canterbury. This new style, which is best seen at Salisbury cathedral itself, has been linked with the well-known canon (and 'Rector of the fabric') at Salisbury, Elias of Dereham. This man, who was also a canon of Wells, was famously one of the two designers of the shrine of St Thomas Becket at Canterbury (completed in July 1220). There has been much debate as to whether he was only an administrator or also an 'architect'.[39] The word 'architect' is really a post-Renaissance term, but it seems that the contemporary evidence shows that Elias was a designer. He is, therefore, the man most likely to have drawn up the designs for Bishop Jocelin's new house at Wells, though his many other activities elsewhere meant that he could not have supervised the work. What is clear is that Bishop Jocelin had, by the 1230s, a fine new residence that was commensurate with his status as bishop and a major figure in the administration of justice in south-west England (Plate 9).[40]

---

[35] U. Engel, *Worcester Cathedral, an Architectural History* (Chichester, 2007), 112–17.

[36] J. Sampson, *Wells Cathedral West Front: Construction, Sculpture and Conservation* (Stroud, 1998), 45–60.

[37] Bishop Jocelin of Wells's own brother, Hugh, also built himself a fine new great hall at Lincoln, after he became bishop there (1209–35). See Chapman *et al.*, *Excavations at the Bishop's Palace, Lincoln*.

[38] Royal Commission on Historical Monuments, *Salisbury: The Houses of the Close* (London, 1993), 53–72.

[39] A. Hastings, *Elias of Dereham, Architect of Salisbury Cathedral* (Salisbury, 1997) sums up the debate about Elias's building activities.

[40] *See* ODNB lviii. 63–4.

6

Bishop Jocelin and His Buildings in Wells

JERRY SAMPSON

This chapter seeks to consider Bishop Jocelin's buildings in Wells from the point of view of buildings archaeology, concentrating on the two prime examples: the cathedral and the Bishop's Palace. While there is probably surviving fabric from Jocelin's period in the Old Deanery, and perhaps in other houses to the north of the cathedral, those remains are slight and have not been studied in detail. The other major survival, the fragments of Jocelin's chamber and chapel at Wookey, lies outside the city. Therefore, what follows is a consideration of Jocelin's work in the cathedral and palace, first by examining the sequence of construction and building styles in the cathedral, and then to see if anything can be learnt by applying a knowledge of those building styles to the thirteenth-century fabric of the palace.

Jocelin's building campaign in the cathedral

Early commentators on the building of the cathedral were wont to credit Jocelin with the whole or the greater part of the building. James Thomas Irvine (whose observation was superb, but whose interpretation was seriously flawed) mistakenly believed the cathedral to have been rebuilt from west to east, and credited Jocelin with the quire, rather than the nave and the west front.

It is, however, salutary to realise that in the famous view of the cathedral from Tor woods to the east, hardly anything built during Jocelin's episcopate can be seen. The east end, chapter house, central tower and Lady Chapel are of the fourteenth century; the western towers are of 1384–94 and 1424+; while the transepts and earliest part of the nave were complete by 1206, when Savaric's obit was celebrated in St Martin's chapel in the south transept.

Over the last twenty years the phases of construction of the cathedral have been clarified – though it is likely that Professor Robert Willis had identified them in the 1870s, but failed to record his observations in detail.

In order to define Jocelin's contribution to the building it is necessary first to look briefly at the constructional history of the church under his predecessors, Bishops Reginald and Savaric.

Rebuilding the church prior to Jocelin's episcopate

Work on the new church must have begun at the east end soon after Reginald's appointment in 1174, with the single-storey eastern retroquire – just as happened at Salisbury in 1220–25. Immediately after this, having established the celebration of the liturgy on site, building-work progressed to the ritual quire, its three bays with the eastern aisles of the transepts and enough of the transept walls to the west to act as buttressing being built by 1184. Next the transepts and the base of the crossing tower were erected, working from north to south, and turning into the nave to provide buttressing against the crossing. Finally the nave was built in two planned phases, with a break at the mid-point.

With each phase of construction the canons and their vicars were provided with a processional doorway which would allow access for the processions required by the liturgy without the need to enter the building-site which lay to the west of the completed parts of the church. In the eastern phases this required the creation of doorways which had no function once the next phase of building to the west was complete, and these doorways were blocked up in the twelfth or early thirteenth century. In the case of the earliest retroquire phase, this door lay in the south wall of the quire aisle, and its blocked scar can still be seen. This bay of the south quire aisle is differentiated from the main quire phase in lacking the corbel table that is universal in the rest of the Early English fabric.

In the main quire phase, the eastern aisles of the transepts opening off the western bays of the quire aisles were necessary abutments to the structure, and these aisles served as processional routes with doors in the end walls of the transepts. The northern door still serves the stair to the chapter house, but the southern is blocked with early masonry, and could not have functioned once the transept chapels divided up the eastern aisle.

A precisely analogous situation exists at Glastonbury abbey – a building very much the twin of Wells – where the end of the north transept's eastern aisle contains an original doorway also blocked with late twelfth- or very early thirteenth-century masonry. Again there is good evidence in the fabric that at Glastonbury the quire formed a separate building phase served by processional doors in the eastern aisles of the transepts.

Close analysis of the fabric of Wells cathedral would be far more difficult were it not for a switch in the provenance of the building stone, from Doulting – whose quarries were owned by Glastonbury abbey – to Chilcote, a greyer, more pebbly limestone of poorer quality. This change in building stone occurs close to the beginning of the second phase of construction, as work began on the transepts, and may have happened in a break in the works immediately following the completion of the quire. It is most clearly visible from the ground in the plinths of the transept end walls, where it forms a vertical toothed break, with Chilcote stone also characterising the stonework between the two western windows above, and rising diagonally towards the south-eastern buttress. It is also clearly visible in the angle between the quire and the north transept at clerestory level, where the Doulting fabric turns onto the transept and terminates with the jamb of the first clerestory window.

Why should Wells suddenly switch quarries in this way?

The most likely reason is that Glastonbury abbey, effectively rebuilt in grand style under Abbots Herlewin and Henry of Blois and with no major building-works projected in the last quarter of the twelfth century, had let its quarries to the canons of Wells, but was devastated by fire on St Urban's Day, 24 May 1184. The account of the fire depicts the monks sifting through the wreckage of the convent for anything worth salvaging, and records that worse than the loss of the buildings was the loss of the relics that they housed. Excavation in the 1920s exposed the nave paving, burned by the intensity of the fire, with lead from the roof having run molten in the cracks caused by the fall of the vaulting and roof timbers.

In the immediate aftermath of the Glastonbury fire the rebuilding of the ancient western Lady Chapel (in a deliberately retrospective style) saw the salvaging of stone of various geological origins, including Bath stone that may have come from Anglo-Saxon contexts. This cocktail of stones occupies the lower five metres of the fabric of the Lady Chapel, but above this the structure is exclusively of Doulting stone with Dundry block used for the fine carving. While the Doulting quarries could supply one cathedral-sized building operation, they could probably not support two at the same time, and the canons of Wells had to fall back on their own quarry at Chilcote.[1]

---

[1]   That this interpretation is correct has recently received support from the discovery of Wells banker masons disappearing from Wells at the start of the Chilcote phase, to be found working stones in the 1184–89 phase of building at Glastonbury. The 'star' mark is particularly interesting, because this mason returned to Wells at the end of the Chilcote phase and is found marking Doulting stone in the high work of the south transept and the east nave.

The construction of Wells cathedral under Bishop Jocelin

Wells fabric studies are particularly fortunate in having not one but two changes in the source of the stone supply, since in the high work of the south transept Chilcote stone disappears and Doulting is once more almost exclusively used. This change is most clearly visible in the south nave aisle, where the stone was cleaned in the 1960s and the colour variation shows up well. As in the quire phase, the break at low level is symmetrical on both sides of the building, but is visible to its full height only on the north side, where the earlier fabric of the Chilcote north transept forms the whole height of the abutment against the crossing. This abutment, comprising the two eastern piers of the nave arcade, one and one-third bays of its triforium and the eastern jamb of the east clerestory window opening, also defines the form of the nave elevation, implying that this was designed while Chilcote stone was still in use.

While the break in construction in the middle of the nave is characterised by at least eighteen changes, the Chilcote phase shows only one major stylistic difference to the rest of the nave – the tympana of the triforium openings being carved as roundels rather than triangular panels. Thus, while we must credit Jocelin's episcopate with the construction of the nave of Wells cathedral, its actual design took place before the second Doulting phase, and the change back from Chilcote to Doulting stone at Wells is probably best explained by Bishop Savaric's seizure of Glastonbury abbey on Whitsunday 1199, the canons of Wells presumably benefiting from their bishops' virtual usurpation of the abbey that owned the best quarry in the district. Thus, if we are to credit Jocelin's period with the design of the nave, it is only really its western elevation for which he can be regarded as responsible.

His episcopate probably saw the completion of the north porch. Its plinth (and therefore its plan) belong to the Chilcote phase, the grey stone clearly visible at the base of the wall; but many aspects of its design – the use of foliate spandrels, intersecting mouldings, deep niches for statuary, and perhaps blue lias shafts in the outer doorway, all prefigure the work on the west front.

Indeed, the fragmentary remains probably deriving from the thirteenth-century cloister – a lost work of Bishop Jocelin's episcopate – serve to show how the Wells masons' yard, once freed from the constraints of the received design of the nave, constantly experiment with architectural form. The physical form of the first cloister can be reconstructed from the rooflines where the thirteenth-century south walk was butted up against the fifteenth-century rebuildings of the east and west two-storey walks, while fragments reused in Bishop Bekynton's west cloister and the chapel of the vicars choral may derive from Jocelin's cloister. The plinth of the west front and the west cloister wall were built in bond, showing that the circuit of its wall was complete in the 1220s.

The early thirteenth-century settlement of the western tower piers

In the preamble to his Ordinance of 1242 Jocelin says that when he became bishop the cathedral building was in danger of collapse. He gives the reason for its precarious state as 'because of age' – which is more difficult to account for. There was certainly an episode of major settlement in the rising structure of the east nave datable to the period around his accession in 1206. If a building is going to suffer from settlement this should become apparent relatively soon after its foundations are fully loaded. Clearly, the western crossing piers settled severely after the central tower was erected in the 1320s, with the famous scissor-arches and other remedial works being undertaken beginning in 1338. However, the loading of the crossing piers in the initial late twelfth- to early thirteenth-century campaign should have been sufficient to cause settlement, and there are signs that this became apparent to the builders at triforium level as the east nave was being built.

All the nave arcade piers in the eastern nave phase of construction have a slight lean to the west, away from the crossing, probably caused by movement in the western crossing piers; but the piers of the west nave phase are all vertical – showing that the movement had been arrested by the 1220s when the construction of the west nave was under way. In the triforia, the elevation of each bay above the aisle vaulting and beneath the roof has a single wide relieving arch over the three triforium openings, but on the south side of the nave, while the first two bays conform to this pattern, the third bay has an individual relieving arch for each opening, and the next two bays (to the mid-nave break) have two such arches – clearly extra reinforcements were being constructed in an attempt to stabilise the structure. The first two bays of the triforium belong to the transept phase of building, and were already wholly (the eastern bay) or partly (the second bay west) constructed by around 1200–2; but the next bays appear to have been strengthened in response to the settlement of the south-western pier of the crossing – the one most seriously affected in 1338. Hence about 1206 the cathedral was, as Jocelin recalled more than thirty years later, in danger of collapse.

Why did Jocelin consider this settlement to be 'because of age'? Modern experience of builders suggests that any misdemeanour discovered by the client is necessarily someone else's fault. Perhaps Jocelin, naturally concerned about the state of the rising church for which he was newly responsible, was told by his master mason that the problem lay with footings which had been laid out in the first phase of construction some thirty years before. Was it

Plate 1. Crozier head found at Wells and now ascribed to the time of Bishop Jocelin. Reproduced with permission of the Dean and Chapter of Wells.

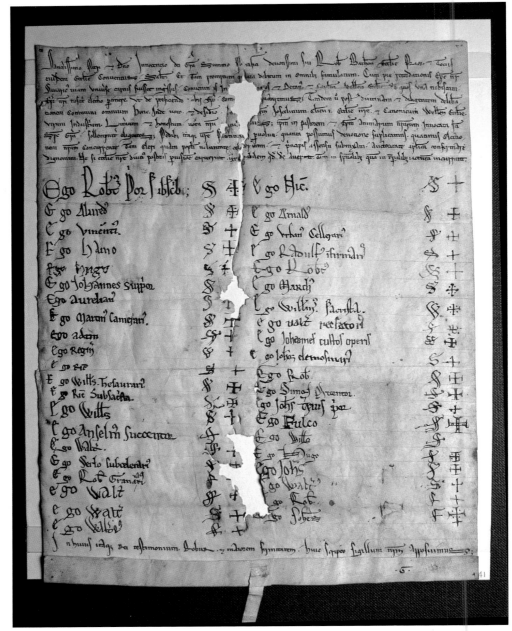

Plate 2. The election of Bishop Jocelin, 1206. Prior Robert and the monks of Bath subscribe to the instrument of election addressed to Pope Innocent III. Wells Cathedral charter 41. Reproduced with permission of the Dean and Chapter of Wells.

Plate 3. The consecration of Bishop Jocelin, 1206. Bishop Jocelin declares that he was consecrated bishop of Bath by William, bishop of London, on Trinity Sunday (28 May) 1206 in the chapel of Our Lady at Reading. Canterbury Cathedral Ancient Charter C107. Reproduced with permission from Canterbury Cathedral Archives.

Plate 4. Seal of Bishop Jocelin, attached to the declaration of his consecration. Canterbury Cathedral Archives Ancient Charter C107. Reproduced with permission from Canterbury Cathedral Archives.

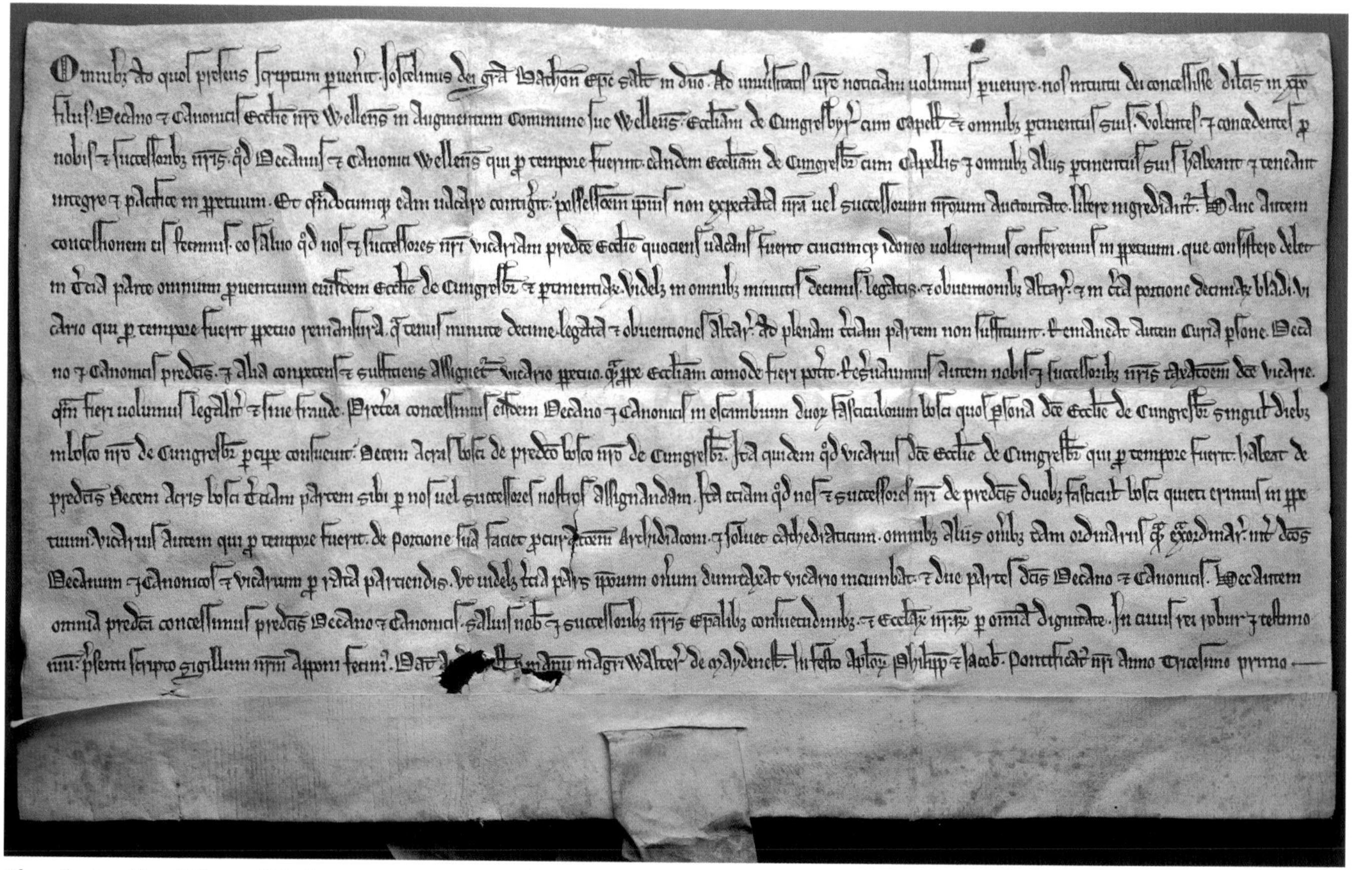

Plate 5. Jocelin, bishop of Bath, in augmentation of their commons, grants to the dean and canons of Wells the church of Congresbury; the feast of SS Philip and James in the thirty-first year of his pontificate (1 May 1237). Wells Cathedral charter 34. Reproduced with permission of the Dean and Chapter of Wells.

Plate 6. Wells Cathedral, west front: hot mastic repairs, a sign of financial strictures. Jerry Sampson.

Plate 7. Wells Cathedral, west front: the west doors and the painting scheme of 1239. Jerry Sampson.

Plate 8. Wells, the Bishop's Palace. Jerry Sampson.

Plate 9. Wells, the Bishop's Palace; Bishop Jocelin's range from the south-east. Mark Horton.

Plate 10. Wells, the Bishop's Palace; two blocked windows with cut-back capitals and abaci restored at the southern end of Bishop Jocelin's range. Jerry Sampson.

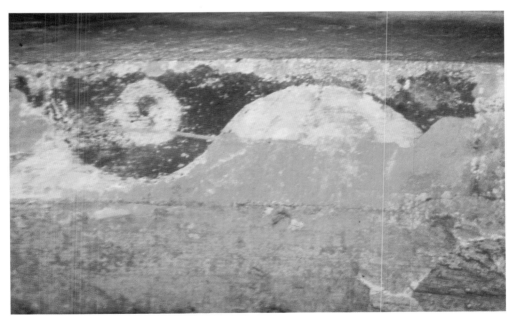

Plate 11a and b. Wells, the Bishop's Palace; ashlar lining and other painted decoration in the roofspace of Bishop Jocelin's range. Jerry Sampson.

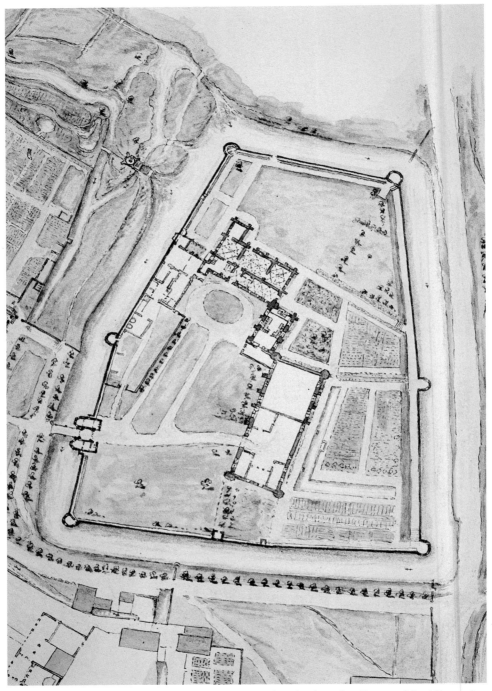

Plate 12. Wells, the Bishop's Palace; extract from the plan by John Carter of the 'General Plan of the Monastical Buildings' at Wells, drawn in 1784 and finished 1808. Reproduced with permission of the Society of Antiquaries of London.

Plate 13. Wells, the Bishop's Palace; excavations on the south side of Bishop Burnell's Great Hall showing the line of the kitchen or service block wall with two internal hearths and floor levels. Mark Horton.

Plate 14. Wells, the Bishop's Palace; culvert to carry water from gardens to moat. Mark Horton.

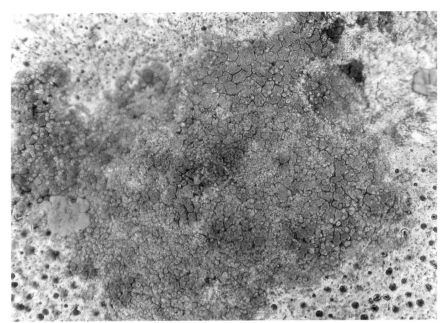

Plate 15. Wells, the Bishop's Palace. *Caloplaca polycarpa* (orange fruiting bodies on ochre thallus) growing on *Verrucaria baldensis* (whitish thallus with black fruiting bodies). *Caloplaca polycarpa* was relatively recently recognised in Britain and is a lichenicolous lichen (i.e. a species growing on other lichens). It can thus only occur later on in the colonising process when its host has become well established. David Hill.

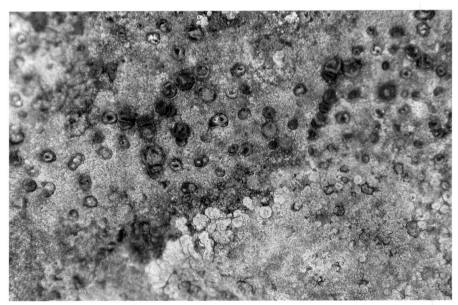

Plate 16. Wells, the Bishop's Palace. *Sarcogyne 'pruinosa'*, a form of *S. regularis*, with black fruiting bodies sunken in the stone with *Caloplaca variabilis* in the bottom right hand quarter. David Hill.

Plate 17. Wells, the Bishop's Palace. The brown lump of lichen with a grey lichen on the top (out of focus) is the nationally rare *Catapyrenium rufescens*. The grey lichen on top is *Physcia* sp. The yellow lichen with orange fruiting bodies is *Caloplaca aurantia*. David Hill.

Plate 18. Wells, the Bishop's Palace. The dark brown lichen in the centre is *Collema confertum*, a nationally rare species. This is a small, button-like growth that can easily be disturbed. It has about five flat, round, fruiting bodies on its upper surface. The yellow lichen on the left is *Candelariella medians* and the yellow one on the right with two fruiting bodies is *Caloplaca citrina*. David Hill.

Plate 19. Wells, the Bishop's Palace; capping stone of rampart wall east of the north tower, showing the weather surface with solution holes. The yellow lichens are species of *Caloplaca* and the white lichen is *Aspicilia calcarea*. Some of the holes have been colonized by plants of ivy-leaved toadflax (*Cymbellaria muralis*). David Hill.

Plate 20. Wells, the Bishop's Palace; Bishop Burnell's Great Hall and chapel from the north-west. Matthew Reeve.

Plate 21. Wells, the Bishop's Palace; Bishop Burnell's chapel from the north. Matthew Reeve.

Plate 22. Wells, the Bishop's Palace; the solar end of the Great Hall. Matthew Reeve.

the age of the foundations which was being blamed by the builders anxious to deflect any blame from their own, more recent, work? Whatever the case, the settlement of the south-west crossing pier fits the date and the circumstances of Jocelin's 1242 report of his earliest involvement with building as a bishop.

The western nave

Remarked on by Professor Robert Willis in the 1870s and formally identified by John Bilson in 1928, the mid-nave break is the most obvious of the phase breaks in the cathedral. The transept phase was provided with the south door to the east cloister as its processional entry and was the main entrance in use when the Anglo-Saxon font was brought in from the ancient minster to the south; the east nave phase was served by the north porch, the 'great gate of the canons'.

Here the line of the construction break is exactly parallel on both sides of the nave, and precisely follows the profile of the Chilcote break on the north side of the nave's easternmost bays. This proves that the line of the mid-nave break was a planned phase break, and not solely dependent upon the Interdict and the bishop's exile in 1209–13. Nonetheless, it is likely that the two events coincided.

A recent dendrochronological date for the east nave roof of 1213 suggests that it was being erected very soon after Jocelin's return from exile, while extrapolation from the 1199 date for the beginning of the second Doulting phase would suggest that the mid-nave break in the masonry took place around 1210, and the number of changes across the line of the break suggests that there was a hiatus during the bishop's absence, and that perhaps there was some delay in continuing with the building of the west nave after the east nave was roofed.[2]

The mid-nave break is traditionally characterised chiefly on a change from small block diagonally tooled, to larger block retooled with a vertical finish, a fashion change which can also be seen at Glastonbury abbey, where the monks built their cloister before they built their nave, erecting the lower part of the south nave aisle wall as the northern abutment of the

---

[2]   There is a possibility that the mid-nave break is not as extreme as it appears, and that work continued with a diminution of output but no real break. In the nave plinths (particularly on the north) the change from small Doulting block diagonally tooled to large block with vertical retooling is not absolute, and passes through a developmental sequence, suggesting that stone was being laid at a much reduced rate. Two masons from the east nave workforce continued to mark stone in the west arcade piers, perhaps men kept on in the reduced circumstances of the 1210s to form the core of a new masons' yard when conditions improved.

cloister in small, diagonally tooled Doulting stone, before adding the south aisle windows above in large, vertically tooled block.

At Wells there are also stylistic changes across the break: the arcade capitals become more extravagant; head-stops disappear in the arcade hood-mouldings, or get bigger in the triforium hood-mouldings; roundels change the form of their surrounds, losing their chamfered margins; and even the joints in the timbers of the roofs develop. In the triforium the tympana change from asymmetrical, often inhabited foliage, to exclusively foliate patterns symmetrical about their centre line – exactly the same form as is seen in the tympana of the west front.

It is no longer apparent, since the foliage patterns on the nave high vaults were repainted in the late1840s to a single template copying a pattern from the west bay, but these patterns also varied between the east and west nave. Recording work carried out from the repair scaffolding in the 1980s showed that the original east nave patterns were of a simpler form and used a slightly different palette.

Within each phase of construction (even though each ended in a diagonal profile) work progressed in a series of horizontal layers, as can be seen in the triforium reinforcements and the leaning arcade of c.1206, and this is also apparent in the distribution of masons' marks. In the west nave the marks left by a mason who used a cross with dotted terminals to 'sign' his work are found only in the arcade and just onto the plinth of the west front. Blocks marked with a mitred corner seem to be restricted to the triforium relieving arches. Another series of marks are found only on the internal flying buttresses beneath the aisle roof, and 'lance' marks are found only on the clerestory jambs above arcade level – perhaps suggesting some subcontracted work.

The sequence of phases in the Wells constructional scheme can be closely paralleled in modern cathedral building – indeed there may be only one way to build a cathedral on a virgin site. At Truro the choir and transepts were erected together, with a temporary wall closing off the crossing. Photographs of the rising building show how precisely the profile of the temporary wall built across the stub of the east nave at Truro conforms to the Chilcote break-line at Wells, where the sloping triforium roof is carried across the stub of the nave from north to south. At Truro, also, the nave rose in horizontal layers, with the west wall an integral part of the rising structure; here, too, the towers were begun only once the nave was weatherproof and the body of the church could be brought into use – a trait which can also been inferred from the structure of the west front of Wells. Again, at Washington DC cathedral, work began with the three-bay east end, followed by the choir, then the transepts working from north to south as at Wells, and then the nave, there divided into three (rather than two) phases.

At Wells the straitjacket of the Chilcote phase nave design could only be sloughed in the tower bases and on the west wall: here volute capitals with round lias abacuses and blue lias shafts replace the frothy west nave foliage and their demi-octagonal Doulting abacus. Originally these changes at the west wall would have been even more obvious; the remodelling of the internal west elevation in the late fourteenth century has masked the high level volute capitals, and the blue lias shafts backed by foliate fleuron decoration of the west front which invaded the window jambs were removed or hacked back and plastered over, probably under William Wynford in the 1380s.

The west front

These stylistic changes in the west elevation belong with Bishop Jocelin's great west front – one of the most remarkable visionary buildings of the Middle Ages, in the design of which Jocelin himself must have been intimately involved.

Once again the geology and the distribution of certain of the decorative and technical features of the building suggest the order in which it was erected. These distributions show such features tending to bunch towards the centre of the facade, suggesting that the builders first closed up the west wall of the nave so that the whole of the church could be brought into operation, before going on to complete the flanking tower bases above the aisle vaults.

Particularly telling is the distribution of a fine-grained white limestone (probably from Beer in Devon, but often referred to in the previous literature on the west front as white lias). This probably represents no more than a single waggon-load of the block, but its distribution is concentrated below and around the west windows of the nave and aisles, and it is not found at all in the tower bases. Its fine texture allowed the carvers to reproduce detail in the stone that would normally have been created by the painters, offering a glimpse of delicate patterns which have been lost elsewhere with the destruction of the painted decoration.

Dundry stone was used for roughly one third of the surviving 297 figure sculptures, the distribution of this material once again concentrated across the centre of the west-facing screen wall. Dundry was a much travelled stone, occurring extensively in Ireland in the first half of the thirteenth century, where the English bridgehead was supplied from Bristol. At Wells, two of the west front figures are carved on blocks jointed together with iron dowels where half the statue is in Dundry stone and half in Doulting – proving that the sculptors' workshop must have been in Wells, the point of delivery for both quarries.

Chilcote stone, having virtually disappeared from the fabric in 1199, reappears briefly in the west gable of the nave – the grey stone clearly visible in the drums of the pinnacles flanking the gable. The west gable must have been amongst the last parts of the facade to have been built; it had a temporary wooden closure, the truss for which has been incorporated into the masonry structure, and it (like the south and east faces of the south tower) lacked sculptures in the thirteenth century, the present figures being of the later fifteenth century, with a new Christ in Majesty with flanking angels added in 1985.

Uniquely on the west front, the Resurrection figures of the upper tier bear incised position marks: to the south of the centre line in roman, to the north in arabic numerals. However, when the time came to fix the carvings it is evident that the base profiles of their niches had been altered from the form expected by the sculptors and that the figures did not fit; it is also clear that the sculptors who numbered the carvings were no longer on site. To the south the fixer masons, recognising the sequence of the roman numerals, simply recut the bases to fit the niches and installed the figures in the correct order. However, no one on site appears to have understood the new-fangled arabic numerals, and from 15 northwards the sculptures have been installed in a completely random order, with the figure on the east-north-east buttress even being installed upside down. The central sequence of figures across the end wall of the nave, however, was installed correctly (presumably while the sculptors were still on site), in niches where the bases matched the sculptures, showing that the nave's west wall was closed first. By the time the niches for the remainder were ready for their installation the sculptors must have gone (probably laid off in the period of financial uncertainty following Jocelin's death) but the fact that they were numbered ready for fixing suggests that the sculptural campaign was complete by 1242, and that the whole output of the Wells carvers' workshop belongs to Jocelin's episcopate.

Another probable signature of work after the end of Jocelin's episcopate is the make-do-and-mend mentality discernible in the last phase of building on the thirteenth-century west front, which again seems to reflect the financial strictures in the period of the dispute with Bath abbey over the relative status of the chapters of Bath and Wells. The medieval hot mastic repairs (see Plate 6), which first appear at Wells in the high vaults of the nave just to the east of the mid-nave break in about 1208–10, occur regularly on the west front, but increase in frequency towards the top of the thirteenth-century south tower – the last part of the facade to be built in the 1240s, as can be seen by the absence of figure carving from its eastern and southern niches, there being no trace of the cramp systems used to hold the thirteenth-century sculptures in place. The lack of any sign that the high vaults were ever installed in the thirteenth-century towers also points to a forced termination of the west front building programme.

Thus we can reconstruct the phases of erection of the west front, rising with the west nave and initially including the tower bases at aisle level; then concentrating on closing the west wall to weatherproof the nave, and with the north side slightly in advance of the south. We may speculate that the west wall of the nave and aisles, together with the tower bases capped off at the top of the aisle vault level, would have been complete for the dedication of the church in November 1239; then, by 1242, work must have been well advanced on the upper parts of the tower bases, with the north side again ahead of the south, but with the Resurrection tier niches still incomplete.

The Bishop's Palace

It is 'certain that to Jocelin must go the credit for the earliest surviving part of the present Palace'.[3] This section of the building comprises the central range, running north–south between Bishop Burnell's chapel and the fifteenth-century apartments at the north and north-west built by Bishop Bekynton. The range incorporates a first-floor hall and solar standing above a vaulted undercroft, both floors having western passageways and a smaller projecting wing at the north-east. The whole was much restored and altered in the nineteenth century when a complete upper storey was added on the western side above the passage.

Jocelin received licence from the Crown to form a park to the south of the cathedral in 1207, and this has often been assumed to represent the date at which the rebuilding of the palace itself began. Assuming that Jocelin was using the same workshop for his work on the palace as was constructing the cathedral itself, with work beginning before the east nave was complete, there should be signs of the cathedral's small, diagonally tooled, Doulting style of construction in the undercroft of the palace, at least. At the base of the western wall on the interior this does appear to be the case, the courses beneath the springers of the vaulting being quite shallow, and certainly in the general range of course-heights seen in the east nave construction phase. However, at the base of the eastern wall of Jocelin's palace the courses are generally considerably taller, and more closely resemble the post-1213 masonry of the west nave. Furthermore, it is possible that the interior ashlar facing of the western wall of the undercroft owes its shallow coursing to the 20 cm-high courses of the two stair turrets at

3   Dunning, 'Bishop's Palace', 229.

Figure 5. Bishop Jocelin's range; extract from the engraving of 1733 by Samuel and Nathaniel Buck.

the western corners of the range (themselves conditioned by the heights of the steps within) being carried through onto the walls to either side, rather than to the east nave style of building. Certainly there is no indication of narrow coursing in the upper parts of the undercroft or the hall above, and if the cathedral masonry styles can be used to date the palace masonry it is clear that the whole belongs firmly in the context of the post-1213 building style. Furthermore, there is no sign of the use of Chilcote stone, which might have been expected if Jocelin's builders were cannibalising a recent stone-built structure on the site for architectural salvage.

Also indicative of a post-Interdict date for the earliest fabric of the palace is the use of blue lias in the bases, columns, capitals and abaci of the undercroft. It is possible that lias was first used in the cathedral in the shafts of the outer portal of the north porch, but its first clear inclusion is in the abaci of the west wall of the nave and the west cloister. The extensive mid-nineteenth-century restoration of the palace has obscured much of the evidence, and the foliate capitals of the first floor have been painted over so that their authenticity is uncertain, but the cut-back capitals and abaci of the blocked windows of the two southern bays of the east elevation show that these were certainly volute capitals with lias abaci of the cathedral west front type (Plate 10).[4]

These two blocked windows, opened up on the interior elevation during repairs in the mid-twentieth century, are quite invisible on the exterior, indicating the extent of the mid-nineteenth-century interventions (Plates 9 and 10).[5] It is evident that amongst other alterations the pitch of the roof of the north-eastern range opening off the northern bay of the thirteenth-century building has been substantially reduced, since the projecting weathering stones can be seen rising steeply above the present eaves on both sides on the main elevation. It is also evident that the main range was completed prior to the erection of the north-eastern range, since within the roof-space of the latter the corbel table of the main range continues uninterrupted. These corbels, however, have their mouldings left incomplete, suggesting that there was only a short period between the completion of the main range and the erection of the extension to the north-east.

Also visible within the roof-space of Jocelin's hall and solar are traces of the early thirteenth-century painted decorative scheme, isolated when the

4   Only one mason's mark has so far been found on the thirteenth-century ashlar of the palace, and this is also consonant with the west nave/west front workshop where marks are also rare. This mark, a capital letter A with a flattened head, has not been certainly identified in the context of the cathedral.

5   This heavy restoration also makes it impossible to know what weight to place on the presence of a section of dog-tooth moulding on the exterior of the west elevation of the undercroft passage. Dog-tooth is only found in the cathedral in the head of the west window, presumably dating from a period very close to the dedication in 1239.

ceilings of the present apartments (or their predecessors) were installed. The wall dividing the solar and hall rose to the full height of the range, and both sides of this retain traces of the red ashlar lining on white limewash which appears (from the additional evidence of the recesses of the southern windows of the east elevation) to have been applied generally over the internal walls. At the apex of both the north and south gables a large quat-refoil window lit the upper part of the chambers, and these also retain much ashlar lining on their surrounds and jambs, as well as areas of richer poly-chromy. The outer quatrefoil frame bears a rich ochre with paler colouration framed in red at the cardinal points, while the inner chamfer of the interior frame retains fragments of a running wave in red and white with counter-coloured roundels at the centres of the waves (Plates 11a and b). No trace survives of the thirteenth-century roof structure, though it is possible that elements from it may have been reused in the later reconstructions.

The episcopate of Jocelin Trotman represents the high point in the crea-tivity of the Wells masons, and their design and construction of the west front of the cathedral – a project in whose detailed design Jocelin himself must have been intimately involved – produced one of the most remark-able buildings of the Middle Ages. Jocelin's palace, shorn of its thirteenth-century chapel, kitchen, offices and ancillary buildings, remains a structure of remarkably high quality, strongly redolent of what has been lost in later rebuilding and restoration. Furthermore, Jocelin's remodelling of the eccle-siastical city to the north of the cathedral, with his provision of houses for the residentiary canons, has been almost entirely lost, but almost certainly was of a commensurate standard of building.

THE BISHOP'S PALACE AT WELLS

7

Geophysical and Geoarchaeological Survey at the Bishop's Palace, Wells*

ALEX TURNER, CHRISTOPHER GERRARD
AND KEITH WILKINSON

Introduction

Geophysical and geoarchaeological surveys were carried out at the Bishop's Palace, Wells in 1998 and 2003–04 by staff and students of King Alfred's College, Winchester (now the University of Winchester) at the request of the Bishop's Palace Archaeological Research Committee. The main objectives in undertaking this work were, firstly, to determine whether buried archaeological features beyond those identifiable in historic cartographic sources exist below the present ground surface and, secondly, to assess whether medieval archaeological remains are buried by thick alluvial or made ground deposits. Resistivity and magnetometer surveys were carried out on the lawns that surround the palace in June and July 1998 to address the first objective, while nineteen boreholes were drilled during two phases of fieldwork in April 2003 and June 2004 to address the second. Here we present the results of the surveys, focusing particularly on the information that the survey data provides with regard to the layout of the eighteenth-century garden and the survival of buried medieval archaeological stratigraphy.

* We would like to thank the Maltwood Fund of the Somerset Archaeological and Natural History Society for funding the borehole studies, Lucy Helmsley for organising logistics for the borehole surveys and Ashley Pooley for his help with the geophysical survey and its subsequent interpretation. A copy of the Carter plan was kindly supplied by Warwick Rodwell.

Methodology: geophysics

The survey covered 0.16 hectares; the available area being laid out with a total station and tapes as a series of 20m x 20m squares. The magnetometer survey was conducted with a Geoscan FM36 fluxgate gradiometer in a series of parallel traverses while the resistance survey was carried out using a Geoscan RM15 with a twin electrode configuration. Each grid was surveyed using zigzag traverses at 0.5m spacings, giving a sub-surface penetration of between 0.75m and 1.0m and a resolution of 1,600 readings per 20m x 20m square. Figure 6 maps the resistivity survey onto a plan of the Bishop's Palace, Figure 7 does the same for the magnetometry data, while Figures 8 and 9 interpret the resistivity and magnetometry results respectively.

Resistivity relies on the ability of materials to conduct an electrical current passed through them. This is linked to moisture content and therefore porosity. Stony features such as walls are recognised as a high response (displayed on Figure 6 in black) while ditches and pits which retain moisture tend to show up as low responses (here in grey or white). High resistance is normally associated with buried structures such as wall foundations, while lower resistance corresponds with infilled features such as pits and ditches. In exceptional circumstances, however, negative features with a rubble or gravel fill can produce a response with a higher resistance.[1]

Magnetometry measures changes in the magnetic field. Anomalies detected by the magnetometer are typically found in silts that infill ditches and pits or which contain higher concentrations of ferrous iron oxides than surrounding soils or sediment, or burnt features, for example, hearths, metalworking areas and concentrations of ceramics. Pedogenesis can also create an enhanced magnetic response, as can infilled ditches or pits when the iron oxides of the fill are magnetically enhanced during the fermentation of decaying organic matter.[2] Human activity sometimes also has the same effect and this is particularly true where features contain large concentrations of magnetic particles of superparamagnetic grain size, generally in cases in which there is an abundance of burnt material within the fill of the feature. The 0.5m x 0.5m resolution of the gradiometer survey used at Wells is capable of detecting relatively small anomalies of the kind along the line of each traverse. In addition, there are also a number of 'spikes', presumably caused by 'ferrous litter' in the topsoil such as nails. In Figure 7 positive magnetic readings register as dark shades of grey.

---

[1]   N. Linford, 'The Application of Geophysical Methods to Archaeological Prospection', *Reports on Progress in Physics*, 69 (2006), 2205–57, esp. 2214.

[2]   C.E. Mullins, 'The Magnetic Properties of Soil and Their Application to Archaeological Prospecting', *Archeo-Physyka*, 5 (1974), 143–347.

Methodology: geoarchaeology

The 2003 and 2004 borehole surveys were carried out using identical methodologies and equipment. During the 2003 study a single north-west to south-east orientated transect of eight boreholes was drilled across the croquet lawn and the lawns to the east of the palace (BH 1–8, Figure 10). In 2004 a north–south orientated transect centred on BH 3 was investigated in BH 9–14, while five further boreholes (BH 15–19) provided coverage of areas of the grounds not included within the two transects. In all cases the location of the boreholes was determined by Alan Thomas, the palace architect, while precise borehole locations were measured in relation to the 1998 geophysics grid and to an arbitrary height datum using an electronic distance measurer. The boreholes were drilled by a third-party geotechnical consultancy which used a track-mounted, petrol-powered percussion auger to carry out the work (Figure 11). This equipment was used to drive a 1m-long auger chamber containing a plastic sleeve to depths of up to 5m below ground surface. Auger chambers of various diameters were employed, but the usual approach was to use heads to decreasing diameters at greater depths down the borehole. After each drill run the plastic sleeve was removed from the auger chamber and cut open. The sediments retained were cleaned and described using standard geological criteria.[3] Descriptive data were combined with positional information within a RockWorks database,[4] and this software was then used to plot the cross-sections reproduced here as Figures 12 and 13.

Results

The croquet lawn fronting the Bishop's Palace

The croquet lawn was investigated by both geophysical and geoarchaeological survey. The resistivity plot suggests the presence of a curvilinear feature on the western side of the croquet lawn and south-east of the gatehouse (A on Figure 3), which is in all probability a metalled carriage drive. The northern stretch of its alignment, that is to say immediately as it emerges south from the gatehouse, is exactly as shown on Carter's plan of 1784,[5] but

---

3   A.P. Jones, M.E. Tucker and J.K. Hart, 'Guidelines and Recommendations', in eidem, eds, *The Description and Analysis of Quaternary Stratigraphic Field Sections*, Quaternary Research Association Technical Guide 7 (London, 1999), 27–76.
4   RockWorks v2006. http.rockware.com (accessed 29 October 2007).
5   Carter's plan, 1784.

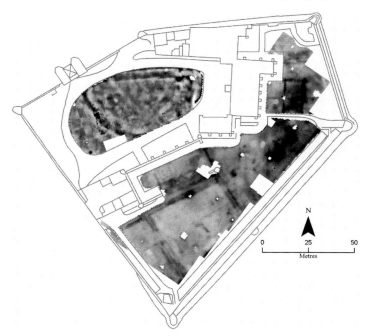

Figure 6. Plot of the resistivity data for the Bishop's Palace, Wells.

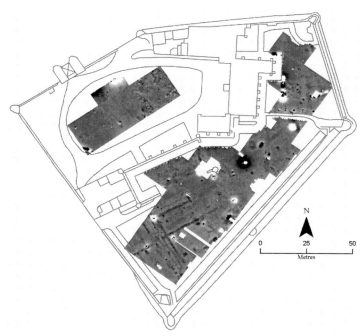

Figure 7. Plot of the magnetometry data for the Bishop's Palace, Wells.

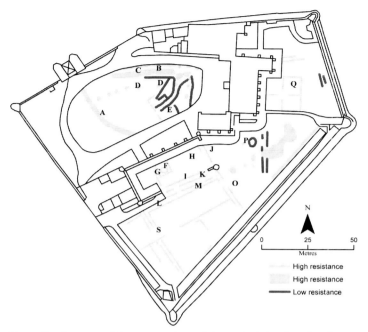

Figure 8. Annotated interpretation of the resistivity data for the Bishop's Palace, Wells.

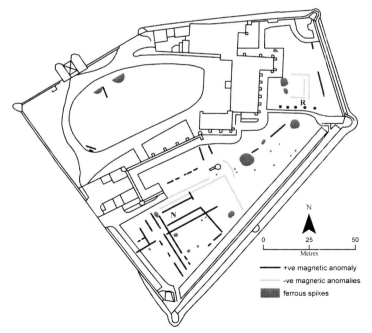

Figure 9. Annotated interpretation of the magnetometry data for the Bishop's Palace, Wells.

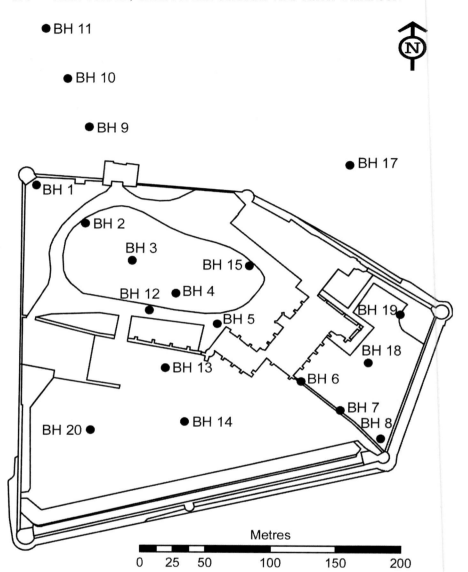

Figure 10. Location of boreholes drilled in 2003 and 2004.

Figure 11. The percussion drilling equipment being used to sample an area of the present croquet lawn.

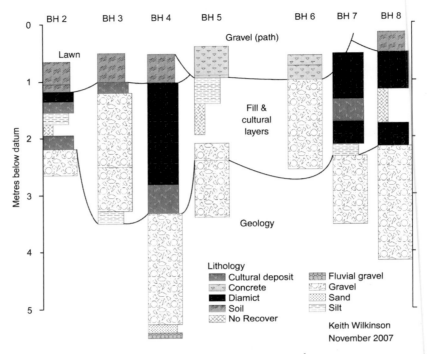

Figure 12. North-west to south-east composite stratigraphic transect.

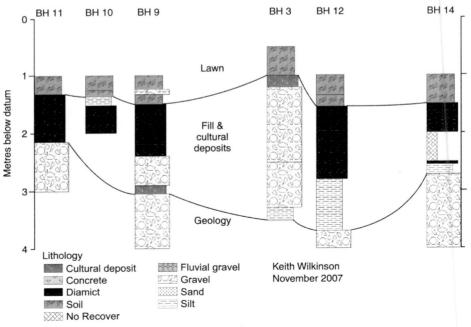

Figure 13. North–south composite stratigraphic transect.

the southern arcs eastwards towards the west end of the chapel. Presumably this represents a reorientation of the lines of access at some time between 1784 and 1888, when the first edition of the Ordnance Survey map shows the lawns and drives as they appear today and a path is seen to continue on through a gap in the north wall of the Great Hall.

On the northern edge of the lawn a linear dark anomaly [B] running east–west is likely to be the southern wall of the northern courtyard shown on the same Ordnance map, while the broader line [C] running parallel a little further south is probably the most northern of the two east–west drives on Carter's plan. The parallel series of black dots [D] a little way to the south are tree boles, perhaps defining the southern of the east–west drives indicated by Carter. Presumably there must have been some kind of avenue of mature trees here approaching the entrance porch from the west. They are certainly too large and widely spaced to be postholes. The geophysics data therefore confirm the circuit of the carriage drive from the gatehouse, forking left (east) down a drive, arriving at the porch, then turning west again to leave along a tree-lined avenue. The data also confirm at least two reconfigurations of the drive between 1784 and 1888: one along the northern side of the Great Hall and another to create the lines of access and movement we see today.

More significant for the archaeologist is the rectangular feature [E] clipped by the southern edge of the lawn. It is possible to see several right-angled alignments here, perhaps two rectilinear 'cells' running to the north-east, which would therefore lie in the same orientation as the Great Hall to the south. They measure about 8–10m across. If they are buildings, their function is unknown. It is possible that they are a coincidental juxtaposition of features of various dates and there is no indication of them on the magnetometry plot (Figure 7). A small-scale evaluation would rapidly establish their importance.

The borehole data demonstrate that 1.5–2.5m of medieval and later sediments overlie the Quaternary alluvial fan deposits mapped by the British Geological Survey as outcropping beneath the site (Figure 12). The latter comprise alternating sets of yellow brown (typically Munsell 7.5 YR 4/4)[6] matrix and clast supported, sub-angular limestone pebble gravels, and well-sorted medium sands. An archaeological sediment sequence unconformably overlies these limestone gravel and sands. The earliest archaeological stratum is a well-sorted silt/clay yellowish brown (Munsell 10 YR 4/2) which is found overlying the gravels in BH 3 and BH 7. The presence of occasional granular and coarse sand-size charcoal fragments attests to human activity whilst the silt/clay was forming, and it seems likely that this stratum is a remnant of a B horizon of a soil that existed on the site prior to the earliest

6   *Munsell Soil Charts*, Munsell Color (New Windsor, NY, 2000).

medieval activity. This palaeosol must have been truncated by medieval and later activity and thereby removed from most of the area now occupied by the palace. Assuming the palaeosol hypothesis is correct, this suggests that initial medieval activity took place at a level between 1.5 and 2.5m below present ground surface. In the case of BH 12 the truncated B horizon was found to overlie a 300mm-thick bed of humic grey-brown silts and clays (Figure 13). The latter might be indicative of sedimentation in a low energy alluvial environment such as a floodplain or a pool. Given the absence of floodplain sediments elsewhere on the site, the latter seems more likely.

The sediment sequence above the truncated palaeosol is complex, but consists largely of diamicts (poorly sorted coarse sediments) of cobble-sized limestone and brick, and pebble/granular-sized mortar and charcoal clasts, in fine sand and silt matrix. Occasionally these coarse-grained deposits are interbedded with moderately sorted silts/clays containing cultural debris such as ceramics and charcoal. The diamicts are obviously deliberate infills that have been dumped to level out a previously undulating ground surface. Much of this fill is likely to be the product of nineteenth-century land-scaping, but the presence of medieval ceramics in fine-grained deposits towards the base of BH 4 may suggest that some of the coarse-grained deposits were present in the medieval period as well.

The stratigraphic sequence discussed above is capped by the present-day lawn, which appears to have been carefully laid on fine-grained deposits containing kitchen waste and ash.

The southern lawn

Within the Great Hall lies a small square garden feature with the lines of gravel paths at right angles to one another in a geometric design with a 'bed' [F] at the centre. The outline of the central anomaly is higher resistance but the level of response is not high enough for it to be a column base. Unfortunately geophysics cannot in itself help to date the features, but this garden cannot predate the mid-sixteenth century when permission was granted to take the hall down. Nor was it present in 1784 when, as Carter observed, the west end of the Great Hall was put to other uses. A nineteenth-century date seems the most plausible.

To the west lies a north–south wall which seems to have separated the service end from the main body of the Great Hall [G]. It too is also clearly shown by Carter. To the east an area of disturbance may well pinpoint Cherry and Drapers' three trenches from 1970 [H]. According to their account,[7] the trenches they dug were four feet square, dimensions which

---

[7]   Cherry and Draper, 'Excavations'.

might easily be mistaken on the geophysics for arcade piers, just as any surviving patches of floor tile might confuse any interpretation in the interior of the hall. Nevertheless, along the south side of the hall there are at least four positive (dark) anomalies on the resistivity plot (Figure 6) which might be interpreted as column bases for the arcade piers of a southern aisle [K]. On the other hand, the southern wall of the Great Hall may have been badly robbed but the crisper line representing the east wall shows that it remains in far better condition under the ground [I].

To the south of the Great Hall lies the east–west canal [L], *c*.4m wide, shown by Carter in 1784. The feature is mostly higher resistance but patches of very high resistance present along its length indicate that the canal is filled with rubble [M]. This is probably demolition material from the Great Hall. Buckle writes that demolition occurred in the eighteenth century[8] and, if so, this would date the canal from after 1735 (it is not shown by Simes[9]) to the 1780s. The very clear straight 'ends' shown on the magnetometer plot [N] may indicate that there were 'compartments' within the canal, perhaps for ease of cleaning or to act as bridges across the water [S and perhaps at O]. The eastern 'arm' of the feature shows clearly on the resistivity plot and, although it is less clear on Carter's 1784 plan, this is likely to be a part of the same water canal feature [south of O]. Within this roughly square moated space the garden paths shown by Carter can be picked out.

Other features visible in the southern lawn include parterres and garden features, perhaps mostly of late seventeenth- and eighteenth-century date [P]. One of the east–west linear anomalies may be the remains of the enclosed gardens shown on Simes or the southern wall of the kitchen court shown by Buckle in 1888.

The borehole survey suggests that the stratigraphy to the north of the Bishop's Palace and on the southern lawn is similar to that described above for the croquet lawn (Figure 8).

The eastern lawn

The main feature here is the clear outline [Q] of the parterre shown on the 1888 Ordnance Survey map. The lines of higher resistance are the paths leading to the central ornamental vase. The line of five magnetic anomaly spots [R] may be garden tags or perhaps the remains of an iron pergola.

---

8   Buckle, 'Wells Palace'.
9   Simes's map, 1735.

Conclusions

Even without the benefit of detailed study of the documentary and carto-graphic sources, the geophysical surveys confirm some detail for the interior of Burnell's Great Hall and suggest at least one demolished building, possibly of medieval date, beneath the croquet lawn. The borehole survey is especially useful here in that it suggests that the latter feature is likely to be buried by at least 1.5m of post-medieval fill. The boreholes, of course, are merely pinpricks in the archaeological stratigraphy and there is some danger in extrapolating the results too far. However, if such a depth of overburden does indeed exist at this location then any medieval features would be too deeply buried to register on geophysical surveys of the kind undertaken in 1998. Our interpretation of a medieval building must remain, at best, very cautious. More positively, however, if parts of the Great Hall were indeed pulled down and dumped into the canals in the last decade of the eighteenth century then medieval architectural fragments may well survive there.

For the post-medieval period the geophysical surveys have produced significant new results suggesting canals and simple geometric parterres with areas of grass dissected by gravel paths. These features are not shown on Simes's map but, nevertheless, they are arguably more typical of the late seventeenth century rather than the mid-eighteenth century and this must call into question the accuracy of the 1735 record. By contrast, Carter's 1784 plan seems to be a very accurate record of many of the buried features revealed during the geophysical surveys. Local parallels for so-called 'Dutch-influenced' water gardens of the kind favoured here at Wells would include Dyrham, Tortworth Court, Low Ham and Ven House near Milborne Port.

8

The Location of Bishop Jocelin's Palace at Wells

MARK HORTON

The Bishop's Palace at Wells is rightly considered to be one of the most important groups of surviving medieval buildings in Britain. Its completeness and modern appearance are, however, the result of long architectural development throughout the Middle Ages, and a certain degree of antiquarian restoration, landscaping and deliberate ruination during the nineteenth century that positioned the palace within its extraordinary setting of gardens, moat and pools.

Understanding the development of this complex site requires the use of a variety of different approaches – documentary, archaeological, antiquarian, architectural and geophysical.[1] Particular difficulties relate to the depth of deposits through the deliberate raising of the ground level to avoid flooding, the intensity of horticultural activity over the years, and the surprising lack of detailed documentary evidence for changes to the buildings and landscapes. The excavation work on the site which took place in 2003–4 was the culmination of a long process of desktop and geophysical survey in order that the scale of invasive archaeology could be kept to an absolute minimum.[2]

This chapter sets out to locate Bishop Jocelin's palace within its landscape and argues that it was much more extensive than the sole surviving range. This conclusion raises the question of the early plan and layout of the site, and more precisely the function of a medieval bishop and his residence.

---

[1] Recent discussions of the Bishop's Palace include Dunning, 'Bishop's Palace'; M. Thompson, *Medieval Bishops' Houses in England and Wales* (Aldershot, 1998), 49–51; N. Payne, 'The Precinct of the Bishop's Place, Wells, Somerset' (unpublished desktop study, University of Bristol, 1999); N. Payne, 'The Medieval Residences of the Bishops of Bath and Wells, and Salisbury' (unpublished PhD dissertation, University of Bristol, 2003), 129–34; A. Emery, *Greater Medieval Houses of England and Wales* (Cambridge, 2006), 669–74.

[2] Undertaken through the auspices of the Bishop's Palace Archaeological Research Committee. The excavations were part of the annual training programme for archaeology students at the University of Bristol.

Figure 14. Engraving of the Bishop's Palace by Samuel and Nathaniel Buck, 1733.

Archaeological and antiquarian investigations

Antiquarian interest in the Bishop's Palace dates from the eighteenth century and by the end of the nineteenth the basic architectural sequence was well known. Key illustrative material includes a view of the palace by Samuel and Nathanial Buck dated 1733 (Figure 14) and schematic details shown in William Simes's map of Wells of 1735 (Figure 15).[3] Of particular importance were John Carter's sketch and plan of 1784 (Plate 12).[4] Nineteenth-century sources include drawings by John Buckler (1825–47) and A.W. Pugin and two important analyses of the architecture by J.H. Parker (1866) and E. Buckle (1888) (Figure 16).[5]

There have been few previous archaeological investigations on the site. George Henry Law, bishop 1824–45, had archaeological interests: he supported John Skinner, rector of Camerton, in various excavations in Somerset, even displaying some of the finds in the undercroft of the palace.[6] At Wells, Law's activities included the demolition of part of the Great Hall c.1824–25[7] in order to create a more 'romantic' ruin, and the enlargement of the springs at some time prior to 1838 to form pools in which the cathedral could be romantically reflected,[8] but there were no recorded archaeological investigations.

The first serious excavations to discover more of the plan of the original building were prompted by Lord Auckland, bishop 1854–69, and involved uncovering the 'fourth' side of the courtyard. Buckle gives a brief account of these digs:

---

[3]   'The South View of Wells Palace in the County of Somerset', plate 263 in S. and N. Buck, *Antiquities of England and Wales*, 2 vols (London, 1774); Simes's map, 1735.

[4]   Carter's plan, 1784; 'North-west view of the outside of the Bishop's Palace at Wells sketch'd 1784, engrav'd and pub'd Jan. 1st 1791 by J. Carter', republished in J. Carter, *Specimens of Gothic Architecture and Ancient Buildings in England* (London, 1824), iii. pl. 88.

[5]   Somerset Archaeological Society, Taunton, collection of wash drawings by J. Buckler, based on original sketches in British Library, Add. MSS.36383–4, 36402, 36409; A.W. Pugin, *Examples of Gothic Architecture* (London, 1836); Parker, 'Bishop's Palace at Wells'; Buckle, 'Wells Palace'; idem, 'Wells Palace: A Correction', *Proceedings of the Somersetshire Archaeological and Natural History Society*, 36 (1890), 200–1. For a comprehensive list of illustrations of the palace see Payne, 'The Precinct of the Bishop's Palace', 63–98.

[6]   For example in the drawing of the undercroft by Buckler in 1835.

[7]   Dunning, 'Bishop's Palace', 242.

[8]   Rodwell, *Wells Cathedral*, 395. In 1999 six evaluation test pits were dug in the allotment gardens to the east of the wells. A large mound remains visible in this area and it was deduced that it was the upcast from the remodelling of the wells in the 1830s. Finds ranged from medieval to early nineteenth century: N. Payne and R. Hoggett, 'Test Pits in the Allotments of the Bishop's Palace, Wells, May–June 1999', unpublished report, University of Bristol.

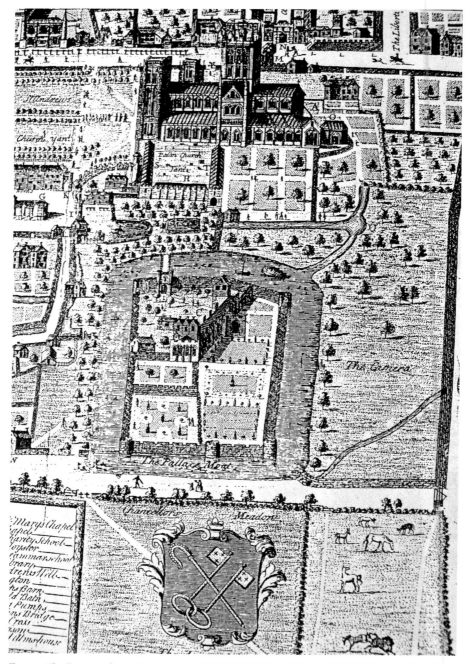

Figure 15. Extract from the map of Wells by William Simes, 1735, showing details of the palace grounds, arranged in compartments with Dutch-style planting.

Some excavations made in the time of bishop Auckland brought to light the foundations of a gate-house in the middle, with a wall extending to the kitchen on one side and the chapel on the other, with a moat and drawbridge on the outside.[9]

These walls may refer to a range, shown in the Buck engraving of 1733 (Figure 14), but demolished by the time of the Carter plan and most likely constructed by Thomas Bekynton, bishop 1443–65. The only other recorded archaeological excavation within the moated area before the present project began was in 1970 when John Cherry and Peter Draper undertook a small excavation in the Great Hall to ascertain floor levels and whether it was an aisled structure with stone piers – an investigation that was largely inconclusive.[10]

Bishop Jocelin's Palace

The oldest surviving section of the Bishop's Palace has, since the nineteenth century, been attributed to Bishop Jocelin on the basis of the *Historia Minor* written by a Wells canon that 'Capellas cum Cameris de Wellys et Woky nobiliter construxit'.[11] On stylistic grounds the work would normally be placed towards the end of his life[12] and was probably a work of several phases.[13]

The ground and first-floor plans of this range remain essentially as they were constructed, and are first shown in detail in Carter's plan of 1784. The main alteration to its medieval appearance was due to the heavy-handed restoration by Benjamin Ferrey in 1846, which resulted in the insertion of a second floor above the western half of the range, refenestration of the west wall and the addition of pseudo-medieval buttresses[14] and rebuilding the main entrance, which had already been moved one bay to the south by the late eighteenth century. On the eastern side of the range, the continuous

---

9   Buckle, 'Wells Palace', 55. Parker, 'Bishop's Palace at Wells', 147, suggests a date of 1860 for this operation when the bishop found 'old drains'.
10   Cherry and Draper, 'Excavations', 52–3. For possible evidence for these stone column bases in the geophysical survey, see p. 135.
11   *Collectanea I*, 55.
12   M. Wood, *The English Medieval House* (London, 1975), 84, gives a date of c.1230–50; N. Pevsner, *North Somerset and Bristol* (London, 1958), 313, gives c.1230. Henry III provided thirty oaks for the building of the palace on 2 August 1233: L.S. Colchester, *Wells Cathedral* (London, 1987), 15, 159.
13   One example is different thicknesses of the west wall. The double windows in the north and south upper walls may also be a little later: Dunning, 'Bishop's Palace', 231.
14   There is little evidence that the west front had buttresses (unlike the east wall); there is only the testimony of the Victorian antiquarians. See Buckle, 'Wells Palace', 60–61, and p. 108.

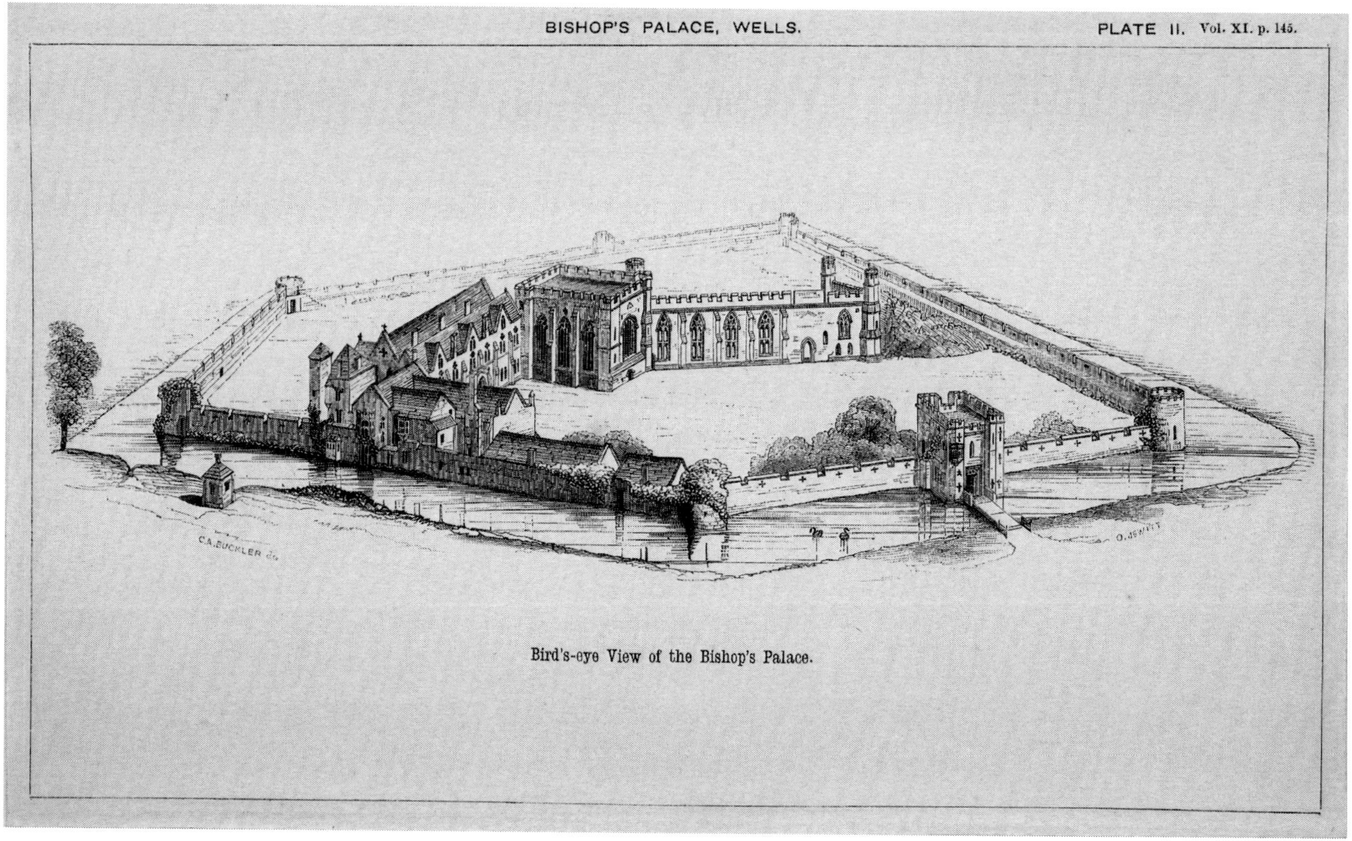

BISHOP'S PALACE, WELLS.

PLATE II. Vol. XI. p. 146.

Bird's-eye View of the Bishop's Palace.

Figure 16. Drawing of the Bishop's Palace by C.A. Buckler, engraved by O. Jewitt, published in *Proceedings of the Somersetshire Archaeo-logical and Natural History Society*, 11 (1861–62), opposite p. 145.

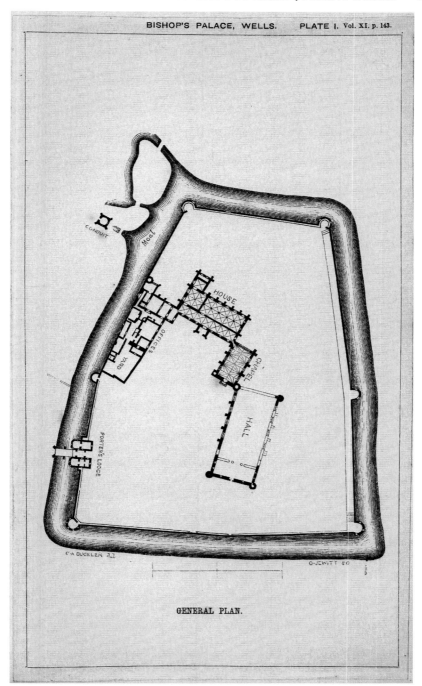

Figure 17. General plan of the Bishop's Palace by C.A. Buckler, engraved by O. Jewitt, published in *Proceedings of the Somersetshire Archaeological and Natural History Society*, 11 (1861–62), opposite p. 144.

corbel table within the roof-space of the north-eastern extension, variously interpreted as a study, garderobe or private chapel, suggests an early addition.[15]

This surviving section of Jocelin's palace was built, as far as can be seen, as a freestanding structure. To the north, Beckington's hall abuts masonry that later replaced the original north-west spiral stair, while in the south-west corner, Burnell's chapel abuts (and refaced) the original south-west stair.[16] The building is an early example of a first-floor hall and solar, with a first-floor gallery divided into three rooms (1:3:3), and undercroft below, following the plan of the upper rooms. There is no trace of a service block. Carter's plan shows a passage that could be interpreted as a screens passage through the building with a doorway in the east wall – although there is no evidence for this in the surviving fabric.

Early topography of the palace grounds

The present plan of buildings within an enclosed and moated area probably dates to the fourteenth century; the earlier landscape of Jocelin's palace would have been very different. The site is a wet and watery place, with at least five large springs in the north-east and a river flowing east–west, known as the Chilcote stream, rising in a series of springs along the Mendip edge to the north and east of the city. In understanding the location of Jocelin's palace, we need to trace how this considerable body of water flowed through or around the site. While these springs were landscaped by Bishop Law in the earlier nineteenth century, their location is confirmed on the earlier Carter plan and their position has probably changed little since the Middle Ages.

Various attempts have been made to reconstruct the early topography and its watercourses, most recently by Warwick Rodwell in the context of his excavations at the cathedral.[17] In the earlier nineteenth century it is

---

[15] Buckle, 'Wells Palace', 54, marks it as a private chapel; Emery, *Greater Medieval Houses*, 669, suggests a garderobe.

[16] There has long been debate about the stratigraphic relationship between Jocelin's range, the bishop's chapel, and Burnell's Great Hall. M. Wood, 'Thirteenth Century Domestic Architecture in England', *Archaeological Journal*, 105 (1950), 108 suggested that the foundations of the present chapel were Jocelin's, rebuilt by Burnell, a view first suggested by Parker, 'Bishop's Palace', 152–3. However, there is little evidence for this in the surviving fabric. The relationship between Great Hall and chapel also remains unresolved although the balance of probabilities suggests that the chapel is earlier and the junction has been modified considerably with the building of the hall.

[17] H. Balch, 'The Old Watercourses of Wells', *Wells Natural History and Archaeology Society, Reports*, 37 (1925), 14–33; Rodwell, *Wells Cathedral*, 30–5, 375–411. For an earlier view, W. Rodwell, 'Anglo-Saxon and Norman Churches at Wells' in *Wells Cathedral, a History*, ed. L.S. Colchester (Shepton Mallet 1982), 1–23, esp. plan 1.

fairly certain that the springs fed both the palace moat itself and a stream that flowed north of the moat, through two pools, to feed the Palace Mill or Upper Mill west of the palace. A weir had been placed in the pools in the Middle Ages to achieve the different levels required. The moat had its main outlet in the middle of its west side (nowadays, it drains in the south-west corner). The Chilcote stream flows towards the springs (its original course) before turning sharply south to avoid the moat, running parallel to it at a slightly lower level and forming the boundary between the palace and the former deer park.

Bishop Ralph of Shrewsbury was granted a licence to crenellate his palace in 1340, implying that the defensive walls and gatehouse were built shortly after this date. While the moat itself could have been earlier, this seems unlikely,[18] given that the walls form one side of the moat itself along the western half of the enclosure. The five-sided irregular plan must derive from the different alignments of Jocelin's range and the later Great Hall, and the need to resolve these visually from the principal gatehouse, constructed by Ralph of Shrewsbury.

The construction of the moat required complex water engineering to ensure that the three mills (the Palace Mill and two town mills) to the west were all supplied with water, while the moat could still be filled. The arrangements can really only be understood in terms of a lost watercourse that passes diagonally across the palace grounds and which has now been infilled and the water used instead to fill the moat.

The idea that water originally flowed in front of Jocelin's palace was first suggested by Buckle who perceptively marked 'old line of stream' on his plan.[19] Rodwell also concluded that a stream ran approximately where Buckle showed it, but slightly to the south and east.[20] The outlet position can be traced back to the eighteenth century and is shown on both the Simes map and the Carter plan, where the moat drained to the west. This outlet is quite distinct from the mill race that fed the Palace Mill and is shown on a pre-1827 map of Canon Grange.[21] This same map also shows the Horse Pond, an area of open water to the north of the palace gatehouse that reflects the line of the more northerly watercourse that avoided the moat and fed this mill (Figure 18). An archaeological evaluation at the Clares Carlton site to the south of the mill site in 1988 recovered the profile

---

[18] Dunning, 'Bishop's Palace', 235. Burnell evidently intended something similar, but did not carry it out. While the walls were undoubtedly intended to impress, the bishop enjoyed far from cordial relations with the town: Dunning, 'Bishop's Palace', 234–5.

[19] Buckle, 'Wells Palace', facing 68.

[20] Rodwell, *Wells Cathedral*, 33.

[21] SRO DD/FCC 10878.

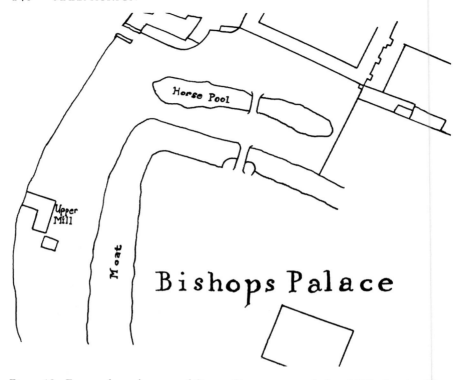

Horse Pool

Upper
Mill

Moat

Bishops Palace

Figure 18. Extract from the map of Canon Grange manor, before 1827, showing Horse Pond and Upper (or Palace) Mill. Tracing by N. Payne from SRO DD/FCC 10878.

of the valley bottom and apparently a revetting wall of the stream predating the laying out of the moat.[22]

There is also some evidence in the fabric of the outer defensive walls of the palace, which have relieving arches at exactly the point where the infilled watercourse would have crossed. These were not culverts, but arches to carry the wall over an area of made-up ground (Figure 19). They remain visible as a pair of arches on the north wall of the palace and in the western wall they are visible when the moat is lowered. This alignment seems also to be suggested by the borehole data, in particular borehole 3 which identified alluvial silts some 3.5m below the present ground surface, and borehole 4 that found fluvial silts and gravels at a depth of 5m[23] suggesting that there are at least 2m of made-up ground in the area in front of the Great Hall and

[22] P. Leach, 'Wells', *Somerset Archaeology and Natural History*, 132 (1988), 235–7.
[23] See p. 132.

Figure 19. Relieving arches along the north wall of the palace enclosure indicating the line of the earlier stream. Mark Horton.

that it and Jocelin's surviving range are sitting on a slightly raised gravel terrace.

The third, most southerly watercourse – the Chilcote stream, which now runs to the south of the moat[24] – forms the northern boundary of the former deer park that lay to the south of the palace. It is shown as such on a nineteenth-century map of the bishop's deer park[25] as well as by Simes and Carter. The artificial nature of its present course south of the palace suggests that it has been diverted, as it has to cut through a small ridge, extending north-west from Tor Hill. Rodwell suggested that originally this stream also flowed through the centre of the valley, linking up with the springs.[26] While it may have been diverted when the moat was constructed *c*.1340, a more likely moment was the creation of the deer park by Jocelin in 1207.[27]

[24] The moat drains into it from its south-west corner, an arrangement present since at least 1886 where a sluice is shown on the 1st edition of the 1:500 OS map.
[25] SRO DD/CC 1150, dated 1838–59.
[26] Rodwell, 'Anglo-Saxon and Norman Church at Wells', 4; compare detail with *idem. Wells Cathedral*, 32, which gives a slightly different course.
[27] C.M. Church, 'Documents Bearing upon Late Excavations on the South Side of the Cathedral Church of Wells in 1894', *Proceedings of the Somersetshire Archaeological and Natural History Society*, 40 (1894), 138.

The canal system

The wet nature of the palace grounds was exploited by the construction of a canal system, which can be traced in the geophysical survey, and by cartographic evidence, and which was the target of excavation in 2003.

Both the resistivity and magnetometry surveys revealed evidence of a masonry structure in the south-west corner of the site.[28] A double wall with a soft infill extended north from the moat, turning parallel to the Great Hall and returning south to the moat. This is clearly the same feature shown on the Carter map, where two of the three arms of the canal are filled with water and the third appears to have been filled in. The rest seem to have disappeared during the time of Bishop Law, when the rubble from the partial demolition of the Great Hall was used as filling. The last trace of the canal system is shown as a culvert built into the bank by the south wall on the 1886 first edition Ordnance Survey map.

The earliest evidence for this canal system is found on the Buck drawing of 1733 which includes a detail of the culvert and part of the canal. It is not shown in the near-contemporary map of Wells by Simes of 1735 which does, however, show a number of walled compartments in this area that may correspond to the additional lines shown in the geophysical survey. Both Buck and Simes depict clipped shrubs in the Dutch fashion planted in this section of the garden, indicating that the canal may have been part of an early eighteenth-century Dutch water garden. The canal apparently cut through Simes's compartments, hinted at in the magnetometer survey south of the Great Hall. Simes's map may be reflecting an earlier arrange-ment in the gardens – possibly derived from drawings made in the 1720s. If so, the Dutch gardens were the product of a longer period of development, of which the canals represent the final stage.

Thomas Ken (bishop 1685–90) and George Hooper (bishop 1704–27) both had contact with the Netherlands in the late seventeenth century as both served as chaplain to Princess Mary while she was resident in The Hague between 1678 and 1680. Either bishop may have been responsible for the introduction of the 'Dutch style' to the gardens at Wells. The balance of likelihood favours Hooper, with his much longer episcopate and the currency of this style during this period.[29]

---

[28] See p. 128.

[29] Bishop Ken is known to have had a keen interest in gardening during his long sojourn at Longleat in exile from his diocese as a non-juror. Also at Longleat at the time was the Revd. George Harbin, another non-juror, who acted as chaplain there from 1699 and who wrote the remarkable *Memoirs of Gardening*: T. Mowl, 'Rococo and Later Landscaping at Longleat', *Garden History* 21 (1993), 56–66; M. McGarvie and J.H. Harvey, 'The Revd George Harbin and his Memoirs of Gardening 1716–1723', 11 (1983), 6–35. Mowl describes the early eighteenth-century gardens at Longleat with their multiple pools as 'Franco-Dutch': T. Mowl, *Historic Gardens of Wiltshire* (Stroud, 2004), 51.

Archaeological excavations 2003–4

The excavations within the palace grounds in 2003 were planned to inves-tigate the canal system, and more generally to locate the nature of archaeo-logical deposits south of the Great Hall. The line of the canal can still be seen as a faint earthwork, so an L-shaped trench 1.5m wide and 7m long was excavated east–west across its line. In 2004, an extension was added at the west end so that overall a T-shaped area was investigated; for the purpose of description both interventions will be considered together. A further small trench was excavated in 2004 to explore where the canal (and culvert) passed below the earthwork known as Bishop Ken's Walk, against the south wall of the palace.

The canal was shown to have been constructed in mortared limestone, in a trench-built feature with a neat internal face. It was 1.8m wide and had been backfilled with rubble presumably from the demolition of the Great Hall. There was no visible base to the canal, although this could not be fully investigated as the excavation reached the water table. Close to the surface part of a stone rainwater drain was found connected to the canal which would have drained the surrounding gardens. Interestingly the canal seems to have been cut into an earlier ditch that was backfilled in the late seventeenth or early eighteenth century. This may have drained water from the Great Hall into the moat, and followed closely the line taken by the later canal.

Further evidence for the nature of the canal comes from the second small trench excavated in 2004. This located the entrance to the culvert that carried the canal into the moat (Plate 14). The culvert was constructed in stone, with a brick roof. The entrance was also built of brick, but was prob-ably a reconstruction of an original stone entrance and tunnel. Traces of the primary stone vault (keyed into the side walls) were clearly visible, and it is likely that the culvert was strengthened in brick soon after its construction. The bricks appear to be mid-eighteenth-century in type. The whole feature was backfilled at the start of the twentieth century; a penny of 1901 was found at its base, and the feature is not visible in the second edition of the Ordnance Survey map of 1904.

The medieval kitchen

The post-medieval features thus discovered cut through significant medi-eval cultural deposits (Plate 13). They survived to the west of the canal and were explored more fully in 2004. The excavation revealed, at a depth of 0.6m, the cobbled floor of a medieval building, with a largely robbed-out wall of mortared limestone that extended diagonally across the trench, and

Figure 20. Detail of the southern hearth on the south side of the Great Hall with a crescent of stones and internal charcoal spreads. Quantities of animal bones were found around the hearth. Mark Horton.

which was 0.80m wide. Only the basal course of the wall was located and in some places even this had been removed, suggesting that the wall had been built without foundations directly onto the ground surface. Clearly this was a fairly insubstantial building; most likely the foundation for a timber-framed structure above.

Two surviving hearths set into the floor determined the function of the building (Figure 20 and Plate 14). These were made with small stones forming a circle (or possibly horseshoe shape) although neither was complete. In the base of each, burnt and carbonised deposits were found indicating that they were hearths. Midden deposits in the base included significant quantities of animal bone. These midden layers also extended around the hearths over the cobbled floor levels. Associated medieval pottery was of the thirteenth and early fourteenth centuries, and was found in the hearths, as well as overlying the robbed-out wall. The conclusion was that this was part of a detached thirteenth-century service block in which food was being prepared on a substantial scale.

Analysis of the bone showed evidence for the three main domestic species (cattle, sheep/goat and pig) and several of the bones showed traces of butchery marks. The sample is too small for detailed statistical analysis, although the assemblage is fully in keeping with meat preparation. A small number of bones might suggest a high status diet; these included two bird bones (one possibly goose), and two small mammal bones (one probably hare).[30]

The alignment and date of this detached kitchen is of interest. While only the west wall was found, it was clearly a building of some size, with sides of at least 5.0m, and was either square or rectangular in plan. The alignment follows exactly that of Jocelin's surviving range, and is therefore askew to the Great Hall that lies between it and Jocelin's palace. The levelling and robbing of the building in medieval times also suggests that it went out of use when the Great Hall was built by Bishop Burnell in the later part of the thirteenth century.

Where was Jocelin's original palace?

There has long been the suspicion that the surviving range of Jocelin's palace is simply a fragment of a wider planned landscape.[31] Hints of this come from the emparkment of the area to the south in 1207 and the suggestion that the Chilcote stream was diverted to form its boundary. The emparkment grant included the diversion of a number of roads, one of which ran east to Dulcote, the course of which is visible on early air photographs.[32] With all this activity taking place in the first decade of the thirteenth century, and the construction of the existing palace block after c.1230,[33] the problem arises as to where any older buildings were located.

The topography suggests that there was a gravel terrace of slightly higher ground immediately to the south of what must have been a wet area separating the site from the cathedral. It would have required a causeway

---

30 I am very grateful to Dr Rachel Scales for undertaking the identification of the animal bones from the excavations.

31 Dunning, 'Bishop's Palace', 233.

32 Church, 'Some Documents', 138; Payne. 'The Precinct of the Bishop's Palace', 48–50 suggests that the line of this road would have passed c.50m east of the moat in the area of the present arboretum.

33 See p. 121 for a comparison of the masonry in the palace and cathedral which comes to a similar conclusion.

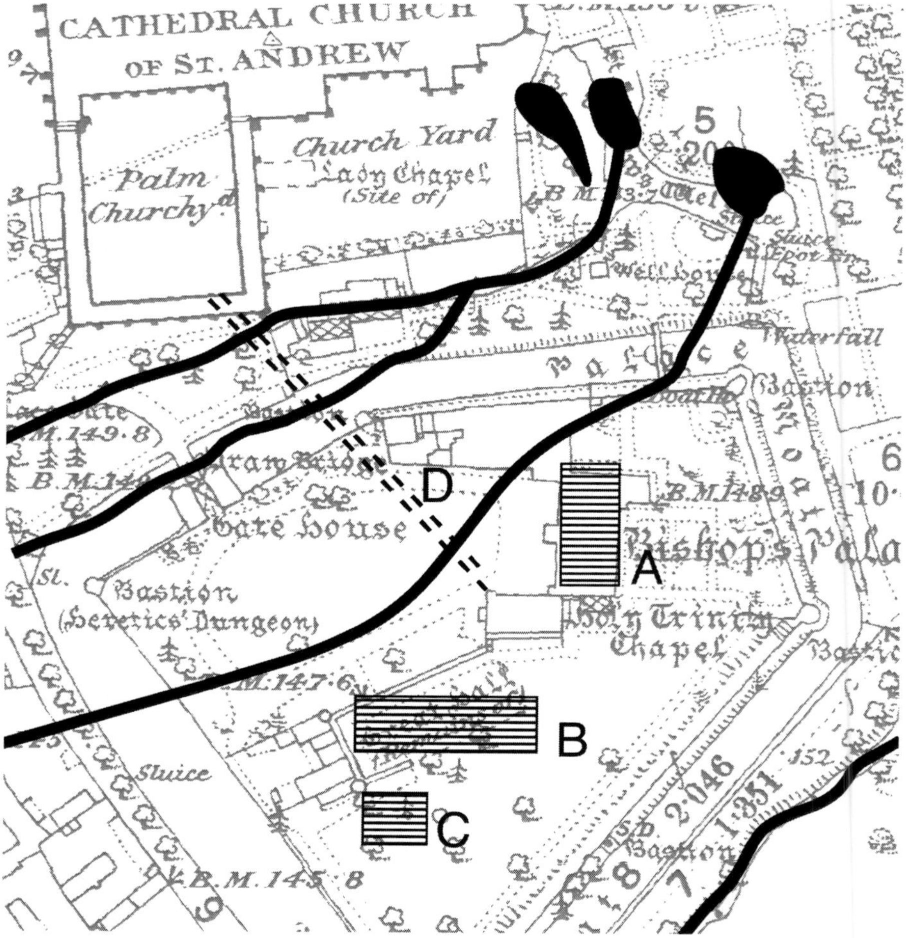

Figure 21. Reconstruction of the topography of the palace at the time of Bishop Jocelin. A = surviving range; B = suggested early hall, with main living accommodation; C = detached service or kitchen range, located in excavations; D = causeway. Basemap Crown Copyright and Landmark Information Group, all rights reserved 2004. An Ordnance Survey/EDINA supplied service.

of around 50m to cross, unless the water was culverted,[34] running in an approximately north-east to south-west direction. The water would have run within a few feet of the north-west corner of the site, making it quite impossible for the service accommodation to be located where the present Bekynton range is and ruling out some kind of claustral arrangement which forms the basis of most of the antiquarian reconstructions.

[34] Might this have been the 'old drains' uncovered in Lord Auckland's excavations in 1860? Parker, 'Bishop's Palace', 147.

The location of what might well have been Jocelin's service block nearly 100m to the south-west of the main range provides a possible solution. It is unnecessarily distant from the surviving range, given that a ridge of higher ground now occupied by the Great Hall lies between the two. That ridge would have been an ideal site for buildings. It faces directly towards the cathedral, across the marshy area that has been identified as the prime position – which of course was recognised by Bishop Burnell. To its south-east lay the newly created deer park.

One possibility is that there is a lost range of Jocelin's palace lying below Burnell's Great Hall, which dates to the earlier part of his episcopate, and which faced directly out towards the new cathedral. In the late thirteenth century this was demolished to make way for the present Great Hall that might of course have reflected, with its anachronistic plan, the form of the earlier structure. Excavation will resolve this hypothesis, and if found, whether it was of timber or stone. Whatever conclusion is finally arrived at, the palace complex at the time of Bishop Jocelin had a very different appearance from that of the present day.

9

Lichens on the Stonework of the Bishop's Palace, Wells*

DAVID J. HILL

Introduction

It may seem rather unusual to have such a chapter as this one within an historical and archaeological book. This arises because I was asked to carry out a survey of the lichens on the walls and stonework of the Bishop's Palace and walls as part of the investigations about the building prior to its development as an historic site for the public to visit. As far as I am aware, this is the first lichen survey that has been done there. The full results have been previously privately reported more fully[1] and this chapter summarises those findings with some additional analysis of the data relating it to the possible age of the stonework. The justification for taking an interest in the lichens (why these of all the possible groups of organisms?) is as follows.

Firstly, the appearance of stone buildings by way of colour and texture is often more to do with the lichens growing on the stone than the stone itself. Indeed, if one were, as if by magic, to remove instantly all the stone substance from the palace, one would still recognise the buildings and walls as they are now by the remaining lichens making their outlines. Secondly, lichens grow in communities (rather like people) but they grow extremely slowly and it takes a long time (hundreds of years) for communities to develop. The consequence is that the large area of stonework on the palace, some dating back to medieval times, is potentially of importance as a reserve of unusual lichen species. And with our commitment to the conservation

* The help of the staff of the Bishop's Palace is gratefully acknowledged, in particular Marion Shaw and James Cross. Lucy Helmsley arranged for the survey to take place. Alan Thomas helped with gaining permission for access to scaffolding. Dr Brian Coppins and Alan Orange very kindly helped by examining specimens of the more unusual lichens.
1 D.J. Hill, 'The Lichens on the Stonework and Walls of the Bishop's Palace at Wells', unpublished report submitted to the Bishop's Palace Archaeological Research Committee, 2006a.

of biodiversity, we should recognise and try to conserve where possible the lichens of the palace for their own sake. This also will conserve the appearance of the buildings and walls. Thirdly, it may be possible to date some of the stonework from the lichens that occur on it. I found from looking at dated gravestones that the lichen communities which had developed on older gravestones were different in their species make up from those on more recent gravestones; the nineteenth-century stones had species on them that were not found on twentieth-cenury stones and some were only found on eighteenth-century and earlier stones.

General information about lichens

There are about 1,850 different species of lichen in Britain and Ireland[2] and about 14,500 species in the world as a whole. They are all composite organisms, being symbiotic associations between species of fungus (to which the name of the lichen applies) and a microscopic alga (or photosynthetic bacterium). The algal partner produces carbohydrate (sugar or sugar-like substance) in the light by the process of photosynthesis and passes it on to the fungus which develops the structure of the lichen thallus within which the alga lives. Lichens are found from the highest mountains to the lowest tidal zone of the seashore, in woodlands, trees and forests and on all kinds of stone or other firm surface exposed to the elements in the natural environment and they have the widest geographical range from the tropics to the arctic and within a few hundred miles of the South Pole. Lichens represent a very diverse group of fungi although they are mostly all belong to Ascomycetes. This diversity is apparent in the range of different colours, structures and textures represented by their thalli some of which can be seen on the walls of the palace (see Plate 15). They are sensitive to air pollution (which is low in Wells) and they grow very slowly (millimetres or fractions of a millimetre a year) so that a circular thallus about 50cm in diameter may be over a hundred years old.

Lichens, like many other groups of organisms, colonise habitats gradually, some species possessing particular features that make them adapted to rapid colonisation of new sites whilst others take considerably longer to colonise; the lichens on a substrate may undergo what is termed a succession, in which the species present change over time.[3] An example can be seen on the twigs of ash trees which can be dated for up to about 10 years from leaf and bud scars and the succession of colonising lichens can be followed over

[2]   B.J. Coppins, *Checklist of Lichens of Great Britain and Ireland* (London, 2002).
[3]   P. Topham, 'Colonisation, Succession and Competition', in *Lichen Ecology*, ed. M.R.D. Seaward (London, 1977), 31–68.

this period.[4] Johansson *et al.* showed that the lichen flora of the rest of the tree changed with time too.[5] Taking the longest living trees, Francis Rose made a long and detailed study of the lichens on the trunks of old trees occurring in ancient woodland and medieval deer parks.[6] He showed that many rare species were only found on the most ancient (medieval) trees that have seen little change in their environment over hundreds of years. He coined the term 'ecological continuity', constructing an index based on how many of a suite of these rare lichens were present, so establishing a scale for a combination of the tree trunks on which lichens grow and the constancy of environmental variables. Lawrey reviewed studies in lichen succession and made the important point that early colonising species, once established, were joined by, and not replaced by, colonising ones which appeared in later years.[7] Despite this, lichen colonisation and succession are areas of research receiving relatively little attention.

The slow growth of lichens has been used extensively by geomorphologists in the study of glacier retreats[8] and provides much of the evidence for the warming of the earth in the historic past. The technique is referred to as lichenometry and involves measuring the diameter of thalli of a long-lived species (usually *Rhizocarpon geographicum* which unfortunately does not grow on the palace) which makes easily measured circular patches on the moraines left by the melting glacier so that the sizes can be correlated closely with the date when the rock on the moraines was exposed to the air. Estimates of how fast the lichen thalli grow is based their size on dated surfaces such as gravestones. Lichenometry has also been used to date rock falls above a main road in Wales.[9]

From an historical and archaeological point of view, the lichens colonising the walls of old buildings present an interesting opportunity for research. As mentioned already, not only does the size of the lichen colonies change with time, but also the range of difference species present. Woolhouse *et al.* made a brief study of succession on acidic rock, showing changes in the lichen

4 G. Degelius, 'Biological Studies of the Epiphytic Vegetation on Twigs of *Fraxinus excelsior*', *Acta Horti Gotoburgensis*, 38 (1964), 11–57.
5 P. Johansson, H. Rydin and G. Thor, 'Tree Age Relationships with Epiphytic Lichen Diversity and Lichen Life History Traits on Ash in Southern Sweden', *Ecoscience*, 14 (2007), 81–91.
6 F. Rose, 'Lichenological Indicators of Age and Environmental Continuity in Woodlands', in *Lichenology: Progress and Problems*, ed. D.H. Brown, D.L. Hawksworth and R.H. Bailey (London, 1976), 279–307.
7 J.D. Lawrey, 'Biotic Interactions in Lichen Community Development: A Review', *Lichenologist*, 23 (1991), 205–14.
8 D.P. MacCarthy, 'Lichenometry', in *Monitoring with Lichens – Monitoring Lichens*, ed. P.L. Nimis, C. Scheideger and P.A. Wolseley (Dordrecht, 2002), 379–83; M.G. Loso and D.F. Doak, 'The Biology Behind Lichenometric Dating Curves', *Oecologia*, 47 (2006), 223–9.
9 V. Winchester and R.K. Chaujar, 'Lichenometric Dating of Slope Movements, Nant Ffrancon, North Wales', *Geomorphology*, 47 (2002), 61–74.

flora as the rock aged.[10] But as a useful tool these methods are very much at an experimental stage when applied to buildings. As with other biological indicators, they have to be calibrated and they are subject to numerous variations and errors. But, given the right questions and the occurrence of appropriate lichens, together with necessary background information, lichens might be able to offer additional evidence to help historians and archaeologists. For example Laundon used the presence of particular species as evidence of the age of stone walls in Bradgate Park in Leicestershire, some of which were of medieval origin.[11] Unfortunately for the present project, that study was of walls constructed of acidic stone (sedimentary and igneous) with lichen flora comprising a completely different group of species from those occurring on the limestones of the Bishop's Palace, and so his study is of little direct help. Neither is there any single species whose growth rate has been calibrated to use in lichenometric methods on the buildings and walls of the palace.

To find out if there are particular lichen species that only colonise older limestone surfaces, the lichens present on dated gravestones in churchyards were recorded.[12] These data only cover a limited period of time because dated gravestones that have been in the same uninterrupted position in a churchyard usually only go back to the eighteenth century. The results indicated that some species were indeed only found on older stones prior to the middle of the nineteenth century. However, this was only a very limited study with only just over fifty limestone gravestones included. With so small a sample, the main problem is that many of the lichens were recorded only on one or two gravestones so that it is not possible to tell if they occurred there by chance rather than because of the age of the stone surface. Therefore any conclusion based on that study should be treated with some caution and use of the results to date other stone surfaces could be subject to considerable error. Another note of caution is that lichens can be used to indicate how long a surface, such as stone, might have been exposed to the elements and not necessarily how old the stonework itself is. For example, if the stonework has been covered at some time in the past, e.g. by render, or deeply shaded by a tree, or if the surface stone has subsequently been replaced, the lichens would not reflect the age of the structure. The opposite also applies in that if some stone was used that had been exposed to the weather for a long time and already had lichens on it, the lichens might indicate a greater age than when a structure was built. Examples of the

---

[10] M.E.J. Woolhouse, R. Harmsen and L. Fahrig, 'On Succession in a Saxicolous Lichen Community', *Lichenologist*, 17 (1985), 167–72.

[11] J.R. Laundon, 'The Use of Lichens for Dating Walls in Bradgate Park, Leicestershire', *Transactions of the Leicester Literary and Philosophical Society*, 74 (1980), 11–30.

[12] D.J. Hill, 'The Succession of Lichens on Gravestones: A Preliminary Study', *Cryptogamic Botany*, 4 (1994), 179–86.

questions we can ask are: is there evidence that some of the wall surfaces have been exposed longer than others, if so where, and are the lichens of sufficient importance that their conservation is important for archaeology as well as biodiversity?

Some lichens are quite small and some are quite cryptic; thorough surveying and accurate identification can be very time-consuming and requires specialist training and considerable experience. However, it is encouraging that there are many common species which are easy to recognise and interesting to get to know. An excellent illustrated guide to the identification of the common British species is by Frank Dobson, who also wrote an guide to churchyard lichens. William Purvis has written a well-illustrated general introductory book about lichens.[13]

Methods

The approach taken at Wells was a preliminary one to find out what species of lichen are present on the buildings and walls in the curtilage of the palace. The aim was to do a rapid survey of as many different accessible parts as possible. This meant that the recording included only lists of species on a first visit and quantitative data not collected included the cover of the different species, the size of particular species of interest, and associations of species. Thus particular areas chosen (sites) were those that might conceivably represent accessible parts of a single structural entity, such as the upper wall of the ramparts accessible from the walkway, or walls around the roof of the gatehouse accessible from the roof. A series of visits was made in April 2006. Field determinations on sight were made for common species but unusual species that required microscopic examination or chemical testing to enable identification were collected as small scrapings representing a matter of square millimetres of thallus. The process did not damage the stonework and was done carefully to avoid leaving a visible mark. Identification was performed as set out in the British Lichen Society guidelines[14] using the standard flora.[15] A stepladder was used to reach up to about 2.5m and a ladder to reach up to c.5m (on the west end of chapel only). Some specimens, those of rare species and one which could not be identified with certainty, were sent to Dr Brian Coppins at the Royal Botanic Gardens as

---

[13] F.S. Dobson, *Lichens: An Illustrated Guide to the British and Irish Species* (Slough, 2005); F.S. Dobson, *A Field Key to Common Churchyard Lichens* (New Malden, 2003); O.W. Purvis, *Lichens* (London, 2000).

[14] D.J. Hill, ed., *Surveying and Report Writing for Lichenologists* (London, 2006).

[15] O.W. Purvis, B.J. Coppins, D.L. Hawksworth, P.W. James and D.M. Moore, *The Lichen Flora of Great Britain and Ireland* (London, 1992).

he is an international authority and has surveyed the natural outcrops of limestone in the Mendips for the National Trust and therefore knows the more unusual species which are likely to occur very well.

In estimating the possible ages of the exposure of the stone surfaces from the lists of species made for each site, the gravestone data from Hill[16] was used as this included lichens growing on limestone and in the same biogeographical area of Britain as Wells. The procedure adopted was as follows: firstly, to exclude all those lichens at the Bishop's Palace that usually occur on moss mortar or stones other than limestone, as these do not usually occur on gravestones. Then the remaining lichens found there and also listed by Hill[17] as occurring on dated gravestones were divided into three separate lists (see Table 9.2): (1) lichens recorded on gravestones up to 100 years old; (2) those recorded from gravestones 100–150 years old but not recorded on younger ones; and (3) those recorded from gravestones more than 150 years old (back to 1684) but not recorded from younger ones. Those lichens whose records had been shown to be statistically significant on older gravestones (*Xanthoria calcicola*, *Aspicilia contorta*, *Caloplaca teicholyta*), even if an occasional record had been made on a slightly earlier one than the divisions above, were moved to the 100–150-year-old list. The dates on the gravestones were regarded as only approximate.[18] Then a fourth list was made of those lichens recorded at the palace but which had not been recorded by Hill (1994) on dated gravestones. Finally the lichens found at each site at the palace were enumerated within these four categories and expressed as a percentage of the total number of species recorded from that site except those growing on mosses, mortar or other substrates (Table 9.1).[19]

Results

Nearly ninety species were found and this represents a rich flora (Table 9.1). The flora (species and communities) is typical of limestone walls of southern Britain. There are some rare species present and this is to be expected on ancient walls.

The lichens of churches and churchyards have been very well studied in Britain. The list of species found in these is prodigious. The Bishop's Palace

---

[16] Hill, 'The Succession of Lichens on Gravestones'.

[17] *Ibid*.

[18] See *ibid*. for discussion.

[19] The names are according to the latest published checklist (Coppins, *Checklist of Lichens*). The conservation status of the species was assessed using R.G. Woods and B.J. Coppins, *A Conservation Evaluation of British Lichens* (London, 2003). Distribution maps were consulted using F.S. Dobson, *Lichen-identifier: A Multi-Access Key to the Lichens of Great Britain and Ireland*,Version 3 (CD and handbook) (New Malden, 2007).

Table 9.1. Numbers of lichen species categorised according to dates of gravestone colonisation (Hill 1994)

Site (see list below)	1	2	3	4	4a	5	6	7	8	9	10	11	12	other
Total number of species.	23	30	38	29	17	22	12	25	41	34	32	30	23	22
Species considered below	20	26	31	28	12	17	10	23	39	31	29	25	22	22
% early species (0–100yrs) (40%)	65	50	48	46	67	53	40	43	56	52	45	40	59	50
% mid-species (100–150 yrs) (18%)	30	35	26	25	33	24	30	22	28	26	28	36	36	23
% late species (150–250 yrs) (10%)	5	11	13	11	0	12	0	6	3	6	7	16	0	14
% not on recorded on gravestones (32%)	0	4	13	18	0	11	30	26	13	16	21	8	5	13
possible age of stone exposure (yrs) based on this data	±150	150–250	250+	250+	<150	250+	? (too shaded)	250+	250+	250+	250+	±250	<150yrs	Mix

1 South end of Bishop's Palace from scaffold up to the roof, 17 March 2006
2 East wall of Bishop Bekynton's range and north wall of Bishop Jocelin's range to roof from scaffold, 17 March 2006
3 Rampart walls, inside south-east wall (facing north-west) and southern part of south-west wall (facing north-east), 3 April 2006
4 East tower battlements, 3 April 2006
4a South tower battlements, 3 April 2006
5 Outside wall of south-east and south-west rampart wall, 4 April 2006
6 West tower and inside wall of rampart going north-east and south-east, 4 April 2006
7 Inside of north rampart wall between Bishop Bekynton's range and north-east tower, 4 April 2006
8 South facing inner walls of battlements on chapel roof and slates, 5 April 2006
9 North facing inner walls of battlements on chapel roof and slates, 5 April 2006
10 West wall of chapel up to height of about 20ft including the sloping ledges and window sill, 5 April 2006
11 Gatehouse roof, 6 April 2006
12 Roof of tower in Bishop Bekynton's range, 6 April 2006
Other Various locations where limited number of common species were found (marked on the map, Figure 22)

Table 9.2. Lichens found at the Bishop's Palace and found on gravestones by Hill (D.J. Hill, 'The Succession of Lichens on Gravestones: A Preliminary Study', *Cryptogamic Botany*, 4 (1994), 179–86)

On gravestones less than 100 years	On gravestones 100–150 years	On gravestones more than 150 years	Not listed by Hill	Species excluded from lists to the left (see text)
Caloplaca aurantia	Aspicilia calcarea	Acrocordia conoidea*	Caloplaca crenulatella	Bacidia sabulatorum
Caloplaca citrina sl	Aspicilia contorta	Agonimia tristicula*	Caloplaca dalmatica	Caloplaca arcis
Caloplaca flavescens	Caloplaca teicholyta	Belonia niderosiensis*	Caloplaca decipiens	Caloplaca flavocitrina
Caloplaca holocarpa	Candelariella medians	Caloplaca chlorina	Caloplaca lactea	Candelariella vitellina
Caloplaca saxicola	Collema auriculatum	Dirina massiliensis var. sorediata	Caloplaca ochracea	Cladonia pocillum
Candelariella aurella	Diploicia canescens	Leproplaca xantholyta	Caloplaca polycarpa**	Collema crispum
Catillaria lenticularis	Hymenelia prevostii	Verrucaria macrostoma f. macrostoma	Caloplaca variabilis	Collema tenax
Clauzadea monticola	Placynthium nigrum		Catapyrenium pilosellum	Lecania cf rabenhorstii
Diplotomma alboatrum	Rinodina gennarii		Catapyrenium rufescens	Lecidella scabra
Lecania erysibe	Solenopsora candicans		Clauzadea metzleri	Lepraria lesdainii
Lecanora albescens	Toninia aromatica**		Collema confertum	Leptogium gelatinosum
Lecanora campestris	Verrucaria baldensis		Hyperphyscia adglutinata	Leptogium lichenoides
Lecanora crenulata	Xanthoria calcicola		Lecania turicensis	Leptogium schraderi
Lecanora dispersa			Leproplaca chrysodeta	Leptogium tenuissimum
Lecanora muralis			Leptogium plicatile	Polysporina simplex
Lecidella stigmatea			Leptogium turgidum	Sarcogyne 'pruinosa'
Phaeophyscia orbicularis			Opegrapha calcarea	Verrucaria viridula var. sorediata
Physcia adscendens			Opegrapha rupestris**	Xanthoparmelia mougeotii
Physcia caesia			Physcia tenella	
Physconia grisea			Physcia tribacia	
Protoblastenia rupestris			Thelidium incavatum	
Sarcogyne regularis			Toninia episema**	
Verrucaria glaucina				
Verrucaria hochsetteri				
Verrucaria muralis				
Verrucaria nigrescens				
Verrucaria viridula var. viridula				
Xanthoria parietina				
28 species	13 species	7 species	23 species	17 species
25% not on gravestones	50% not on gravestones	59% not on gravestones	0% on gravestones	

* lichens found associates with rising damp; ** lichen parasite or starts as a lichenicolous lichen.

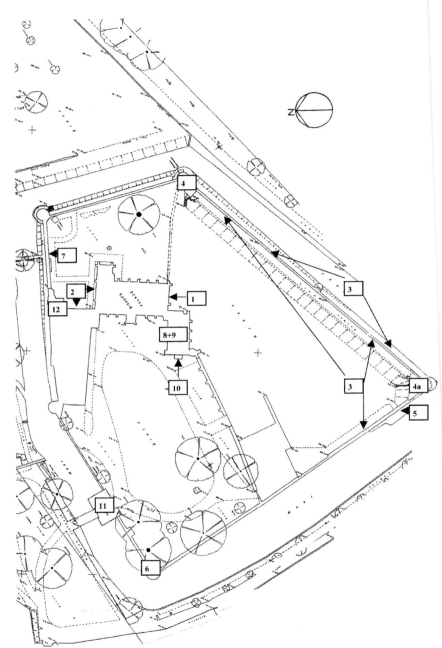

Figure 22. Plan showing locations of the sites referred to in Table 9.1.

at Wells is a building not dissimilar to numerous churches built of limestone across lowland Britain. The fact that rare species have been found in this survey indicates that the Bishop's Palace is indeed a valuable site for lichens. Lichen floras of churchyard and church have frequently been known to exceed 100 species exceptionally up to 150 species.[20] This large number is usually based on a large variety of memorial stones made of different geological types, as well as old trees. In comparison, the ninety or so species found in this survey just on the limestone walls and buildings (with only a few found on slate which is normally quite poor in species) represent a very rich site and include four nationally rare and four nationally scarce species.

The main sites studied are treated in turn. At the first visit there was scaffolding on the south elevation of Bishop Jocelin's range (see Figure 22, Sites 1 and 2). This was a valuable opportunity to survey the walls of that building higher up than is possible even with a ladder. Here the stonework was mostly ashlar, but the rather dry vertical surface had a poor lichen flora because lichens need water and some mineral nutrients as well as light. The species seen were all common ones and were mostly present on stonework at an angle or jutting out on the sloping tops of the buttresses where the stonework catches the rain.

Then the rampart walls were surveyed and proved most interesting but more extensive than could be studied in great detail. Access is a problem, the easiest being the stretch (Site 3) from the south tower (Site 4a) to the east tower (Site 4). Even so, the south-east side could only be sampled by leaning over the parapet between the battlements (a very limited view and impossible to examine closely with a hand lens). On the top, the capping stones in the sun and the stones in the north face of the wall in the shade and the damp decaying mortar presented a range of micro habitats to explore. A list of about fifty species was fairly easily obtained, from the tower in the corner in the south and along the terrace towards the tower and entrance in the east corner. The top of the sunny south-east face could be seen by leaning carefully between the battlements where there were patches of *Collema auriforme*, a lichen whose photosynthetic partner to the fungus is a cyanoacterium instead of an alga. This is only physiologically active when wet with rainwater. In contrast, some species such as *Diplotomma alboatrum*, *Leproplaca* spp., and *Diploicia canescens* can absorb water directly from humidity in the air and hence are able to grow where rain hardly ever falls. On the north wall in damp crevices there is *L. lesdainii* – an almost glowing powder-green felt growing deep in the cracks between the stones, a species named after the extraordinary French lichenologist M. Bouly de

[20] T. Chester, 'Top Twenty Churchyards Challenge!' *The British Lichen Society Bulletin*, 69 (1991), 22–4.

Lesdain who described many new species to science. His herbarium was destroyed during the allied invasion of France in the Second World War so lichenologists are not sure now what lichens his names refer to. Collections of named specimens (such as at the Natural History Museum and Kew) are of enormous scientific importance in getting the names of organisms correct. Without correct names, research in biology and ecology is worthless.

The bottom of the rampart wall was accessed from the strip of land along the inside bank of the moat and is included as a separate site (Site 5) as it was a very different habitat. Here occurred mostly the commoner limestone species with a few additional species (not included) growing on the fruit trees trained against the wall.

On the inside of the north rampart wall between Bishop Bekynton's range and the north-east tower the capping stones (Site 7) are of weathered limestone. The lichens on the south facing sloping sides included the lichenicolous species *Caloplaca polycarpa* (Plate 15) and *Opegrapha rupestris* (growing on *Verrucaria baldensis*) as well as *Caloplaca ochracea*, three species which are not common and are of special note. Like those in other places with older weathered capping stones with solution holes dissolved in them, these stones represent older masonry that has had time to accumulate rarer species of lichen over hundreds of years. Previous studies on gravestones have shown that some quite common species do not appear to colonise stone until it has been exposed for 100–200 years.[21]

The walls of the rampart towers are of similar construction to the rampart walls between the towers and have a similar flora. The east tower (Site 4) with some twenty-six species is notable in that the capping stones like those on the rampart wall at Site 7 are old weathered limestone. Here three uncommon species of note were found: *Hymenelia prevostii* (with minute pink fruiting bodies sunken in the limestone rock), *Caloplaca polycarpa* (on *Verrucaria baldensis*) and *Sarcogyne 'pruinosa'* (Plate 16) (*S. 'pruniosa'* is an unusual and distinctive form of *S. regularis* with its fruiting bodies also sunken into the limestone but it is doubtful that it is a different species from the common *S. regularis* to which it is similar in all other ways and may have this appearance due to the great age of the thallus). *Caloplaca polycarpa* has only recently been listed as occurring in Britain but has been found by Brian Coppins to be locally common in the Mendips. The east tower (Site 4) appears to have a completely different lichen flora from the south tower (Site 4a). The tower and the rampart walls in the west are shaded by trees and the lichen flora was rather limited. Other species found at these sites (Sites 4 and 7) and nowhere else in the palace included *Caloplaca ochracea* and *Clausadia metzlerii*.

21 Hill, 'The Succession of Lichens on Gravestones'.

The roof of the chapel (Sites 8 (south facing aspect) and 9 (north facing aspect)) was particularly rich in lichen species with as many as fifty or so being found. Although there were a few common species on the slates, most of the lichens listed were on the inside of the walls around the roof. Some species such as *Catapyrenium rufescens* (Plate17) were of special note. This species is designated nationally rare and enjoys the lack of disturbance at this location where there are few people who can easily knock it off the stone surface. The richness of the lichen flora here is probably due to the stonework being ancient and undisturbed.

The west end of the chapel (Site 10) is also of considerable interest. The gargoyles from the roof discharge water that apparently splashes parts of this wall. The window- sill was just reachable with a 20ft ladder and on it the minute lichen *Leptogium turgidum* grows and in amongst this is another potentially interesting species *Leptogium tenuissimum*. These species are not frequently recorded and are regarded as nationally local or rare and may become threatened. On the drip-course beneath the window was *Collema confertum* (Plate 18) that is also nationally rare, having been found only in a few places in England and Ireland previously. Like *Catapyrenium rufescens* this grows as a small brownish button-like structure that can easily be knocked off. Species of *Leptogium* and *Collema* contain cyanobacteria as the photosynthetic partner in the symbiosis with the fungus and can only function if the cells are irrigated with liquid water such as rain and drainage water; they therefore tend to grow with mosses on angled surfaces which catch the rain. Most other lichens contain microscopic algal cells as the partner; they can function by absorbing water from humid air and therefore do not need liquid water.

The gatehouse roof (Site 11, the inside of walls around the roof) was also very rich (thirty species) and had a similar flora to the chapel roof although the area was smaller. Here *Catapyrenium pilosellum* (which is very similar to *C. rufescens*, differing in having very fine white hairs growing out of the tips of the lobes, a feature reflected in its name) and *Collema confertum*-like thalli were found (the latter was damaged by browsing invertebrates). The walls on the roof of the tower above the bishop's residence had a fairly rich flora but, as they represented a smaller amount of stonework, the number of species was correspondingly lower (twenty-three species) and no notable ones were found here.

Other locations were also examined very briefly. No species of conservation importance were found in these places but the lichens give character to the stonework and are in their own right valuable contributions to the biodiversity that the palace supports.

Conclusions

This preliminary survey indicates that there are some parts of the palace that may contain more important lichens than others. The main areas so far found are:

- the chapel roof (battlements) and west wall (elevation above reachable height standing on the ground) of the chapel;
- the east tower battlements. Some of the capping stones of the ramparts appear to be eroded and have the richest lichen flora. This seems to be the oldest stonework and I would suggest that it is at least 300 years old;
- the gatehouse roof battlements;
- the battlements of the rampart wall between Bishop Bekynton's range and the east tower. Here, the capping stones, like some of those on the east tower, are eroded and have a rich lichen flora. It is only on these stones that *Caloplaca ochracea*, *Clausadea metzlerii* and *Caloplaca polycarpa* were found.

These are the locations where nationally rare and scarce species are present.[22] Therefore, in assessing the importance of the palace in supporting lichen biodiversity, we must conclude that it is not only of local and regional importance but nationally also. The rarer species are found on natural outcrops in the Mendips, but finding them on a building is very unusual.

Turning to the archaeological aspects, lichen floras take time to develop. As Rose (1976) found with lichens on trees, richer floras with rarer species are only found at sites where there has been a long continuity of uniform ecological conditions.[23] Similarly with rock and stone, the longer the exposure of the surface the more opportunity rarer species have to colonise and become established. Therefore, comparing the various locations that were surveyed on the palace buildings and walls, the areas where the stonework is likely to have been exposed for longer are those with the richer floras, i.e. those listed above. The oldest stonework, based on lichenological evidence, was certain capping stones of the ramparts on the east tower and by Bishop Jocelin's range (Site 7). The dating is extremely uncertain with the limited sample sizes in the research that has been done. The small number of occurrences of many of the species did not allow statistical analysis which would determine whether they were present as a result of the age of the stone or just on older stones by chance. However some species are clearly early colonisers and some appear only later. For example, *Toninia aromatica* was only found on gravestones more than a hundred years old and *Caloplaca teicholyta*

---

[22] Woods and Coppins, *A Conservation Evaluation of British Lichens*.
[23] Rose, 'Lichenological Indicators of Age and Environmental Continuity in Woodlands'.

was only found on stones more than eighty years old. *T. aromatica* was found at most of the locations examined on the walls within the palace and *C. teicholyta* at more than half. It is therefore concluded that the stonework of most of the walls is possibly nineteenth-century or older. But further than this, estimates of age are less certain.

Despite this we can compare all the lichens found on the stonework, rather than individual species, with those Hill recorded as occurring on dated gravestones (Table 9.2).[24] We can thus suggest possible periods when the palace stonework might have been constructed (Table 9.1). Although this is fraught with uncertainties, it may be helpful in indicating whether such a lichenological approach to dating stone surfaces is of any value. The three main uncertainties are (a) the incompleteness of the data in Hill based on too few gravestones; (b) that walls of buildings represent a very different habitat for lichens from gravestones; and (c) we do not know if the walls had in the past been covered (e.g. by ivy or enclosed in now demolished buildings). Therefore we have assumed that the gravestone data is reliable, that the buildings and walls on the site are like gravestones and have had an uninterrupted exposure to the elements.

The results (Table 9.1) would indicate that much of the stonework surveyed might be older than the eighteenth century. The exceptions are 2, 4a and 12 on the south wall of Bishop Jocelin's range (Site 1) which adjoins the east end of the chapel, the north wall at the other end of the same building and the contiguous east-facing wall of Bishop Bekynton's range (Site 2). The tower above it (Site 12) and the south tower of the ramparts were indicated as the most recent (less than 150 years). Comparing the amount of erosion of the stonework, the oldest stonework appears to be that on capping stones of the ramparts on the east tower and by the palace (Plate 19) that correlates with the lichen flora. These walls may therefore represent original medieval stonework.

Further possible research

The present brief survey was inended to explore the lichen flora of the walls and buildings within the curtilage of the Bishop's Palace to identify whether the lichen flora was worthy of conservation. Now that this is clearly demonstrated, more detailed examination of the lichen flora is recommended as there may be additional species, with the real possibility of unusual ones, still to be discovered. A further project is needed to explore the possibility of dating the surfaces and to provide more precise locations and more information about the lichens present. Such a project would involve working

---

[24] Hill, 'The Succession of Lichens on Gravestones'.

with archaeologists to demarcate areas of stonework that form units, iden-tifying the lichens present, estimating their cover abundance and, using lichenometric techniques, measuring the sizes of some of the species which are able to form larger thalli. Such an approach would provide more reliable evidence than is offered in this present cursory study.

10

Robert Burnell and the Transformation of Bishop Jocelin's Palace

MATTHEW M. REEVE

The sequence of Decorated buildings associated with Robert Burnell, chancellor of England 1274–92 and bishop of Bath and Wells 1275–92, including the chapter house and staircase in his cathedral at Wells and the monumental additions to Bishop Jocelin's palace there, together with related buildings at Acton Burnell in Shropshire and Nantwich in Cheshire, have been justly celebrated as 'one of the most coherent and interesting' sequences in English Decorated architecture.[1] These buildings have hardly gone unnoticed by scholars of medieval architecture, but to date the majority of attention has focused upon Acton Burnell castle and the additions to the cathedral, leaving Burnell's additions to the palace largely unstudied. Yet Burnell transformed that palace into a monumental fortified residence that included a new aisled hall, a chapel and a range of outbuildings, the whole probably surrounded by crenellated murage.

Burnell's work at the palace is admittedly fragmentary as compared with the chapter house and its staircase but the significance of the palace buildings is not in doubt: they are among the 'most impressive English domestic buildings of the Middle Ages', and Jean Bony awarded them a seminal role in the development of the Decorated style and in the introduction of a fortified vocabulary of architectural design into English architecture

[1] J. Maddisson, 'Building at Lichfield During the Episcopate of Walter de Langton', in *Medieval Art and Architecture at Lichfield*, British Archaeological Association Conference Transactions (London, 1993), 65–84. The most important accounts of the sequence include P. Draper, 'The Sequence and Dating of the Decorated Work at Wells Cathedral', in *Medieval Art and Architecture at Wells and Glastonbury*, British Archaeological Association Conference Transactions (Leeds, 1981), 18–29, and T. Ayers, *The Medieval Stained Glass of Wells Cathedral*, Corpus Vitrearum Medii Aevi, iv (Oxford, 2004). This paper derives from the author's doctoral thesis 'The Episcopal Palace at Wells c.1207–1465: An Architectural and Institutional History', Cambridge University 2003.

(Plate 20).[2] The purpose of this chapter is to survey for the first time the range of archaeological, documentary and antiquarian evidence for Burnell's additions to the palace, beginning with a discussion of his patronage and motives. There follows consideration of form, function and sequence.

Patronage

Robert Burnell was by birth a member of a prosperous landholding family in Shropshire and he seems to have been more secular aristocrat than committed prelate. He had long served Edward I as prince and his preferment was sought by the king, twice to the archbishopric of Canterbury and once to the see of Winchester. In the event Burnell was only modestly rewarded in the form of the bishopric of Bath and Wells, which he seems to have secured against further opposition to promotion by resigning benefices and making over his secular landholdings.[3] Perhaps in the light of his second failure for promotion to Canterbury in 1278, Burnell began in 1279–80 to repossess his estates.[4] Documentary evidence for work at Acton Burnell begins to occur with frequency from 1279–80, suggesting that the return of his estates allowed a large-scale campaign of building, which coincided with Burnell's work at the palace at Wells.

Burnell had several reasons for building on a monumental scale at Wells. The age-old requirement of a residence to reflect the pretensions of its owner was clearly significant and cannot be underrated in the light of his aspirations for the country's highest ecclesiastical office. Jocelin's palace must have been considered an unassuming residence indeed for the chancellor of England: by the 1280s it was not only outdated but probably also diminutive compared to the recent court-related building projects such as the episcopal palaces at Worcester and London and the new Welsh castles, with which Burnell was personally involved. Viewed in this context, the expansion of the palace at Wells can be seen to fulfil a single aim: to enhance the prestige of Wells as an episcopal centre and thus to celebrate Burnell's personal power and status.

2   G. Webb, *Architecture in Britain: the Middle Ages* (London, 1956), 158; J. Bony, *The English Decorated Style: Gothic Architecture Transformed 1250–1350* (Oxford, 1979).
3   Burnell's career has recently been studied by Richard Huscroft, 'The Personal and Political Life of Robert Burnell', unpublished PhD thesis, University of London, 2000.
4   *Ibid.*, 202; *Rotuli Ricardi Gravesend Diocesis Lincolnensis*, ed. F.N. Davis (Oxford, 1925), 63, 69, 126; *CPR 1272–81*, 90; *CCR 1272–79*, 521 is an order of 1279 by which the manors of Acton Burnell, Winstanton and other Shropshire estates were returned to Burnell, having been given to his nephew Hugh Burnell 'to hold of the bishop during the bishop's life and after the bishop's death'.

It is also likely that the expansion of the palace was a matter of some necessity, both in order to accommodate possible court visits and to house what must have been a burgeoning episcopal household. Perhaps for the first time, the building was consciously designed to provide for large-scale hospitality. Little is known about Burnell's own entourage,[5] but in general there was a substantial increase in the size of episcopal households over the course of the thirteenth century. Burnell's see palace was the first of a number that would be expanded in the late thirteenth and early fourteenth centuries.[6] Edward I's two other episcopal advisors, Anthony Bek, bishop of Durham 1284–1310, and Walter de Langton, bishop of Coventry and Lichfield 1296–1321 and treasurer of England, also expanded the ceremonial spaces of their palaces, constructing comparably large halls.[7] Cumulatively, those buildings may be illustrative not only of the important role of court-based builders, but also of the expansion and growing sophistication of episcopal governments formed during the twelfth and thirteenth centuries.

Burnell's secular buildings at Wells continued the programme begun by Bishop Jocelin to re-establish his administrative centre at Wells. Contemporary with the inception of Burnell's plans to enlarge Jocelin's palace was a parallel plan to diminish and eventually to destroy the episcopal residence at Bath. In 1280 he granted a plot of land bordering on the palace there to the citizens of Bath.[8] The grant was first of a number that would see it eventually destroyed. It is thus not surprising that Burnell is only once recorded as having visited it.[9] Burnell's building at Wells clearly endowed the cathedral

---

5   Huscroft, 'The Personal and Political Life of Robert Burnell', 207–14. See also U. Hughes, 'A Biographical Sketch of Robert Burnell with Materials for his Life', unpublished B.Litt thesis, Oxford University, 1934, chapter 4.

6   A late thirteenth-century date has been plausibly suggested for the destroyed hall at Chichester, but this has yet to be confirmed by stylistic or documentary evidence: T. Tatton-Brown, 'The Buildings of the Bishop's Palace and Close', in *Chichester Cathedral: An Historical Survey*, ed. M. Hobbs (Chichester, 1994), 229.

7   The hall block was twice altered in the Middle Ages: around 1350, Bishop Hatfield lengthened, or more likely rebuilt, the southern chambers; and at the end of the fifteenth century they were separated by a cross wall erected by Bishop Fox, and subsequently divided into separate apartments. I follow here the most recent commentator who opined, 'it is likely that he [Bishop Hatfield] did not simply stretch the hall to an inordinate length of 131 feet but rather replaced or built anew a two-storied *residential block* under the same roof-ridge as the hall': A. Emery, *Greater Medieval Houses of England and Wales 1300–1500* (Cambridge, 1996), i. 79. On the Romanesque undercroft see M. Leyland, 'The Origins and Development of Durham Castle to AD 1217: The Archaeological and Architectural Record', unpublished PhD thesis, University of Durham 1994, 15–18.

8   *Ancient Deeds Belonging to the Corporation of Bath*, ed. C.W. Shickle, Bath Record Society 6 (Bath, 1921), 42; M. Chapman, P. Davenport and E. Holland, 'The Precincts of the Bishop's Palace at Bath, Avon', *Archaeological Journal*, 152 (1995), 99; E. Lucas, 'Documentary Evidence Relating to the Bishop's Palace', in *Archaeology in Bath*, ed. P. Davenport (Bath, 1991), 96–7.

9   Huscroft, 'The Personal and Political Life of Robert Burnell', 232; 10 June 1281.

precinct not only with aristocratic accommodation and ceremonial space of the highest order, but also significantly enhanced the general prestige and visual glamour of Wells as an episcopal centre.

The buildings: site and subsidiary structures

Burnell's additions, chapel, Great Hall and attached kitchens, were built in a sequence against the south-west corner of Bishop Jocelin's range, with the chapel abutting its south-west corner and the hall attached to the south-west angle of the chapel. Connected at eccentric angles, the additions form a dogleg with the pre-existing buildings. The Great Hall was positioned roughly on an axis with the cathedral church, creating two walls of a courtyard, and possibly three walls if there were buildings extending from the north-west corner of Jocelin's range. It has been suggested that Burnell's additions are descendants of the twelfth- and early thirteenth-century fashion for building aisled halls attached to chamber blocks to form a courtyard.[10] While it is possible that such an arrangement was planned, the location and orientation of the new buildings were initially dictated by the presence of a watercourse that ran in front of Jocelin's buildings, prior to its diversion in the fourteenth century.[11]

Burnell's hall and chapel represent the ceremonial and devotional centres of the late thirteenth-century palace. The bishop's household and guests required housing, stabling and service buildings. By the nature of their construction, probably in wood rather than in stone, the buildings were susceptible to decay, ruin and frequent rebuilding. A survey of the buildings dated 1340–42[12] records several structures 'covered in stone' as opposed to the lead of the hall, chapel and other chambers, including kitchen, brewery, bakery and larder; and outside the new walls a granary, barn and other agricultural buildings. A gateway 'towards the town' was flanked by two ranges including halls and chambers 'set aside for visiting lords' and a prison.[13] It

---

[10] J. Blair, 'Hall and Chamber: English Domestic Planning 1000–1250', in *Manorial Domestic Buildings in England and Northern France*, ed. G. Meirion-Jones and M. Jones, Society of Antiquaries Occasional Paper (London 1993), 11.

[11] Rodwell, *Wells Cathedral*, 33.

[12] A.J. Scrase and R.W. Dunning, 'The Bishop's Palace, Wells', *Somerset and Dorset Notes and Queries*, 35, 52–5, based on an MS in Wiltshire and Swindon Record Office, Chippenham, 161/142.

[13] Buckle, 'Wells Palace', 72. Buckle drew attention to the appearance of parch marks running parallel to the south wall of the Great Hall at the west end. He suggested that these may represent foundations of previous service buildings on site. It is more likely, however, that they are in fact the foundations of the later gardens evident in Carter's plan: N. Payne, 'Historic Landscape Desktop Study: The Precinct of the Bishop's Palace, Wells, Somerset', unpublished MA thesis, University of Bristol, 1999, 48–50.

is possible that they may have been part of Burnell's works. The prison was certainly there in 1329[14] and one was required from 1262 when all bishops were enjoined to have one or two prisons within their bishoprics for 'the safekeeping of criminous clerics'.[15] In the sixteenth century the prison had two chambers above it.[16]

Burnell's expansion of the Bishop's Palace probably involved the construction of a perimeter wall and gatehouse, which must have been superseded by the present fourteenth-century fortifications. The house of a cathedral canon was described by Bishop Drokensford in 1312 as 'extra portam curiae nostrae et eidem curiae contiguam' and in 1321 as 'extra portam manerii nostri'.[17] The 1340–42 survey states that a turret (*turrellum*) was built over the common entry to the palace (*super portam communam*) in which there were private apartments and small chambers, all of which were covered in lead.[18] Fortification of the palace by Burnell would accord with a pattern established at Worcester and Exeter, where palace precincts were recently fortified, and would also accord with Burnell's own works at Acton Burnell, where a gatehouse extended over a wet moat.[19] Burnell in 1286 received a licence to wall and crenellate the cathedral churchyard at Wells and also the precinct of the canons' houses, but no reference was then made to the palace.[20]

The buildings: the chapel

Possibly like its early Gothic predecessor, the chapel was freestanding (Plate 21). Many castle chapels were located within keeps, gates or walls, but episcopal chapels were typically semi-detached structures built off the main ceremonial space.[21] One reason for this tradition may have been

---

[14] *Reg. Drokensford*, 298.

[15] J. Shinners and W.J. Dohar, *Pastors and the Care of Souls in Medieval England* (Indiana, 1998), 268. Such prisons were also built at the palaces at Worcester, Durham, Exeter and Chichester in the late thirteenth century: Emery, *Greater Medieval Houses of England and Wales*, ii. 464.

[16] *Wells MSS* ii. 263. A possible analogy for the prison is the fourteenth-century archiepiscopal prison at Hexham, which similarly featured two cells on the first floor and chambers above: Emery, *Greater Medieval Houses of England and Wales*, i. 101–2.

[17] *Reg. Drokensford*, 51, 196.

[18] Wiltshire and Swindon Record Office, 161/142.

[19] Worcester: *CPR 1266–72*, 580; Exeter: *CPR 1281–92*, 393. On the gatehouse and perimeter fortifications at Exeter see J.F. Chanter, *The Bishop's Palace Exeter and Its Story* (London, 1932), chapter 7, esp. 66; Anon. 'Shropshire: Acton Burnell', *Medieval Archaeology* 8 (1964), 272–3.

[20] *CPR 1281–92*, 229.

[21] N. Pounds, 'The Chapel in the Castle', *Fortress*, 13 (1991), 13–21; J. Bony, 'La chapelle épiscopale et les apports lorrains en Angleterre après la conquête', *Actes du XIXe congrès*

to increase the visual prominence of the chapel within the palace, thus standing as a signifier of a bishop's dual role as secular lord and spiritual pastor. Contrary to the tradition of earlier, two-level episcopal chapels, Burnell's was a single open space, articulated internally by expansive traceried windows and covered by a stone vault. Although *comparanda* are hardly abundant, there appear to be few precedents for open chapels of this sort, with the closest extant parallel at Chichester, built by Ralph Neville (which was originally freestanding but has now been subsumed into the other palace buildings). Ralph's chapel is a rectangular space built in four bays, covered with two bays of sexpartite ribbed vaulting.[22] Bishops built single-storey chapels, albeit in a collegiate rather than palatial context: the parish church of St John the Baptist, Oxford, from 1292 the chapel of Merton College, Oxford,[23] employs a similar array of alternating tracery designs in the lateral windows. The design of Burnell's chapel inspired at least one follower: that of the Benedictine priory at Spalding, Lincolnshire. Built in 1311, it was probably meant be a private chapel for Prior Clement of Hatfield (prior 1294–1318).[24] Like Burnell's chapel, Hatfield's is a squat, flat-topped structure in three bays with alternating tracery patterns, the east wall terminating in a broad traceried window. The notable similarities between the buildings leaves little doubt that Burnell's chapel was the principal source of inspiration.

The buildings: the Great Hall

Unlike the chapel, which survives remarkably intact, the Great Hall was subject to several campaigns of destruction and spoliation after the Middle Ages, leaving the fabric evidence fragmentary. At present, it retains the

---

international d'histoire de l'art (Paris, 1958), 36–43. This is not to suggest, however, that there were not related projects in non-episcopal residences, for example, the castle chapel at Ludlow: G. Coppack, 'The Round Chapel of St Mary Magdalene', in *Ludlow Castle: Its History and Buildings*, ed. R. Shoesmith and A. Johnson (Woonton, 2000), 145–54.

[22] There has been some discussion regarding the date of the bishop's chapel at Chichester. It has traditionally been attributed to the remodelling of Seffrid II (1180–1204), with the possibility of a remodelling of the vaults in the early thirteenth century: I.C. Hannah, 'Bishop's Palace, Chichester', *Sussex Archaeological Collections*, 52 (1909), 5; T. Tatton-Brown, 'The Buildings of the Bishop's Palace and Close', in *Chichester Cathedral: An Historical Survey*, ed. M. Hobbs (Chichester, 1994), 228. However, a comparison between the moulding profiles in the door jambs, the vault ribs and the work on the south porch (the bishop's liturgical entrance) suggests that the chapel was built in a single campaign by Bishop Ralph Nevill (1224–44).

[23] *VCH Oxford* (1979), iv. 384.

[24] Emery, *Greater Medieval Houses of England and Wales*, 323–4; D.M. Smith and V.C.M. London, eds, *Heads of Religious Houses, England and Wales, II, 1216–1377* (Cambridge, 2001), 193.

full height of the north and west walls, fragments of the south wall at the western end, and the south-east turret. The best evidence for the original form of the complex is the view by Samuel and Nathaniel Buck of 1733 (Figure 14)[25] which represents the only visual record for the form of the vaulted, two-level porch[26] originally attached to the north side, the upper parts of the south elevation and the kitchens attached to the west wall. Despite the destruction of much of the fabric, the internal arrangements can be reconstructed with some accuracy. Internally it was divided into two clearly articulated spaces: the Great Hall occupied the first five bays, while a private chamber occupied the westernmost bay separated by a stone wall, raised over services. Over the course of the thirteenth century the ceremonial porch became ubiquitous in princely residences as the symbolic place of entry for the lord.[27]

No documentary evidence exists to show the hall in use during Burnell's episcopate, but later evidence confirms that, like all secular halls, it was intentionally multifunctional.[28] Edward III's court was in residence from Christmas to Epiphany 1331–32, though Bishop Ralph of Shrewsbury himself was on the move elsewhere in his diocese.[29] Unfortunately that is all that we know about the royal visit except that the celebrations were *mirabilia sumptuosa*.[30] In 1337 Bishop Ralph himself staged an elaborate feast for ten gentlemen and their retinues, with the bishop's own people a total of 268, at which 86 gallons of wine, 280 gallons of ale, 672 loaves of bread, and a variety of fish were served. The occasion was to settle a dispute of political and financial significance to the bishop.[31]

The hall might also be used for formal legal proceedings where its grandeur could be used to effect. Bishop Ralph of Shrewsbury met the cathedral chapter there in 1338 to settle a dispute between them[32] and there was

---

25 'The South View of Wells Palace' in *Buck's Antiquities and Venerable Remains* (1774), pl. 263; above, Figure 14.

26 The evidence for vaulting derives from William Worcestre, who saw the hall complete c.1470 and noted that the hall had 'a beautiful porch with a vault': William Worcestre, *Itineraries*, ed. J.H. Harvey (Oxford, 1969), 288.

27 Undoubtedly inspired by the episcopal palaces at Lincoln and Canterbury, in 1244 Henry III gave order to 'have an entrance which befits such a palace' made for the palace at Westminster 'so that the king may dismount from his palfrey with dignity and make his way beneath it: CCR 1242–47, 273.

28 On the forms and functions of the great hall in the Middle Ages, see M.W. Thompson, *The Medieval Hall: The Basis of Secular Life, 600–1600* (Aldershot, 1995).

29 CPR 1330–34, 225–6, 228–31, 233–4; CCR 1330–33, 383, 387, 390–1, 416–17; CFR 1327–37, 291–2; *The Register of Ralph of Shrewsbury*, ed. T.S. Holmes, Somerset Record Society 9 (1896), xxiv, xxxi.

30 *Chronicles of the Reigns of Edward I and Edward II*, Rolls Series (London 1882), i. 356.

31 'Household Roll of Bishop Ralph of Shrewsbury 1337–8' in *Collectanea I*, 102–4.

32 *Wells MSS* i. 543.

evidently pressure from royal justices and other officers to use it without the bishop's permission.[33]

Contrary to the contemporary fashion for two-level halls like those built into fortified perimeter walls in the royal works at Caernarvon or Conway, or in the contemporary episcopal palace at Lichfield, Burnell's Great Hall was built in emulation of a line of late twelfth- and thirteenth-century free-standing aisled halls built at ground floor level. Although no evidence has come to light confirming the size or form of the arcade piers at Wells, their original placement was noted by William Worcestre, who confirms that it was a traditional aisled structure, divided internally into a nave with side aisles (*duos elas*).[34] It is clear that it followed the most ambitious great halls of the thirteenth century by having clustered marble piers, a precedent that had been established in episcopal and royal halls during the 1220s and 1230s such as Henry III's hall at Winchester castle, and the archbishop's hall at Canterbury.

Features of the planning of Burnell's hall, however, indicate that it derives from a single source: the Great Hall at the bishop's palace at Lincoln, built by Hugh de Wells c.1221–25.[35] Both are 'end halls' with a hall space and a separate solar raised over lower chambers in the end bay. Both buildings have polygonal corner turrets containing analogously placed stair turrets and garderobes. Contrary to the predilection for kitchens positioned to one side of great halls and attached by an L-shaped pentice as at Canterbury and Clarendon, the kitchens servicing the halls at Wells and Lincoln are attached directly off the end wall. Passage between the buildings was gained through a portal in the centre of the end wall at ground-floor level, which led into the kitchen range and into the chambers beneath the solar. Attached to the penultimate bay of those halls was a two-level porch with a vaulted lower section. At Lincoln and Wells there is evidence of a former stair turret in the angle of the hall and porch, allowing access to the upper chamber and to a series of parapet walks. Although the hall at Lincoln is one bay shorter, and the end chambers are on three levels due to the sharply sloping ground, there can be little doubt that the designer of the Wells hall, and perhaps Burnell himself, were familiar with the hall at Lincoln.

33 *CChR 1341–1417*, 52.
34 William Worcestre, *Itineraries*, 289: 'Memorandum the Hall of the Bishop's Palace at Wells is about 80 paces long by estimation and about 40 paces wide, including its nave and two aisles.' Small-scale excavations were conducted in the 1970s to determine the position and form of the arcade piers, but no evidence was uncovered: Cherry and Draper, 'Excavations', 52–3.
35 The relationship of the end bay of Lincoln to Wells has not gone unnoticed in the literature: H. Chapman, G. Coppack and P. Drewitt, *Excavations at the Bishop's Palace, Lincoln* (Sleaford, 1975); P. Faulkener, 'Lincoln Old Bishop's Palace', *Archaeological Journal*, 131 (1974), 340–4.

Built some sixty years after Lincoln, Burnell's was to be one of the last free-standing aisled great halls built in medieval England.

Burnell's hall departed from Lincoln in one signally important aspect, namely its size. With overall internal dimensions of 43.05m x 16.22m, it was conceived on a monumental scale.[36] In terms of size, the most recent precedent was the archiepiscopal hall at Canterbury (61m x 19.5m). The halls built after Canterbury, such as Henry III's hall at Dublin castle (36.6m x 19.8m) and the great hall at Winchester castle (34m x 16.8m), were built on a humbler scale.[37] After the archbishop's hall, and more distantly William II's hall at the royal palace at Westminster, Burnell's was the third largest secular hall in England. The size of great halls was frequently remarked by medieval commentators, leaving no doubt that they constituted an important sign of aristocratic power and influence.[38] Emphasising that fact, the floor of the Wells Great Hall was originally decorated with tiles featuring a variety of heraldic devices including those of Plantagenet, Poitou, and de Clare.[39]

It is worth noting that the design common to Wells and Lincoln was adopted again in the construction of Bishop Salmon's palace at Norwich (1299–1325). It is very close to Burnell's in size, 36.57m x 18.29m, and appears to have shared similar internal planning.[40] The loss of that hall is particularly unfortunate, as it clearly reflected awareness of Burnell's hall, and would undoubtedly have illustrated much about the comparative context of Burnell's works. The sequence of the halls at Lincoln, Wells and

---

[36] The measurement presented here was taken on site by the author. The dimensions most frequently quoted in the literature follow from the erroneous figures of 115' x 59' 6" offered by A. Pugin, *Examples of Gothic Architecture in England* (London, 1839), ii. 53. Pugin's measurements include only the hall proper, and not the raised space at the western end identified as 'the kitchen'; see Buckle, 'Wells Palace', 69. For a list of approximate sizes of aisled halls (where this error is repeated), see M. Wood, *The English Medieval House* (London, 1994), 45–8.

[37] In size if not in format, Burnell's hall was comparable to Henry of Blois' hall block at Wolvesey palace, Winchester; 44m x 23.47m including the hall space and attached apartments: M. Biddle, 'Wolvesey: the *domus quasi palatium* of Henry of Blois in Winchester', *Chateau Gaillard*, 3 (1966), 28–36.

[38] For example, the famous comment of William Rufus that Westminster was 'too big for a chamber, not big enough for a hall': *The History of the King's Works*, ed. H.M. Colvin (London, 1963), i. 45.

[39] The tiles were discovered in 1975 and are now in Wells Museum: Cherry and Draper, 'Excavations', 52.

[40] E. Fernie, *An Architectural History of Norwich Cathedral* (Oxford, 1993), 182–3. Fernie suggests a model was the archbishop's hall at Canterbury. However, comparison with the hall at Wells leaves little doubt that it was the singular point of reference in both planning and size: A. Wittingham, 'The Bishop's Palace, Norwich', *Archaeological Journal*, 137 (1980), 365–8; H. Harrod, 'Excavations Made in the Gardens of the Bishop's Palace, Norwich', *Norfolk Archaeology*, 6 (1864), 27–37. The lateral wall of the bishop's solar is shown on an eighteenth-century engraving, which illustrates that, like Wells, it was built over services leading to the kitchen: Harrod, 'Excavations', 30.

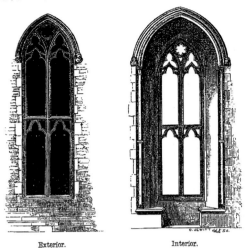

Exterior.   Interior.

Windows of Bishop Burnell's Hall, c. 1280?

Figure 23. Windows of Bishop
Burnell's Great Hall, drawn and
engraved by O. Jewitt, published
in *Proceedings of the Somersetshire
Archaeological and Natural History
Society*, 11 (1861–62), opp. p. 155.

Norwich appears not only to illustrate the selective longevity of the 'end
hall' plan throughout the thirteenth and fourteenth centuries, but it may
also suggest that the specific plan incorporated in the three buildings was
part of a recognised formula for bishops' halls.

The architectural details of the Wells hall owe a debt to the development
of a new ecclesiastical vocabulary employed in the design of secular buildings from the early years of the thirteenth century. Appearing first in the
halls of reform-minded prelates in the 1220s, and subsequently emulated in
the halls of Henry III, the transfer of forms from ecclesiastical architecture
to the secular sphere is apparent.[41] The most significant borrowings at Wells
are the soaring windows in the lateral walls (Figure 23). They span almost
the complete elevation of the hall and are set within deep, broadly splayed
window casements flanked by *en delit* blue lias shafts that rise from the sill
to the springing of the window head. The lower register, below the transom,
originally contained shutters, while the upper register and window heads
held glass.[42] Composed of two lights divided by a transom already enjoyed a
long genealogy in secular halls by the last quarter of the thirteenth century,
first appearing in the archbishop's hall at Canterbury, complete by 1220.

---

41   On these issues, see M. Reeve and M. Thurlby, 'King John's Gloriette at Corfe Castle',
Journal of the Society of Architectural Historians, 64:2 (2005), 168–85; P. Crossley, 'The
Nave of Stone Church in Kent', *Architectural History*, 44 (2001), 195–211.

42   C.E. Davis, 'On the Bishop's Palace at Wells', *Journal of the British Archaeological Associ-
aition*, 13 (1857), 184–5 noted the presence of hook irons in the window jambs, which
he took to indicate that both the upper and lower registers were originally covered by
shutters. Hook irons are still visible on the western solar window.

Figure 24. Window in the church at
Nantwich, Cheshire. Matthew Reeve.

The height and sheer surface area of the windows must have provided a
sense of luminosity to the interior of the hall, which could hardly fail to
evoke comparison with contemporary church architecture.

However, while within a tradition of vernacular design, Burnell's hall
windows are significant in that they represent one of the earliest examples
of linked-panel tracery in English architecture. Within each window bay
the tracery is treated as a four-unit composition with four identical trefoil-
headed panels that are tightly arranged within the linear gridwork of the
central mullion and lateral transom. While the ultimate source for this mode
of articulation is French *Rayonnant* architecture, within an English context,
the other early example of this mode of fenestration is found in Burnell's
own church at Nantwich, Cheshire. John Maddisson has shown that it was
built by Walter of Hereford (Figure 24), who had also been employed in

the royal works.[43] At Nantwich, tall two-light windows are separated into panels with trefoil cusping in the heads of each panel. Although based on a rather less formal design, the Nantwich windows may nevertheless illustrate an aspect of Burnell's taste.

The west end of Burnell's hall is significant as an early example of the developed screens passage in English secular architecture, indicated by the placement of paired doorways in the west hall bay that allowed passage through the hall without entering the hall space proper. The screens passage would have been divided by a wooden screen, shortening the hall by one bay.[44] The position of a screen at the west end indicates that the high table was positioned against the east wall of the hall where the end bay is some 50cm longer than the central bays.

Beyond the western screens passage was the private solar 16.22m x 7m (Plate 22).[45] The floor level of that space is indicated by a continuous off-set of masonry directly above the three service doors at the bottom of the western wall, about 3m above the ground level, that would have supported a wooden floor.[46] John Carter's plan of 1784 (Plate 12) shows that this space was raised over two rectangular rooms formed by stone walls, between which a passage led through to the central door in the west wall, giving

[43] John Maddisson, 'Decorated Architecture in the North-West Midlands: An Investigation of the Work of Provincial Masons and their Sources', Unpublished PhD thesis, Manchester Univ. 1978, 36–46.

[44] It may be (pace Hamilton Thompson) that a screen was referred to in the fourteenth-century Household Roll (Collectanea I, 102, n. 1) which records provision for candles 'ad cameram domini J. Carleton I li pro parchiis'. Hamilton Thompson considered parchiis or perches to refer either to candlestick stands formed by beams projecting from the walls, or more likely to the screens at the end of the hall. W. Phelps, History and Antiquities of Somersetshire, 4 vols (1836), ii. 89–90 stated that the western end of the hall contained offices and apartments 'with the music gallery, mentioned by an old writer'. I have been unable to locate the source for this information.

[45] Older scholarship referred to this space as the hall kitchen: N. Pevsner, The Buildings of England: North Somerset and Bristol (Harmondsworth, 1958), 315. Pugin, Examples of Gothic Architecture in England, ii. 45 similarly identified the solar as 'kitchen'. W.Phelps apparently believed that the kitchen was beneath the solar: 'a portion of the building at the Western end seems to have been partitioned off to form a kitchen, and requisite offices; and over them was a saloon and other apartments': Phelps, History and Antiquities of Somersetshire, ii. 89–90. The division between hall and chamber is indicated in the 1340–42 survey of the palace, which records an aula and a camera, a distinction also reflected in the Household Roll of Ralph of Shrewsbury of 1337–38, which makes provision for candles 'ad cameram domini' under the accounts for the bishop's hall: Collectanea I, 97–8.

[46] Parker, 'Bishop's Palace at Wells', 155 supposed that the space was vaulted in stone, but this cannot be confirmed from the present evidence. What Parker interpreted as springers can only have functioned as offsets for wooden flooring: were there to be evidence for springers at this point, they would rise far too high to allow adequate space between the solar floor and roof.

access to the kitchen, and John Parker noticed 'the remains of the buttery and pantry, with the passage between them'.[47]

The Great Hall was originally served by a kitchen range that stood immediately to the west of it, and was probably attached to it by a short pentice.[48] The 1340–42 survey noted 'two separate and spacious buildings covered in stone, of which one for the kitchen, brewery and bakery, and the other for larder and other necessaries'.[49] If the 1733 view by the Bucks is to be trusted, the original kitchen was a spacious single-storied building, covered by a low-pitched roof, and entered through a door in its north wall and possibly through another in the south wall.[50]

A single portal in the centre of the west wall of the Great Hall allowed food to be brought in under the bishop's solar. That room was separated from the cross-passage by a stone dividing wall, the remains of which are still visible on the north wall. It is clear that this wall rose above the parapet level to support the original western gable. The division of this room from the hall was also articulated externally where there is a noticeable change in the design of the windows. There is also a change in the level of the crenellated parapet that has been dropped about 50cm below the level of the hall parapets.

Consideration of the internal arrangements of the bishop's chamber suggests that it was a well-appointed apartment, intended to be a place of seclusion from the hall. It was roofed in a separate span, running transversely to the east–west orientation of the hall roof. In the end wall are the remains of a fireplace and chimney flue in the thickness of the wall, which would have provided the main source of heat.[51] Two elegant windows filled with tracery now ornament the north and west walls, and Carter's plan shows that the south wall also had two windows.[52] The tracery patterns in those windows are softened versions of the tracery in the Great Hall, being composed of two rounded trefoils impaled by trefoil-headed arches with a sexfoiled roundel in the heads. Rebates in the tracery show that they originally held glass.[53] The door at the south-west corner of the apartment

[47] J.H. Parker, 'Remarks on the Medieval Architecture of the City of Wells', *Archaeological Journal*, 36 (1879), 366.
[48] Parker, 'Bishop's Palace at Wells', 366.
[49] Scrase and Dunning, 'The Bishop's Palace, Wells', 55.
[50] *Buck's Antiquities*, pl. 263; Figure 14.
[51] A drawing by John Buckler in the Somerset Archaeological Society's Pigott Collection representing the sixteenth-century Tudor fireplace in the first floor of the central range suggests that it was removed from the Great Hall.
[52] Plate 12.
[53] Burnell owned a house in Westminster with glazed windows: *Records of the Wardrobe and Household 1285–6*, ed. B.F. Byerly and C. Ridder-Byerly (London, 1977), 24. On Burnell's chambers at Westminster see Colvin, *King's Works*, i. 103.

led into the garderobe, which was located in the usual position off a lord's private chamber.[54] It is an elegant octagonal cell housed within the corner turret, vaulted with a sexpartite, domical rib vault carried on eight turned capitals (Figure 25).[55]

The bishop's chamber in the western bay of the Great Hall reflected the traditional division between the public and private aspects of the medieval household. Some sense of the privacy of that space can be gleaned from an analysis of the parapet passages that gave access to it: the system of parapet walks, undoubtedly intended as service passages, allowed travel from the chamber to other parts of the palace without entering the hall space. The chamber could be serviced separately from the rest of the hall.

It has long been assumed that the fourteenth century witnessed a gradual shift of the lord's dining space from the high table, in view of the entire court, to the private chamber. Scholars have typically turned to a passage in Langland's *Vision of Piers Plowman* (c.1360) in which the lord is chastised for not dining in hall.[56] What has eluded commentators is the fact that Langland's criticism was not an actual chronicle of recent events, but rather part of a long-standing literary *topos* on proper lordly conduct in great halls. It was an established aspect of aristocratic decorum that lords, and particularly bishops, should appear in hall in order to present a splendid vision of their lordship and wealth to their court and visitors. Medieval etiquette dictated that retreating from hall was not only dishonourable but also cowardly, carrying with it the air of suspicion and secrecy. In his *Household Rules* (c.1242) Robert Grosseteste, bishop of Lincoln, warns that lords should not withdraw to 'hiding places and chambers' to dine away from the household, as this is wasteful and will bring dishonour to the lord. Elsewhere he suggests that a great lord should be seated at all times in the middle of the high table so that the lord's presence is clearly visible and the lord can earn 'great fear and reverence'.[57] Rather than indicating a shift in the fourteenth century away from the great hall to the solar, the change

54 Davis, 'On the Bishop's Palace at Wells', 186 n. 1 records excavations conducted in the floor of the garderobe that discovered a drain leading to the moat. Those excavations were not published and no other evidence has come to light to confirm the reference. A possible source for the vaulted garderobe is that at Winchester built by Henry III 'in the fashion of a turret' with double vaulting (*duplice vousura*): Wood, *The English Medieval House*, 379–80.

55 The internal arrangements of this cell have been altered: the present doorway at ground level was added or enlarged, and the cell lined with new stonework that removed any evidence for post-holes or other flooring: Parker, 'Bishop's Palace at Wells', 155.

56 (Book X, 97–101): 'Elynge is the hall each day in the week / There the Lord nor the Lady liketh to sit. / Now hath each rich a rule to eat by himself / In a privy parlour ... / Or in a chamber with a chimney, and leave the chief hall / That was made for meals, for me to eat in, / And all to spare to spill that spend shall another.'

57 D. Oschinsky, *Walter of Henley and Other Treatises on Estate Management and Accounting* (Oxford, 1971), 403, 407.

seems to have happened as early as the twelfth century, and possibly earlier still. There is every reason to suggest that the bishop's chamber (and the related chamber at Lincoln) was always intended to be a space for separate dining with the bishop and his associates.[58] As a model of good conduct, St Hugh, bishop of Lincoln, was known to withdraw after dining to his private chamber (*camera*) where he entertained his more distinguished guests with improving stories of famous men from history.[59] The extent to which the bishops of Bath and Wells lived up to the social ideal of lordly display within the hall will never be known, but it is likely that the solar was never used for more than small dinners or meetings between the bishop and his familiars.

The bishop's hall and chapel were designed to incorporate a system of parapet walks that allowed for passage around the rooflines of the bishop's hall into the battlements in the corner turrets, into the upper storey of the hall porch and into the bishop's chamber. The merging of the hall and chapel at some point during their construction (discussed below) meant that the chapel parapets continued onto the hall parapets, allowing passage between the two buildings. At each corner of the hall, the parapets led to small crenellated battlements located within the tops of the corner turrets. Although clearly representing a quotation from military architecture, these turrets do not seem to have been designed to function in a defensive capacity. The parapets also allowed access into the bishop's chamber. The north-west battlement leads to a passage within the wall thickness of the west wall directly into the chamber. The chamber could also be accessed through the former staircase on the west side of the hall porch that led directly to a door in the north wall of the chamber, and probably also into the room over the north porch. The functional implications of this system meant that one could enter the chamber either via the exterior of the hall, or via the north range–chapel–hall parapets without entering the hall space proper. Such an arrangement suggests a remarkably clear separation between the hall and chamber.

[58] A feature that has been little discussed in the historiography of medieval planning is the relationship of divisions in secular spaces to household divisions. It is tempting to suggest that the emancipation of the 'home' from the 'travelling' court in the thirteenth century was the rationale behind the formation of 'end halls': the planning of these structures allowed the entire court to gather within one building, but in two different rooms, dictated by their status and proximity to the bishop. According to Blair's reconstruction, the earliest example of an end hall with storied chambers appears to be the bishop's hall at Hereford, built by Bishop de Vere (1186–98). J. Blair, 'The Twelfth-Century Bishop's Palace at Hereford', *Medieval Archaeology*, 31 (1987), 59–72.

[59] *Magna Vita Hugonis*, ed. and trans. D.I. Douie and H. Farmer, 2 vols (London 1962), 202.

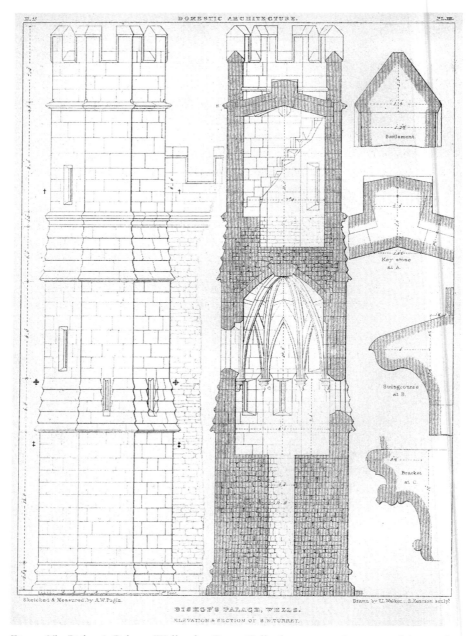

Figure 25. Bishop's Palace, Wells, the Great Hall: elevation and section of the south-west turret, sketched and measured by A.W. Pugin, drawn by T.L. Walker, engraved by E. Kennion for A.C. Pugin, *Examples of Gothic Architecture* (1831–38).

The sequence of construction and the evidence of a change in plan

All writers on the palace have pointed to the awkward conjunction of the hall and chapel as the crucial evidence for interpreting the constructional sequence. The archaeology is complex, particularly when read in the context of the Decorated sequence at Wells as a whole, and it has accordingly inspired a range of frequently opposite interpretations. What those interpretations have in common, however, is that they were based on an insufficiently close reading of the fabric. Because an understanding of the archaeological evidence has wider implications for interpreting the morphology of the palace as a whole, it is worth reviewing the evidence as it now stands.

John Henry Parker proposed in 1861 that the chapel preceded the hall by some ten years, but considered the lower section of the chapel was the work of Bishop Jocelin.[60] Richard Morris considered it to have been 'well under way' before the hall was started but made no assumption that the lower levels belong to the early Gothic campaign.[61] In 1888 Edmund Buckle reversed Parker's sequence, and stated that the hall was begun before the chapel, which was squeezed into the space between the hall and Jocelin's range, but that the chapel was begun soon afterwards, and that both buildings were constructed together at the top of the turret.[62] Buckle's opinion has met with acceptance in recent discussions of the Decorated sequence at Wells.[63] The implications of those assessments have been to suggest that Burnell's work was begun well into the 1280s and was completed in the episcopate of his successor William de Marchia (1292–1302). The present writer's reading of the evidence agrees most closely with Parker's assessment in insisting that the construction of the chapel preceded that of the hall, but also agrees that the chapel and hall were integrated at the level of the parapets. There is good evidence to suggest not only that the construction of the hall followed that of the chapel, but that it represents an important change to the original design. That a hall was intended from the begin-

---

[60] Parker, 'Bishop's Palace at Wells', 153–4.
[61] Dunning, 'Bishop's Palace', 232, personal communication.
[62] Buckle, 'Wells Palace', 73.
[63] T. Ayers, 'The Painted Glass of Wells Cathedral 1285–1345', unpublished PhD thesis, University of London, 1996, 32–5. Ayers's assessment follows from P. Draper, 'The Sequence and Dating of the Decorated Work at Wells', in *Medieval Art and Architecture at Wells and Glastonbury*, British Archaeological Association Conference Transactions (Leeds, 1981), 19. A misreading of the evidence led Margaret Wood to place the chapel after the hall due to its 'more developed' window tracery: M. Wood, 'Thirteenth-Century Domestic Architecture in England', *Archaeological Journal*, 105 (1950), 76. Pevsner, *South and West Somerset*, 314–15 suggested that the chapel was the work of Robert Burnell, but stated that due to ogee detailing in the cusping of the chapel windows, the hall must have been completed after 1300.

Figure 26. Junction between the south-east turret of the Great Hall and the south-west corner of the chapel. Matthew Reeve.

ning is likely, but the change in style between the hall and chapel and the awkward synthesis of the buildings suggests that the hall represents an important change mid-way through the campaigns.

The most significant evidence favouring the construction of the chapel in advance of the hall is the blocked-up doorway in the south wall of the chapel at the west end (Figure 26). The blocking was the result of the construction of the hall turret against the south-west angle of the chapel: the intimate relationship of those two structures demanded that the original hood moulding over the chapel door was chiselled off to accommodate the bulk of the hall turret against the southern flank of the chapel corner. Although the specific liturgical function of the door is unclear, it was an integral part of the chapel's design, and the merging of the hall against the angle of the chapel rendered it obsolete. Above the blocked door is the second blocked doorway on the north-east hall turret, half-way up its east side. Again, the function of the door is unclear, but it may have led to a wooden platform on the east side of the hall, or it may have worked in some other way with the east elevation that we can no longer realise.[64] The archaeological evidence suggests that the doorway was used throughout the Middle Ages, and blocked up afterwards.[65]

The archaeological evidence thus suggests that the chapel was built in advance of the hall, and that the construction of the hall demanded significant alterations be made to the fabric of the chapel. The exact point at which the hall began relative to the completion of the chapel is more difficult to determine. That the chapel was in an advanced stage of construction is indicated by the change in profile of the moulded stringcourse that runs above the chapel windows to join with the hall turret on the west and south sides, indicating that the chapel was complete at least to its rooflines. The construction of the chapel vault, which rises from low springers on the lateral walls, would imply that the vault was also built at that time. The point at which the hall was constructed seems to be indicated by a notable

---

[64] Davis, 'On the Bishop's Palace at Wells', 183. Davis suggested that the door formed an entrance to a wooden pulpit or stage. Analysis of the masonry immediately below the door shows two small postholes that may have formed some sort of walkway that projected outward from the door. My thanks to Jerry Sampson for discussions with me on site.

[65] Davis, *ibid.*, noted the presence of (now lost) hinges on the blocked door, suggesting that it was in use throughout the Middle Ages. Draper suggested that the blocked doorway was the decisive evidence indicating that the hall was built prior to the chapel. He proposed that the chapel wall was constructed 'to allow some light to an existing window on the turret that would otherwise have been blocked': Draper, 'The Sequence and Dating of the Decorated Work at Wells', 28, n. 13. It seems unlikely that the desire to allow light onto this small portal dictated the orientation of the existing buildings, which were most likely built in accordance with the pre-existing stream, as discussed above.

disturbance in the masonry on the inside of the north-east hall turret about 15 ft above ground. The synthesis of those two phases occurs at the level of the parapets. In order to accommodate the parapet walks the turret was built not only with a spiral stair leading to the hall parapets, but also with a doorway that gave access from the chapel roof. The regular coursing of the stonework on the crenellations of the hall turrets and chapel parapets and the uniform height of the hall and chapel crenels indicate that the addition of the crenels on both buildings was part of a single campaign of construction commenced at the point of the completion of the Great Hall. That would help to explain another anomaly of the design, namely the high parapets that rise above the (now altered and more steeply pitched) chapel roof. The height of the parapet was based on matching the height of the crenels on the hall turrets, with the intention of endowing the hall and chapel with a continuous crenellated silhouette. Significant modification of that sort to an original design during the construction of medieval secular buildings was commonplace.[66] However visually incongruous, the merging of the hall turret with the chapel was not the result of an architectural miscalculation; it was intended to accommodate the fluid system of parapet passages that connected the Decorated buildings to their early Gothic predecessors.

Design sources

The interpretation of the archaeological evidence offered here accords well with the stylistic evidence of the buildings themselves. The apparent break between the chapel and hall is also reflected in a change in architectural language. Consideration of the stylistic sources suggests that the design of the chapel relies primarily upon recent West Country Decorated buildings of the early 1280s, while the architectural sources of the hall indicate that it was brought up to date with contemporary court-based building of the mid-1280s and 1290s. While it might be suggested that the stylistic differences are related to their different functions as devotional and ceremonial spaces, the changes between the buildings are pronounced, and many of the architectural sources for the buildings can be clearly identified.

It has long been agreed that Burnell's works at Wells are intimately related to another building under his patronage, namely his own manor house and church at Acton Burnell, Shropshire, probably built c.1279–

---

[66] On the process of design in medieval secular buildings, see M. Hislop, 'Bolton Castle and the Practice of Architecture in the Middle Ages', *Journal of the British Archaeological Association*, 149 (1996), 10–22.

83.[67] Richard Morris's analysis of the architectural mouldings has shown that the Wells chapel was built by the same masons as Acton Burnell, an observation that also extends to the contemporary work at the cathedral involving the chapter house staircase and vestibule.[68] The palace chapel and Acton Burnell also share a handful of distinctive features such as bowed triangles in the window tracery with internal cusping, and heavy square corner turrets that are crossed by string courses. The similarities between Burnell's two building projects in Shropshire and Somerset leave little doubt that they were produced by a common atelier of masons and, more speculatively, by a single architect. The connections mean that we must imagine one significant patron wielding a substantial workforce that was employed between two building projects.

In contrast with the diversity of motifs in the chapel, the hall reflects a tighter, more formalised design. The architectural details of the hall, and particularly its window tracery, indicate that it was updated to incorporate many of the *Rayonnant*-inspired features fashionable in court building in the mid-1280s and 1290s.[69] An important source for the design of the bishop's hall was the palace chapel of St Etheldreda in Holborn, built by Burnell's associate John Kirkby, bishop of Ely, completed in or before 1286.[70] This in itself is significant, as Bony has awarded St Etheldreda's a seminal role in the development of the court style of the 1280s and 1290s.[71] The main borrowing from Holborn appears in the lateral windows of the hall: the tracery patterns with impaled pointed trefoils, Y-tracery and a sexfoil oculus

---

[67] *CPR 1272–81*, 521; *1281–92*, 108; *CCR 1279–88*, 219; *1281–92*, 157. It is probable that Acton Burnell was substantially complete by autumn 1283 when the court met there for five weeks when the *Statuta de Mercantoribus* was passed: C.H. Hartshorne, 'On the Ancient Parliament and Castle of Acton Burnell', *Archaeological Journal*, 2 (1845), 334–5. An early date for the castle is suggested by the very terminology of the licence to crenellate, which appears to refer to an existing house: 'License to R. Burnell Bp. etc., *to crenellate his dwelling house* of Acton Burnell': *CPR 1281–92*, 10. The singular problem with accepting 1283 as a *terminus ante quem* is that the documentation shows that work was again under way in 1286: *CPR 1281–92*, 126, 228. The nature of those works is unclear, but rather than referring to the castle proper, it is more likely that they were made for the enclosure of the castle within a moat and curtain wall, which followed on from the licence to crenellate in 1284. A similar opinion has recently been expressed in Emery, *Greater Medieval Houses of England and Wales*, ii. 502–4, but without recourse to the documentary evidence.

[68] R.K. Morris, 'The Remodelling of the Herford Aisles', *Journal of the British Archaeological Association* 37 (1974), 21–39.

[69] Bony, *The English Decorated Style*, 10–13.

[70] The documentary evidence for the dating of the Holborn palace was first noticed in C. Wilson, 'The Origins of the Perpendicular Style and its Development to c.1360', unpublished PhD dissertation, University of London, 1980, 31, n. 9. It has since been summarised in J. Schofield, *Medieval London Houses* (New Haven and London, 1994), 191–2. Bony proposed that the chapel might have been built in the two-year period between 1284 and 1286 when Kirkby was treasurer: Bony, *The English Decorated Style*, 12.

[71] *Ibid.*

Figure 27. Windows of the palace chapel of St Etheldreda, Holborn.

in the heads are almost identical to those in the lateral windows of the hall (Figure 27).

The other source of inspiration for Burnell's works was clearly the contemporary royal castles in North Wales, and related works in the north-west Midlands. The windows in the bishop's chamber may be compared with the windows in the east wall of the great hall at Conway Castle, built between 1284 and 1286.[72] The now badly deteriorated two-light windows on the ground floor of Acton Burnell, with a quatrefoil in the heads with sharply pointed trefoil-headed arches below, are also comparable to the windows in the north wall of the great hall at Conway Castle.[73] Further connections are also suggested by the semi-circular heads of the window frames in the domestic block of Acton Burnell, which recall those in the great hall at Conway, the gatehouse at Harlech, and the Queen's Gate at Caernarvon.[74] The complex vaulting in the south-west tower also suggests a connection to the Welsh castle projects: here the domical vault is formed from eight intersecting planes, with roughly hewn stones set in a radiating pattern. Vaults of that sort first appeared in the octagonal chapel of the Eagle Tower

---

[72] A.J. Taylor, *The Welsh Castles of Edward I* (London and Rio Grande, 1986), 50.
[73] S. Toy, 'The Town and Castle of Conway', *Archaeologia*, 86 (1936), 186.
[74] A.J. Taylor, 'Castle Building in Thirteenth-Century Wales and Savoy', *Proceedings of the British Academy* 63 (1977), 267.

at Caernarvon, and similar vaults at Acton Burnell can surely be explained by direct influence from the Welsh castle projects, if not direct involvement of architects and masons in the orbit of the royal works in North Wales.

Although there are notable changes in the style of the Wells chapel and hall, the problem with apparently simple stylistic change is the marked similarity in the architectural mouldings of both buildings. Comparison of the range of moulding profiles in the chapel with those in the hall demonstrates either the reuse of templates or, where new profiles were employed, inspiration from the former chapel designs. Thus, contrary to the stylistic evidence, the mouldings may illustrate continuity at the level of craftsmen in both structures, suggesting that the same workforce was employed in the construction of the chapel and subsequently the Great Hall. The updating of the bishop's hall in the light of recent architecture is interesting because it seems to reflect Burnell's awareness of, and keen interest in, up-to-the-moment architectural design. While it is possible that the design of the hall reflects the work of a second master who was familiar with work in both North Wales and London who employed the same masons from the chapel, a more likely solution is that the updating of the designs was achieved through the arrival of new architectural drawings.

The evidence of the architectural mouldings suggests that the ultimate sources for Burnell's campaigns at Acton Burnell and Wells lie in the royal works in Wales and related court building in the north-west Midlands. The Welsh castles and other royal works there introduced two significant features into the architectural repertoire: the sunk chamfer and the wave moulding.[75] Sunk chamfers were used in both hall and chapel at Wells, and the mouldings of the chapel piscina represent one of the earliest examples of wave mouldings outside the Welsh castle projects.[76] Close connections between Wells and Caernarvon are evident in the curvilinear plinth profiles of the hall, which are related to Acton Burnell but almost identical to those on the great hall at Caernarvon (built 1283–92). Connections are also evident with Acton Burnell church: the jamb mouldings in the south transept of Acton Burnell church compare closely with the hall windows jambs at Conway. Although it is not now possible to pinpoint a single source for the Decorated work or to name a single architect, it seems clear that there was a fluid exchange of ideas and architects between Burnell's works and the royal projects in North Wales.

The connection between Burnell's patronage and the royal works is not difficult to explain. John Maddisson's attribution of Nantwich to Walter of Hereford indicates that Burnell had already borrowed architects from

---

[75] Maddisson, 'Decorated Architecture in the North-West Midlands', 91–2.
[76] *Ibid.*, 92; R.K. Morris, 'The Development of Later Gothic Mouldings in England *c.*1250–1400, Part 1', *Architectural History*, 21 (1978), 22–3, 27.

the royal works for his own commissions. Burnell's itinerary shows him frequently residing at the Welsh castles throughout the 1280s, and his correspondence records that he was in communication with the master masons.[77] Burnell's association with the royal works in fact began in the 1270s when he and Edward I built new towns or bastides.[78] Burnell witnessed the laying of the foundation stone of Edward's new Cistercian abbey at Vale Royal in Cheshire in August 1277, built by Walter of Hereford; in his role as executor of the will of Queen Eleanor of Castile, Burnell was partially responsible for the placement and orchestration of at least one of the nine Eleanor Crosses. The scale of Burnell's works in the 1280s, involving the Wells palace additions, the cathedral works and the works at Acton Burnell, suggests that an extensive workforce was assembled for their construction. The history of architectural patronage in the court of Edward I has yet to be written, but such a project would surely illustrate a fact that is becoming increasingly stated in the literature: building in the last quarter of the thirteenth century was characterised by intimate workshop connections, and it is clear that there was considerable interchange between a number of significant contemporary building projects.[79]

Iconography: the militarisation of the Bishop's Palace

Burnell's additions announced an important change in the architectural iconography of the palace. Aside from the physical expansion, the hall and chapel introduced for the first time a fortified aesthetic, by which it took on the guise of a fortified castle. That was achieved principally through the addition of heavy crenellated parapets around the rooflines; it was an aspect of the building's iconography that was significant in the minds of its users and viewers, since it was specifically addressed in the fourteenth-century survey, which states that Burnell's buildings were 'built in the form of a castle' (*ad modum castri constructum*).[80] Although the additions possessed

77 Huscroft, 'The Personal and Political Life of Robert Burnell', 232–9. For Burnell's involvement in the finance of the Welsh castles: TNA SC1 22/19. On Burnell's correspondence with Richard le Engineer: TNA SC1 23/53; 29/208; 48/177; 61/28.
78 J.P. Trabut-Cussac, 'Date, fondation et identification de la bastide de Baa', *Révue Historique de Bordeaux*, 10 (1961), 133–44.
79 V. Jansen, 'The Design and Building Sequence of the Eastern Arm of Exeter Cathedral, c.1279–1310: A Qualified Study', in *Medieval Art and Architecture at Exeter Cathedral*, British Archaeological Association Conference Transactions (London, 1991), 44: 'the picture that is emerging in this period [is] of the closest interconnections among the London workshops and other sites: Oxford, Wells, Exeter, and elsewhere. It seems as if nearly every mason and patron knew of all the significant building in England and at times farther afield – perhaps even at the design stage.'
80 Scrase and Dunning, 'The Bishop's Palace, Wells', 55.

all the obvious signifiers of castle architecture such as turrets, crenellations and parapet walks, they were clearly not designed with defence in mind. Analysis of the chapel parapets show that the crenels were used for visual effect, serving to shield the rooflines from view and crowning the building with an embattled silhouette.[81] If defence was a factor at all in Burnell's campaigns, it is possible that perimeter defences satisfied that need.

The significance of Burnell's additions lies in their position amongst the earliest examples of a type of quasi-fortified architecture that was to become ubiquitous in the later Middle Ages, which possessed no offensive and few defensive features, but borrowed freely from military architecture, particularly in the frequent use of crenellated parapets. In that, Burnell's additions must be classed among a handful of secular palaces built within a generation or so, such as the manor house at Little Wenham in Suffolk built c.1290, the palace of the bishop of Saint David's at Llawhaden, Markenfield Hall, and the late thirteenth-century additions to Ludlow castle. Burnell's work also parallels some of the earliest uses of that aesthetic in religious architecture, such as the eastern arms of Exeter cathedral, and of St Augustine's abbey, Bristol. Although Burnell's additions to the palace were by no means unique, his patronage may, as Bony has suggested, have been important in disseminating a martial aesthetic.[82] His other architectural commissions also borrowed from the vocabulary of castle architecture: Acton Burnell has low horizontal, crenellated parapets and, as Maddisson's reconstruction of Nantwich church has shown, it was among the first examples of a hall-church, probably also with crenellated parapets.[83] The castle-like appearance is emphasised by the curious exorcism of external sculptural ornament and the use of thick, unadorned walls into which delicate bar-tracery windows are set. Contrary to the rather more richly decorated Romanesque palaces at Castle Rising or Hedingham, both of which use lavish external embellishments in the form of sculpture, rich mouldings and blind arcading, the late thirteenth-century additions at Wells are remarkably austere and their essentially rectilinear form of compact, squared-mass buildings also endowed them with the look of an embattled castle.

Although Burnell's role in the validation of this mode of militaristic display is clear, the origins of the style are not. It has been assumed from royal documents that the 'domestication' of crenellations originated within the royal court of Henry III[84] from the 1230s, such as the hall and chapel at Woodstock (whitewashed to highlight their effect), the queen's ward-

---

[81] It may also be at this time that a crenellated cornice was added to the roofline of Jocelin's early Gothic block, now visible only in Buck's view of 1733.

[82] Bony, *The English Decorated Style*, 17.

[83] Maddisson, 'Decorated Architecture in the North-West Midlands', 41–6.

[84] Bony, *The English Decorated Style*, 17.

robe at Winchester, and the palace at Westminster.[85] Crenels also adorn the rooflines of Westminster Abbey after the model of Rheims.[86] The peculiar preservation of royal buildings and documents, however, has served to bias the evidence in favour of royal initiative. Were there ornamental fortifications of that sort on episcopal palaces? That question cannot be answered, but there seems every reason to suggest that crenellations may have been employed with some frequency in bishops' palaces in the early thirteenth century, among them possibly at Lincoln.[87] As the planning of Burnell's hall illustrates, the important and apparently innovative buildings of the Decorated style could rely strongly on previous models, even perhaps extending to decorative and iconographic formulae.

Only one reading of the military symbolism of the late thirteenth century palace additions has been offered. Morris has suggested that the iconography may have been responding in some way to the local cult of King Arthur at Glastonbury abbey, and more broadly to an 'Arthurian micro-climate' based around the exhumation of Arthur's remains.[88] Following that interpretation, the Wells Great Hall becomes an evocation of the great hall of Arthur, the mythic West Country king. While Arthur enjoyed a well-known flourishing of popularity in the court of Edward I,[89] a specifically 'Arthurian' interpretation of the Bishop's Palace does not stand up to scrutiny. In the first place, there is no evidence whatsoever of Burnell's interests in the Arthurian legend. Significant as such explanations are in elucidating the wider symbolic meanings of aristocratic residences, and particularly the literary manifestations of chivalry, romance and the cult of warfare, they are simply too narrow as criteria to encompass the wider meanings of the Bishop's Palace or fortified buildings in general.[90] As a category of domestic building that became adopted in most great houses in the thirteenth century and

85   T. Hudson Turner, *Some Account of Domestic Architecture in England* (Oxford, 1851), 201, 214, 229, 239.

86   P. Binski, *Westminster Abbey and the Plantagenets: Kingship and the Representation of Power 1200–1400* (New Haven and London, 1995), 36.

87   A. Gibbons, 'Parliamentary Survey of the Bishop's Palace at Lincoln, taken in 1647', *Lincoln Diocesan Magazine* (1889–90), 153. Crenellations, but of an unknown date, were noticed on the roof of the thirteenth-century hall.

88   R.K. Morris, 'The Architecture of Arthurian Enthusiasm: Castle Symbolism in the Reigns of Edward I and his Successors', in *Armies, Chivalry, and Warfare in Medieval Britain and France*, ed. M. Strickland (Stamford, 1998), 63–81. See also *idem*, 'European prodigy or regional eccentric? The rebuilding of St Augustine's Abbey Church, Bristol', in *'Almost the Richest City': Bristol in the Middle Ages*, ed. L. Keen, British Archaeological Association Conference Transactions (Leeds, 1997), 41–56, 51.

89   R.S. Loomis, 'Edward I, Arthurian Enthusiast', *Speculum*, 28 (1953), 114–27. For a less optimistic view of Edward's Arthurianism, see M. Prestwich, *Edward I* (London, 1988), 120–2: 'Arthur was probably no more than a conceit [Edward] toyed with occasionally.'

90   This interpretation has already been queried by C. Coulson, 'Fourteenth Century Castles in Context: Apotheosis or Decline?' in *Fourteenth Century England I*, ed. N. Saul (Woodbridge, 2000), 138.

beyond, the castellated house or palace resonated with a wider range of meanings.

In a real sense, fortification signified aristocracy, and the privilege of crenellation was in part a phenomenon of *arrivisme* that affected the propertied classes. Indeed, the process of gaining licence to crenellate suggested entry into an elite sector of society.[91] That last factor must have been especially apposite in the reign of Edward I, characterised as it was by a scrutiny of such licences.[92] The tight controls on the privilege must have given crenellated buildings the air of royal approval, a sign of close allegiance of the grantee with the court. It is not surprising that Edward's court bishops received some of the earliest such licences. By the fourteenth century, however, and particularly into the fifteenth, licences were granted freely, and crenellation became a universal symbol of nobility, gracing many palaces, parish churches and tombs. For the present purpose, the dissemination of military ideals from early sites such as the Bishop's Palace serves to remind us of the significance of the architectural projects of elite courts in the formulation of aesthetic and cultural ideals.

But taste for martial display should not lead us to interpret Burnell's buildings in solely secular terms. Military symbolism enjoyed a wide context in mystical writing, hagiography and romance literature deriving ultimately from biblical sources such as Psalm 18 ('The Lord is my rock, my fortress and my deliverer / my God is my rock, in whom I take refuge / He is my shield and the horn of salvation, my stronghold'). Castles and fortifications were common symbols for Christian fortitude and religious authority.[93] Grosseteste, for example, allegorised the sacrament as 'the most safe protection of a castle', around whose walls of Confession and Penance flow the waters of Baptism, and from whose midst rises the mighty Keep of the Holy Sacrament of the altar, with seven ascending steps. 'With these defences', he continues, 'you who are spiritual kings, defend your subjects strenuously against the spiritual powers of wickedness, with fasting and alms, offering up, without ceasing, lauds and spiritual hymns.'[94] Perhaps the most telling

---

[91] C. Coulson, 'Structural Symbolism in Medieval Castle Architecture', *Journal of the British Archaeological Association*, 132 (1979), 73–90; *idem*, 'Hierarchism in Conventual Crenellation: An Essay on the Sociology and Metaphysics of Medieval Fortification', *Medieval Archaeology*, 26 (1982), 69–101; *idem*, 'Freedom to Crenellate by Licence: An Historiographical Revision', *Nottingham Medieval Studies*, 38 (1994), 86–137.

[92] D. Williams, 'Fortified Manor Houses', *Transactions of the Leicestershire Archaeological and Historical Society*, 50 (1974–75), 5–6.

[93] This material has been discussed at length in C. Whitehead, 'Castles of the Mind: An Interpretive History', unpublished D.Phil. dissertation, Oxford University, 1995.

[94] G.R. Owst, *Literature and the Pulpit in Medieval England* (Oxford, 1961), 78; Whitehead, 'Castles of the Mind', 107.

conceit of the castle as an embodiment of Christian virtue is an early four-teenth-century illumination in the De Lisle Psalter, representing the Tower of Wisdom in the guise of a fortified castle.[95]

This chapter has argued that Robert Burnell's additions to the Bishop's Palace at Wells deserve far more attention than they have hitherto received. A complete assessment of the buildings and their complex archaeology has not been possible, but aspects of its style, date, and sequence have been explored. Burnell's additions now stand as a powerful testament to the changing nature of bishops of Bath and Wells, from Jocelin the reformer to an overtly secular, aristocratic lord with fewer personal ties to his cathedral church. Burnell's buildings were amongst the most lavish of the period, and it is not surprising that within a generation Bishop Ralph of Shrewsbury felt the need to circle the palace with substantial fortifications and a wet moat, a sign of further change in the nature of his office.

95   BL MS Arundel 83, fo. 135; L.F. Sandler, *The Psalter of Robert de Lisle in the British Library* (Oxford, 1983), 82.

Index

Abingdon, Edmund of, archbp of
  Canterbury 10
Acton Burnell (Salop), castle 170, 173,
  188–9, 189n, 190–1, 193
  manor 170n
Adam, archdn of Oxford 46
Alardus, Master 18
Alexander, bp of Lincoln 105n
  dean of Wells 27n
Alfoxton see Holford
Alhampton (Somerset) 13
Aller (Somerset), see Sampford Brett
Allerton (Somerset) 13, 14n
Alphege, archbp of Canterbury 73 and n
Amesbury, Michael of, abbot of
  Glastonbury 43n
Angouleme, Isabella of 23
Archenfield (Herefs) 18
Athelney (Somerset) abbey 49n; abbot
  54n, 57
Attebere, Richard de 48
Auckland, Lord, bp of Bath and Wells 139,
  141, 152n
Avalon, Hugh of, bp of Lincoln 15, 183
Axbridge (Somerset) 87, 93, 95

Banwell (Somerset) 13, 101n
Barlinch, Brompton Regis (Somerset),
  priory 16n
Barrow Gurney (Somerset), priory 16n, 48
Bath, Robert of, abbot of Glastonbury 43n,
  50
Bath (Somerset), abbey (cathedral priory)
  25, 43n, 44, 50, 53, 72, 84n, 87, 96
  bp's house at 20, 90, 171
  monks 18n, 25, 53–4, 73
  prior 44, 89n, and see Robert
  synods at 44, 71
Bath (Somerset) 78–9
  Barton (hundred) 80n, 84n, 85
  borough 73
  burgesses 73
  charters 78–9
  citizens 18n, 83–4, 171
  coronation 73n
  guild 78, 81
  hospitals 16n; St John's 82n, 91, 96

  mayors 82
Bath (Somerset), archdn see Blois, Peter of
  bps 13, and see Lewes; Tours
  see 72–5
Bath and Wells, bp see Auckland;
  Bekynton; Bitton; Drokensford; Giffard,
  Walter; Hooper; Ken; Law; Marchia;
  Mountagu; Salisbury; Shrewsbury
Bathampton, Hilary of and his w Hilaria
  Trotman 14n
Batheaston (Somerset) 73
Bec-Hellouin, abbot 57
Bedford, castle 40
Bek, Anthony, bp of Durham 171
Bekynton, Thomas, bp of Bath and Wells
  113, 119, 141
Biddisham (Somerset) 63n
Bitton, William de I, bp of Bath and Wells
  45n, 63n
Blacman, John 1
Blois, Henry of, abbot of Glastonbury, bp of
  Winchester 104, 112, 177n
  Peter of, archdn of Bath 56
  William of, bp of Lincoln 12, 28
Bohun, Jocelin de, bp of Salisbury 105
Bridgwater (Somerset), hospital 48
Bristol 18n, 38, 74, 85
  castle 17, 39, 85
  St Augustine's abbey 193, 194n
Bruton (Somerset), priory 46
Buckland, Durston (Somerset), Hospitallers
  16n, 46, 48
Burgh, Hubert de 39–40
Burnell, Hugh 170n
  Robert, bp of Bath and Wells 11, 79,
  108, 119, 144n, 145n, 169ff, 181n,
  189n

Caernarvon, castle 176, 190–1
Camera (fitz Robert, or of Wells), Simon
  de, archdn of Wells, bp of Chichester
  15–16, 16n, 18
Cannington (Somerset), priory 16n, 48
Canonsleigh (Devon), canons 46
Canterbury (Kent), archbp's palace 102–3,
  175n, 176–7, 178n

archbp *see* Abingdon; Alphege; Corbeuil; Lanfranc; Langton, Stephen; Walter
monks 2
see 170
Carlingcott (Somerset) 49
Castle Rising (Norfolk) 193
Chard (Somerset) 87
Charlton Mackrell (Somerset) 48
Cheddar (Somerset) 41, 63n, 87–8, 101n
hundred 93
Chesney, Robert de, bp of Lincoln 105
Chew Magna (Somerset) 46, 55n
and see Norton Hawkfield
Chewton Mendip (Somerset) 46, 57n, 63n
Chichester, Peter of 44, 57n
Chichester (Sussex), bp *see* Camera; Poore; Seffrid
bp's chapel 174 and n
bp's palace 171n
bp's prison 173n
chancellor *see* Tournai
Chinnock (Somerset) 50
Churchill (Somerset) 13n
Clarendon (Wilts), palace 108, 176
Claverton (Somerset), park 85, 87
Combe St Nicholas (Somerset) 60
Compton Bishop (Somerset) 43n
Congresbury (Somerset) 63n
Conteville, Ralph de 14n
Conway, castle 176, 190–1
Corbeuil, William of, archbp of Canterbury 104n
Courtenay, William de 48–9
Coventry and Lichfield, bp *see* Langton, Walter
Cranborne (Dorset) 17–18
Cranmore (Somerset) 94–5
Curry, North (Somerset) 18n, 63n, 87

Dereham, Master Elias of 57, 109
Devizes (Wilts), castle 104
Dogmersfield (Hants) 12, 20n, 35, 41, 87
Dorchester (Dorset) 17
Draycott (Somerset) 93; Figure 3
Drokensford, John, bp of Bath and Wells 173
Dublin, castle 177
Dunster (Somerset) 42
Durham, bp of *see* Bek; Hatfield; Poore; Puiset
bp's prison 173n
bp's residence 104–5
Elias the chaplain 57n
Ely, bp *see* Kirkby
Essex, earls, 16 and n

Evercreech (Somerset) 17n, 49, 60, 91n, 94, 101n
Exeter (Devon), bp's palace 173
bp's prison 173n
cathedral 192n, 193

Farrington Gurney (Somerset) 2
Ferrey, Benjamin 141
FitzGeldewin, Savaric, bp of Bath and Glastonbury 12, 25–6, 50, 54–5, 60, 78–9, 113
FitzJocelin, Reginald, bp of Bath 12, 18n, 54–5, 57n, 57n, 58, 60, 75–7, 87, 91, 93n, 96, 108
FitzPeter, Geoffrey 17
FitzUrse, Reginald 49
Fox, Richard, bp of Durham 171n

Gaunt, Maurice de 87
Giffard, Walter bp of Bath and Wells, 43n
William, bp of Winchester 105
Gildeford, Master Philip de 44
Giso, bp of Wells 22, 53
Glastonbury (Somerset), abbey 26, 43n, 49–50, 194
abbot 44, *and see* Amesbury; Bath, Robert of; Herlewin; St Vigor
building 111–12, 115–16
monks 12, 26
see 79–80
Gloucester 10, 39
Godley, John de, dean of Wells 65
Gower peninsula 13
Gray, John de, bp of Norwich 38n
Grestein (France), abbey 49
Grey, Walter de, bp of Worcester, archbp of York 11, 43–4, 55
Grosseteste, Robert, bp of Lincoln 182

Hammes, William de 57n
Hampton (Somerset), manor and hundred 86
Harbin, George 148n
Harlech, castle 190
Hatfield, Clement of, prior of Spalding 174
Thomas, bp of Durham 171n
Hereford, Walter of 179, 191–2
Hereford, bp *see* Lorraine; Vere
bp's palace 105, 183n
hospital 48
Herlewin, abbot of Glastonbury 112
Hexham (Northumb), prison 173n
Hildebert 53
Holford (Somerset), Alfoxton in, 14n
Hooper, George, bp of Bath and Wells 148

Hugh of Wells, brother of Jocelin, bp of
      Lincoln 11–12, 15, 37, 67, 86 and n,
      91, 93, 95
   career 17, 28, 54
   children 20 and n, 21n, 32n, 36n
   clerk in government 18 and n, 23–4, 31
   exile 38
   lands 94
   relations with Wells 19, 95–6
   Rome 41
   will 13 and n, 16, 17n, 21, 38, 48, 91,
      93–4
   death 41
Hugh the bishop:
   election and consecration 28, 32, 38, 91
   episcopal administration 43–4
   household 57
   house and palace 40n, 109n
   relations with Wells 19, 95–6

Ickford, Master John de, official of Bp
      Jocelin 45n, 84n
Ilchester, Richard of, bp of Winchester
      14–15, 16n, 91n
Ilchester (Somerset), hospital 16n, 49
Ivo, dean of Wells 59n

Jocelin (of Wells; Trotman):
   ancestry 13 and n, 14 and n, 64, 86 and
      n, *and see* Ilchester; Poore; Trotman
   birth and early years 10–12, 34, 37, 54
   early career 12, 17–19, 27, 35
   possible child 20
   tomb 3, 34, 65
   tributes 33, 40, 51 and n, 66
Jocelin the bishop 34–52
   administration 43–51, 57
   appropriations 49
   consecration 13 and n, 14, 30–1; Plates 3
      and 4
   courts 46, 86
   devotion to BVM 55–6
   election 22, 25, 27–30, 54, 80 and n;
      Plate 2
   estates 87
   houses 40, 101n, 102, 108–9, 141; Figure
      4
   officials 45n
   ordinances 46–7, 64–5; Figure 2
   pastoral staff Plate 1
   relations with chapter 53–66
   relations with religious 49–51
   relations with towns 50–1, 79–80, 88–9,
      97
   seal 55; Plate 4

   see title 80–1
Jocelin the builder 63, 110–22
   chapel 185
   dragon 1
   finance 90
   hospital of St John, Wells 90–1, 94–6
   houses 101n, 102, 108–9, 141; Figure 4
Jocelin the courtier 10–11, 18, 23–4, 35–7,
      39–40, 87, 109; Figure 1
   exile 31n, 32, 38, 57, 60, 91
   interdict 38
   relations with pope 41–2
John, count of Mortain, king 2, 17–18,
      18n, 22–3, 26, 28, 31, 37

Ken, Thomas, bp of Bath and Wells 148
      and n
Kent (Ken, Keu), Ric of (de) 13n, 14n
Keyhaven (Hants) 87
Keynsham (Somerset), abbey 9, 49
Kingsbury Episcopi (Somerset) 60, 87
Kirkby, John, bp of Ely 189 and n

Lanfranc, archbp of Canterbury 69, 103
Langton, Stephen, archbp of Canterbury
      10, 24, 32, 37–9, 102
   Walter de, bp of Coventry and Lichfield
      171
Law, George Henry, bp of Bath and Wells
      139, 144
Lechlade, Master Ralph of, archdn of
      Taunton, dean of Wells 57 and n, 59n,
      86, 91
Leonius, Master, dean of Wells 59
Lewes, Robert of, bp of Bath 3, 25, 37, 53,
      58, 60, 63n, 74–5, 75n, 76–7, 87, 96
Lichfield, bp's palace 176
Lidiard, Master Geoffrey de 46
Lincoln, archdn of 43n
   bp of, *see* Avalon; Alexander; Blois,
      William of; Chesney; Grosseteste;
      Wells, Hugh of
   bp's palace 104–5, 175n, 176–7, 194
   chapter 12, 19, 58, 54
   see 12, 18, 32, 35
Llawhaden (Carms) 193
London 43n, 91n
   bp's palace 170
   bps' houses in 101–2
   council of 69
   Holborn, St Etheldreda's 189; Figure 27
   Old Temple 48n
   Tower of 16
Lorraine, Robert of, bp of Hereford 105
Lovell, Thos 17n

Ludlow (Salop), castle 174, 193
Lugwardine (Herefs) 18, 35
Lusignan, Geoff de 24
    Hugh de 23

M, scholar 42
Maidstone, Master Walter of 44
Malmesbury (Wilts), castle 104
Mandeville, Geoffrey de and family 16
Marchia, William de, bp of Bath and Wells
    185
Marden (Herefs) 35
Margam (Glam), abbey 13
Mariscis, Master Robert de 46n
Markenfield Hall (WR Yorks) 193
Marlborough (Wilts), castle 17
Marshwood (Dorset) 16
Martock (Somerset) 60n
Mauger, bp of Worcester 36
Medicus, Master Alexander, dean of Wells
    56, 58, 59n, 63n
Melun 38
Merton, Master William de, dean of Wells
    64
Milverton (Somerset) 61
Monkton Farleigh (Wilts), priory 16n
Montacute (Somerset), priory 49
Mountagu, James, bp of Bath and Wells 97
Mowbray, Robert de 73
Muchelney (Somerset), abbot 57
Mudford (Somerset) 49, 63n

Nantwich (Cheshire), church 179–80, 191;
    Figure 24
Neville, Hugh de 24
    Ralph, bp of Chichester 36, 40n, 174
    and n
Norton Hawkfield (Somerset), in Chew
    Magna 93
Norton sub Hamdon (Somerset) 49, 63n,
    93
Norwich
    bp see Gray; Ralegh; Salmon; Walton
    bp's palace 103–4, 177 and n
Nunney (Somerset) 63n

Old Sarum (Wilts) 11; and see Salisbury
    bp's house 104–5, 108
Oxford 192n
    archdn of see Adam
    Merton college chapel 174
Pandulf, legate 39, 51, 80
Paris, abbot of St Victor 42
    schools 37
Periwood (? county) 87

Pilton, Thomas of 47
Pilton (Somerset) 13, 47, 60
Plympton (Devon), priory 16 and n
Poore, Herbert, bp of Salisbury 11, 15, 58
    Richard, bp of Chichester, Salisbury,
        Durham 10–11, 15, 36–7, 39–42, 45,
        58 and n, 71, 109; Figure 1
Poulton (Cheshire), abbey 16n
Pucklechurch (Glos) 41, 87
Puiset, Hugh de, bp of Durham 105

Quarr (Isle of Wight), abbey 16n

Rackley (Somerset) 87
Radstock (Somerset) 87
Ralegh, William de, bp of Norwich and
    Winchester 57
Reading (Berks), Jocelin's consecration at
    30n
Reginald, bp of Bath see FitzJocelin,
    Reginald
Richard, Henry son of 48
    official of Bp Jocelin 45n
Robert, dean of Wells 59n
    prior of Bath 12, 27n
Roches, Peter des, bp of Winchester 11, 32,
    38, 42, 102, 108
Rochester (Kent) castle 104n
Roger, bp of Salisbury 105
    chaplain of Chewton 57n
Rowberrow (Somerset) 93; Figure 3

Salisbury, Roger of, bp of Bath and Wells
    81, 97
Salisbury (Wilts) 11
    bp of see Bohun; Poore, Herbert and
        Richard; Roger
    bp's palace 109
    cathedral 4
    chapter 54–5, 58
    earl of 23
Salmon, John, bp of Norwich 177
Sampford Arundel (Somerset) 46
Sampford Brett (Somerset) 46
    Aller in 46–7
Sancta Fide, Master William de, precentor
    of Wells 55
Sandwich (Kent) battle 10; Figure 1
Savaric, bp of Bath and Glastonbury see
    FitzGeldewin, Savaric
Seffrid II, bp of Chichester 174n
Selwood (Somerset), hospital 16n
Shaftesbury (Dorset) 17
    abbey 21
Shapwick (Somerset) 49

Shepton Montague (Somerset) 46
Sherborne (Dorset), castle 39, 104
Shrewsbury, Ralph of, bp of Bath and Wells 145, 175, 180n, 196
Skinner, Revd John 139
Slebech (Pembs), preceptory 13
Spalding (Lincs), priory 174
St Vigor, William of, abbot of Glastonbury 43n
St-Martin-de-Garenne (Ile de France) 16, 38, 91
Stanley (Wilts), abbey 16n
Stavensby, Alexander of, bp of Coventry 42n
Stawley (Somerset) 63n
Stogursey (Somerset), prior 46
Stowey, Over (Somerset) 46
Stratton, William de 21
Studley (Oxon), priory 16n

Talland (Cornwall) 46
Taunton, Master Gilbert of 44
Taunton, archdn see Lechlade; Wrotham
Templo, John de 44
Tournai, Hugh de, chancellor of Chichester Figure 1
Tours, John of, bp of Bath 14, 25, 53, 72, 90
Trotman (Tortesmains, Trotem(an)), Edward see Wells, Edward
  Elias 13 and n
  Henry 13 and n
  Hilaria w of Henry, later w of Hilary of Bathampton 14n
  Jocelin see Jocelin
  Ralph 12, 14, 21
  Thomas 13n, 14n
Turri, Jordan de 16, 17 and n, 91 and n, 93, 95n

Vale Royal (Cheshire), abbey 192
Vere, William de, bp of Hereford 105, 183n
Vivon, Hugh de 88–9

Walter, Hubert, archbp of Canterbury 16n, 26, 28n, 35, 37, 102
Walton, Simon of, bp of Norwich 21
Wedmore (Somerset) 58n, 60–1
Wellington (Somerset) 46, 55n, 87
Wells, Edward of 12, 14–15, 19, 21, 35, 45, 67, 86 and n, 93 and n, 96
  Herbert of 92
  Hugh of, archdn of Bath 91–2
  Hugh of, bp of Lincoln see Hugh
  Jocelin of, bp see Jocelin

  Jocelin of, chaplain 54n, 86n
  Master Nicholas of 20, 36, 64, 92n
  Osbert of 92n
  Roger of 92
  Simon of see Camera
  William of 92
  family 19
Wells, archdn of 28, and see Camera
  bp of see Giso
Wells (Somerset), Bishop's Palace 20, 41, 119–22, 171; Plates 8–12; Figures 5, 14–17
  archaeology 137–53
  chapel 172–4; Figure 26
  Edward III at 175
  excavations 139, 141, 149–53; Plates 13–14; Figure 20
  garden 148
  Great Hall 172, 174–84; Plates 8, 20, 22; Figures 23, 25–6
  lichens 154–68; Plates 15–19
  mills 145–6
  moat and walls 145, 147, 173
  park 1–2, 20, 41, 87, 90, 119, 147
  plans Figures 4, 17–18
  prison 173
  surveys 125–36, 172–3, 181
Wells (Somerset), borough 19, 67n, 72, 76, 82
  city 85
  charters 77–8
  courts 86
  fairs and markets 12, 19, 76–8, 78n
  fulling mill 93
  hospital of St John 16, 48 and n, 49, 86, 90, 93–7
  King John at 20
  Launcherley 86
  men of 19
  St Cuthbert's church 60
Wells cathedral (collegiate church, minster) 12, 25, 53, 75n, 76
  building 54–5, 63, 110–11, 113–19
  canons 18 and n, 25, 36, 72–3, 112, 173
  canons' houses 53
  chancellor see Winsham
  chapter 46, 53–66
  chapter house 169
  constitution 58–9
  dean 44, and see Alexander; Godley; Ivo; Lechlade; Leonius; Medicus; Merton; Robert
  dedication 63 and n
  defences 173
  finance of building 61, 63, 86; Figure 2

Lady Chapel 55
light of St Andrew 46
liturgy 55–6, 64
prebends 60
precentor *see* Sancta Fide
quire 55
St Mary by cloister 65
school 12
service of BVM 46
sub-dean 86
vicars 55, 64–5
West Front 11, 117–19; Plate 7
Wenham, Little (Suffolk) 193
Westminster 181n
  abbey 15, 194
  abbot and monks 42
  royal palace 108, 175n, 177 and n, 194
Whitchurch Canonicorum (Dorset) 63n
Williton (Somerset) 46
Winchester (Hants), bp see Giffard,
    William; Ilchester; Ralegh; Roches
  bp's house (Wolvesey)104–5, 177n, 193

  castle 176–7, 182n, 193–4
  see 170
Winscombe (Somerset) 13, 35, 63n
Winsham, Master Roger of, chancellor of
    Wells 55, 58
Winsham (Somerset) 27, 60
Winstanton (Salop) 170n
Winterstoke (Somerset), hundred 93
Witham (Somerset), priory 1–2, 15, 50
Woodspring (Somerset), priory 48–9
Woodstock (Oxon) 193
Wookey (Somerset) 61, 101n, 110, 141
Worcester, bp *see* Grey; Mauger
  bp's palace 170, 173
  bp's prison 173n
  cathedral 22
Wrotham, Master William of, archdn of
    Taunton 28n, 31, 55
Wynford, William 117

York, archbp *see* Grey

Other Volumes in
Studies in the History of Medieval Religion

I: Dedications of Monastic Houses in England and Wales 1066–1216
Alison Binns

II: The Early Charters of the Augustinian Canons of
Waltham Abbey, Essex, 1062–1230
Edited by Rosalind Ransford

III: Religious Belief and Ecclesiastical Careers in Late Medieval England
Edited by Christopher Harper-Bill

IV: The Rule of the Templars: the French text of the Rule of
the Order of the Knights Templar
Translated and introduced by J. M. Upton-Ward

V: The Collegiate Church of Wimborne Minster
Patricia H. Coulstock

VI: William Waynflete: Bishop and Educationalist
Virginia Davis

VII: Medieval Ecclesiastical Studies in honour of Dorothy M. Owen
Edited by M. J. Franklin and Christopher Harper-Bill

VIII: A Brotherhood of Canons Serving God: English Secular
Cathedrals in the Later Middle Ages
David Lepine

IX: Westminster Abbey and its People c.1050–c.1216
Emma Mason

X: Gilds in the Medieval Countryside: Social and
Religious Change in Cambridgeshire c.1350–1558
Virginia R. Bainbridge

XI: Monastic Revival and Regional Identity in Early Normandy
Cassandra Potts

XII: The Convent and the Community in Late Medieval England:
Female Monasteries in the Diocese of Norwich 1350–1540
Marilyn Oliva

XIII: Pilgrimage to Rome in the Middle Ages: Continuity and Change
Debra J. Birch

XIV: St Cuthbert and the Normans: the Church of Durham 1071–1153
William M. Aird

XV: The Last Generation of English Catholic Clergy:
Parish Priests in the Diocese of Coventry and Lichfield in
the Early Sixteenth Century
Tim Cooper

XVI: The Premonstratensian Order in Late Medieval England
Joseph A. Gribbin

XVII: Inward Purity and Outward Splendour:
Death and Remembrance in the Deanery of Dunwich, Suffolk, 1370–1547
Judith Middleton-Stewart

XVIII: The Religious Orders in Pre-Reformation England
Edited by James G. Clark

XIX: The Catalan Rule of the Templars:
A Critical Edition and English Translation from Barcelona,
Archito de la Corona de Aragón, 'Cartes Reales', MS 3344
Edited and translated by Judi Upton-Ward

XX: Leper Knights:
The Order of St Lazarus of Jerusalem in England, c.1150–1544
David Marcombe

XXI: The Secular Jurisdiction of Monasteries
in Anglo-Norman and Angevin England
Kevin L. Shirley

XXII: The Dependent Priories of Medieval English Monasteries
Martin Heale

XXIII: The Cartulary of St Mary's Collegiate Church, Warwick
Edited by Charles Fonge

XXIV: Leadership in Medieval English Nunneries
Valerie G. Spear

XXV: The Art and Architecture of English Benedictine Monasteries, 1300–1540:
A Patronage History
Julian M. Luxford

XXVI: Norwich Cathedral Close: The Evolution of the
English Cathedral Landscape
Roberta Gilchrist

XXVII: The Foundations of Medieval English Ecclesiastical History
Edited by Philippa Hoskin, Christopher Brooks and Barrie Dobson

XXVIII: Thomas Becket and his Biographers
Michael Staunton

XXIX: Late Medieval Monasteries and their Patrons:
England and Wales, c.1300–1540
Karen Stöber

XXX: The Culture of Medieval English Monasticism
Edited by James G. Clark

XXXI: A History of the Abbey of Bury St Edmunds, 1182–1256:
Samson of Tottington to Edmund of Walpole
Antonia Gransden

XXXII: Monastic Hospitality:
the Benedictines in England, c.1070–c.1250
Julie Kerr

XXXIII: Religious Life in Normandy, 1050–1300:
Space, Gender and Social Pressure
Leonie V. Hicks

XXXIV: The Medieval Chantry Chapel: An Archaeology
Simon Roffey

XXXV: Monasteries and Society in the British Isles
in the Later Middle Ages
Edited by Janet Burton and Karen Stöber